The Splendid Five

A MEMOIR OF WWII

The Splendid Five

A True Story About the Splinter Fleet in the Pacific During WWII

Wesley Hall

Writers Club Press

San Jose New York Lincoln Shanghai

The Splendid Five
A True Story About the Splinter Fleet in the Pacific During WWII

Writers Club Press
an imprint of iUniverse.com, Inc.

For information address:
iUniverse.com, Inc.
620 North 48th Street, Suite 201
Lincoln, NE 68504-3467
www.iuniverse.com

ISBN: 0-595-13196-4

Printed in the United States of America

Dedication

To the officers and crew of the USS SC-995:
William F. Schmidt, Lt., the Skipper
Lt.(jg) Lowery, the Exec.
Lt.(jg) Cleary, Third Officer
Ace McCormick, QM1c
Victor Donato, BM1c
Kwaitkowski, CCS
Leafdale, CPhM
Vanderveen, MoMM1c
Bill Cody, GM1c
Rex Henderson, SoM2c
Jean Chalmer Taber, SM2c
Hutchinson, RdM2c
Harold D. Jines, RM2c
Milleson, MoMM2c
Eddie Jake Groth, SM1c, the Messcook
Carpenter, SM1c
Julius Anthony Roucloux, SM1c
Johnny Olson, QM3c
Pop Law, SM1c
John Leavy, SM1c

Gilberto Martinez, SM1c
Beck, FM2c
Dowell, FM2c
Blair, FM2c

Epigraph

Our real enemy in the Pacific War was a boatswain's mate named Baldini, but in the end we realized he had saved us from something far worse than death…

Contents

List of Illustrations

Introduction

Before me lies an old photograph of the Subchaser-995 crew, taken in Hollandia, New Guinea, in the summer of 1944. At the time this picture was taken there were only seventeen men and three officers left of the original crew. And in the eyes of everyone of my old shipmates I see something that bothers the hell out of me. How long has it been, fifty, going on sixty, years? And I still haven't published the story of the five subchasers and their epic journey into Jap-infested waters.

Ace McCormick laughingly dubbed the five wooden ships *The Splinter Fleet* when they were converted to *LCC's* down in New Caledonia in the summer of 1944, but because of the Walt Disney artwork on their bridges they were already being called *The Donald Duck Navy* at the U. S. Naval Supply Base on Ile Nou Island, where they were converted.

There was no promise on my part that I would write the story. But I guess I seemed like the logical one to do it because I spent so much time in my bunk writing. Which everybody knew was a journal, not letters home to Mom, as I pretended. And I was the bookworm on the ship, no question about that. I belonged to two book clubs, both of which sent out hardback Greek and Roman classics; and my mother saw to it that these reached me, come hell or high water. Nobody on the ship wanted to read my Plato or my Homer or my Æeschylus, despite the fact there was absolutely nothing else on the ship to read. Of course, that was perfectly all right with me because I liked to take care of my books (There are no dog-eared classics in my library). The thought of one of my shipmates getting his grimy hands on *The Republic* or *The Iliad* was enough to ruin my day.

Through all the island-hopping and *kamikaze* raids and typhoons, when nobody was betting on ever seeing the States again, my shipmates just plain came to expect me to tell their story. More than one of them said so in no uncertain terms. If I didn't do it, who would? Who else but a crewmember of one of those five wooden subchasers would have the know how, not to mention the interest, to write what the hell the *Splinter Fleet* was all about? It was obvious to everyone that no professional writer was going to come along and do it.

All through the years I've kept busy doing other things, thinking about those days like someone with a great secret. But that's all I did, think about them and keep it all to myself. And the crazy thing is I remember what we went through as though it all happened yesterday.

The picture before me is one of those group things *Life* photographers did for the little ships in the War Zone, when they had nothing better to do. What I mean is, they had no intention of using such pictures in their stories home, even though they bragged to us they would. Battleships and cruisers and aircraft carriers were their meat. But what the hell? This one was taken when we were in Hollandia, New Guinea, just before we landed on the Palaus. I remember because it was the only picture anybody ever took of us until we reached Pearl, after the war was over.

We were bunched on the bow of the *995* and Bill Cody and Carpenter were sitting on the bucket seats of the forty millimeter gun and Gilberto Martinez was in the port elevation seat right beside them with his head blocking part of the Bugs Bunny *logos*. Cody's face, which I still know better than I do my own brother's, is saying, "I knew you would never do what you said you was goin' to do."

I never said I was going to write a word about them. They thought that up themselves. They're standing there looking disappointed, as though they knew I'd let them down, and some of them have that *I told you so* look on their faces.

Carpenter, our yeoman-striker, is saying, "Yeah, sure, I'll believe it when I see it in a second-rate bookstore."

Martinez, the guy that knew he was going to die and came damned close to doing just that, is next to Leafdale, our old sour pharmacist's mate and philosopher, who, in the end, was closer to me than my own father. He used to tell Martinez he was a dead man, that he had a dead man's look on his face and that one of these days his number was going to come up. And despite all the cursing and reviling Martinez directed at Pills, I guess he came to believe him. Pills had it all worked out in his mind why some men and ships made it through the war unscathed while others paid a visit to Davy Jones' Locker. He called it his *Number Theory*.

In a world gone crazy it made a lot of sense to me.

Of course, if you bought the entire theory, as I did for a time, you had to accept the fact that any minute your number was likely to come up and there wasn't a damned thing you could do about it. I finally gave up on that theory because I am basically an optimist and believe in good luck, not bad. And I came to believe that being careful and not taking unnecessary risks was better than waiting around for your number to come up.

Ace McCormick is standing down front with his arms across his belly, fingers locked around his elbows. He, more than any of the others, wanted me to write about the wooden subchasers. I tried to tell him that the only writing I ever did was V-letters home, but he would laugh and clap a long bony arm around my neck and say, "Listen, Pinky, there aint nobody else in this world can write about us like you can! Hell, kid, you read guys like Plato and Aristotle! We don't expect anything fancy like that, you understand. Just tell it the way it was, the good with the bad."

Our Skipper, Lt.(jg) William F. Schmidt, is grinning at me in the picture. He looks likes a big good-natured kid, but he was our rock. Through three island invasions, countless *kamikaze* attacks, a typhoon that dang near ran us into a carrier, and the constant threat of submarines he never once wavered. If he was aware of our vulnerability, he never let on. He called the shots from deep in the heart of the South Pacific to Saipan Island, in the Marianas, and somehow he managed to keep two dozen looney-toons from killing each other when boredom and apathy and a diet of graham crackers and cling peaches just about got the best of them.

Wherever the man is, I love him dearly.

Mr. Cleary, the Third Officer of the *SC-995* and fresh out of an Ivy League ninety-day-wonder V-12 program, is the serious one in a white skivvy shirt (It should have been tie-dyed, since we were in the War Zone) beside the Skipper in the picture. He reminded me of a yachts-man that had somehow stumbled aboard our little ship by mistake. He was the only officer or enlisted man I ever knew personally that came out of the war exactly as he had gone into it. Like everybody else, he knew you couldn't hide from bullets on that subchaser; but when we'd go in close to the beach to act as a liaison between the LCVP landing barges and the troop transports and the Japs'd begin to do a little target practice in our direction, he showed absolutely no trace of fear.

I keep looking for Benito Baldini, the boatswain's mate and our own personal nemesis. Is he lurking about someplace just beyond the cam-era's window? More life-threatening than the Japanese, more persistent and irritating than the day-to-day boredom of convoy duty, and more debilitating than a steady diet of cling peaches and graham crackers, Baldini was our particular albatross. But his absence, I suddenly remember, was not caused by shyness, because he was the least shy human being I ever knew. Nor was it an oversight on the part of the cameraman because by the time this picture was taken he had gone down to Davy Jones' Locker, sent there by the crewmember who drew the shortest straw.

Now, after a good deal of time to think about it, I realize that had it not been for Baldini everyone of us would've surely gone mad long before the war was over. We spent so much time and energy hating him we had little of it left to expend on ourselves and our hopeless lot.

I swear I can smell Eddie Jake there on my left. I'm the one wearing the white golfball cap (It should have been tie-dyed) in the upper right corner of the picture; and Eddie Jake Groth, from Alice, Texas, is the big wavy-haired messcook beside me. His arms are folded across his gut but even so I can smell his underarms.

*   *   *

I've often wondered what became of this salty crew. Very likely they're pushing up daisies if their luck held out, or dealing with the Big Nurse if not. We vowed we'd keep in touch with Christmas cards and maybe have a re-union someday, but we never did. We spent sixteen months of hell together, and I swear they came to mean as much to me as my own family. Maybe more.

I saw July Roucloux in San Antonio in 1946, about a year after I escorted him to the Mare Island brig for attempting to mail a Navy Colt .45 pistol to his folks. He was dating a señorita across the river in the Latin-American quarter, and when we shook hands at the end of my visit we both knew it was *so-long, pardner*.

July (generally pronounced *Julie*) was my loader on the starboard twenty millimeter antiaircraft gun, and to look at him you'd think he was just a big awkward kid. But behind that soft Texas drawl and big flat chest was one hell of a man. He was as tall as Ace but heavy built through the shoulders and back; and he could toss a ninety-five-pound ammo canister around like it was a basketball. In eight seconds flat he could remove the smoking barrel of my twenty, ram it into a cooling tube, and replace and lock it in. Not only did he keep me loaded and going hot but he could spot planes better than I could. And, using a little routine we worked out with me pulling the trigger and following the tracers (instead of trying to use the big, useless gunsight) and him yelling directons at me, we did something no other subchaser gunners ever did in the annals of U. S. Naval warfare: We actually brought down two Japanese aircraft.

I dare anybody to prove me wrong on this.

You would have to be aboard one of those one-hundred-ten-foot bottle corks during a skirmish to realize how unlikely that was. And because of the extraordinary circumstances in one of the cases, the U. S. Navy brass awarded our ship a Presidential Unit Citation. Roucloux told me he had no interest in medals when I was presented with a Bronze Star, but I could read his face like a book and it was plain he felt that he should have received some recognition for those two kills. I felt exactly the same way, because I could not have done it without him. Both of us would eventually receive Philippine Liberation ribbons and Asiatic Campaign ribbons and three tiny bronze stars for the three invasions (and, of course, Good Conduct Medals, since we had had no opportunities to fuck up).

Jean Chalmers Tabor is over on the extreme starboard, next to the lifeline, and his face and whatever it is he's holding about navel-high are obscured. But I know exactly what the expression on his face was because he happened to be a Blackfoot Indian and his face never changed, even when he slept. He was the best poker player the South Pacific ever saw and indisputably the best signalman that ever stood a bridge watch. No battlewagon hotshot ever got ahead of him, and many's the time he put those boys on the big ships to shame with a blinker light.

Also at the bottom of the picture but on the opposite side from Tabor and stooping, is our cook, Kwaitkowski, who is smiling warmly at me, saying, "Hey, kid, you were young and pink and there hadn't been any saltpeter for a long time. Don't blame me. Blame it on where we were and our circumstances. Blame it on the war. You were such a neat kid I just couldn't help myself."

Harold Jines, in a baseball cap, seems to be pausing for the picture, perhaps on his way to the radio shack. After Fletcher rotated back to the

States and DiAugustino transferred to RS-31, the U. S. Navy Receiving Station, he and I handled the whole radio operation by ourselves, the sixteen Army transceivers, in addition to our own Navy equipment. Split-phone watches on the Navy frequencies and half a dozen different speakers going at the same time on the Army frequencies. Somehow he was able to remain calm in the midst of that bedlam. And while he was perhaps the sanest man aboard the ship, after the Skipper, there was a side to him that I couldn't make up my mind about, that put me on my guard whenever we were alone and made me suspect that beneath his mild and affable exterior there lurked a streak I cared not to see. But I knew I could depend on him, come hell or high water.

In the center of the picture in a white Navy skivvy shirt smoking a cigarette is Mr. Lowery, our Executive Officer and a fine Southern gentleman, the coolest man under pressure I ever knew. Tabor was cool but he had a high temper where other signalmen were concerned, Jines was cool most of the time but Baldini could get his goat any hour of the day or night. The Skipper, who wasn't afraid of the devil himself, turned red in the face and flared up when he thought the Japs were about to sink us, or Mr. London, of the *SC-1318*, was trying to pull something. But Mr. Lowery was simply unaffected by what was going on around him. A knock-down, drag-out fistfight between two of the men would perhaps cause him to say affably, "Now, fellows, do yall really want to battah each otha like that?" He moseyed about the ship in skivvies, sometimes in cut-off dungarees and a tie-dyed undershirt, smiling and speaking in his soft Southern voice. And while we respected and idolized the Skipper, we genuinely liked him.

After the war was over and we were soaking up the sun on Saipan Island, waiting to take the subchaser back to the States, the Skipper received orders to go to Pearl for reassignment, leaving Mr. Lowery in command of the ship! Even with his new brass lieutenant (jg) bars, we weren't certain he could get us all the way back to the States!

But he just smiled and told Ace McCormick, our quartermaster, to follow the leader (in the convoy), and somehow one day we passed under the Golden Gate and found ourselves back home.

*   *   *

Subchaser duty was not for the timid or the sickly, and so the Navy brass laid down some rules before assigning personnel to the various berths. Most important, only volunteers were to be used. And next in importance was the length of duty any individual, officer or man, would be expected to serve before rotation to the States. The maximum length was set at nine months.

In the case of the *SC-995*, however, I was the only volunteer in the crew, and I know for a fact that after we left New Caledonia none of us was ever rotated back to the States.

The crews of the other subchasers may have been volunteers, and it is possible that some of them were rotated after nine months; but I doubt it. The motley group that checked aboard the *995* in New Caledonia had one very important characteristic in common: They were independent as hell. And after the initial shock of finding themselves aboard a ship that did not pay any attention to Naval Regulations (Officers did not wear uniforms and therefore did not have to be saluted, there were no Captain's Inspections or bugles (or even whistles) with which to sound *reveille*, chow was served in plates instead of trays, and there was never a 'uniform of the day'), they began to realize that they had found their proper niche in the Navy. And once they discovered they were being led by a man who had the guts to follow his own dictates even when they clashed with the big brass, they just quite naturally became one hell of a crew.

The story my shipmates wanted me to write would have taken a thousand pages and no publisher would have touched it, even if I had been capable of doing it right. They wanted the world to know what it was like to travel twenty thousand miles in a small wooden ship in wartime; and in their version there would have been no bigger-than-life heroes, no great triumphs over the enemy, no final romantic twist that would put the whole thing into perspective and send a message to the world. They wanted it to be a story about the absurdity of war, especially as seen from the unsteady deck of that small ship, about the absolute nothingness that occupied most of their days at sea, about a diabolical boatswain's mate who deliberately set out to drive the men beneath him nuts, about malnutrition and sailors becoming toothless at the age of twenty on a persistent diet of graham crackers and cling peaches, and about the creeping rot of insanity brought on by boredom and apathy and fear and hopelessness.

Most of all, I think, they wanted me to explain how a crew of misfits could come to feel a closeness for each other that transcended blood and family.

Truth to say, no James A. Michener or Herman Wouk ever experienced such a life, never knew what it was like to go into battle against the mighty Japanese in a ship that had a flank speed of twelve knots and the firepower of a PT-boat, in a ship built to chase submarines but which could not defend itself against one, in a ship that was expected to make long ocean voyages with no storage space for fresh water or food supplies, in a ship that was always last in line with the supply ships.

*   *   *

The Officers and Crew of the SC-995 (New Guinea, 1944)

TOP ROW, left to right: Cody, Carpenter, DiAugustino, Leafdale. SECOND ROW: Jines, Olson, Mr. Lowery (Exec), Hall, Groth, Roucloux (in front). THIRD ROW: Law, Leavy, McCormick, Mr. Schmidt (the Skipper), Mr. Cleary (3rd Officer), Henderson, Tabor. FRONT ROW: Kwaitkowski, Martinez, Hutchison. Seven unaccounted for: Vanderveen, Milleson, Beck, Baldini, Blair, Klinger, and Smith.

1

Comseronsopac

The only thing lower than a messenger boy at Admiral Halsey's service squadron in Noumea, New Caledonia, had to be a messcook, something in a dirty apron that peeled potatoes, washed pots and pans, and filled the trays at chow time. But even these unsailorlike menials had it made in the shade here. There were so many of them and so few potatoes and pots and pans no one actually had much to do, and there were few limitations and restrictions upon what they could do between meals.

The drivers at the Comseron Motor Pool, handpicked by the brass for their inability to do anything to a Jeep or automobile except wreck it, belonged to an infinitely higher level of society. At least in their own opinion. They had struck the Mother Lode, hit Pay Dirt, found by pure luck the Best Duty the Navy could provide outside the continental bounds of the United States. They had never done anything in their lives, either in the Navy or in civilian life, to deserve this laid-back style of living. On their undress white uniforms there were no petty officer patches or hashmarks, nor likely to be, since the one would require serious study and application to a trade and the other six years in the service.

The noncommissioned officers (yeomen and radiomen and other old salts who could type that had had their ships shot out from under them) were the work horses of the outfit, the ones who did their eight hours a day behind desks, giving reason and meaning to the whole idea of a Comseronsopac. They did essentially the same thing typists and secretaries did the world over; and with the single exception of the uniform they had to wear to work, they might very well have been civilians working for some insurance firm back in the States.

It was a very small thing, but the messenger boy of this outfit did have one distinction. He was only one of his kind.

No rules had been laid down at all for when I should get up in the morning or go to bed at night; and since my single reason for existence was to deliver the mail twice daily from A to B (that is, from the headquarters building to the row of quonset huts below the hill), the freedom I enjoyed was right up there with the very birds that accompanied me on my rounds.

The officers at Comseron were, for the most part, high-ranking and no nonsense. For them, this was a holiday from the spit-and-polish of shipboard life. They dressed in khakis with no markings, and in the afternoons some of them would put on shorts and tennis shoes and stroll about among the enlisted. In the evenings, all of them put on their uniforms and campaign ribbons and went to the Comseron movie. No one could predict when an admiral, even Bull Halsey himself, might show up at one of these events.

A great deal of water had gone under the bridge before I arrived at this high water mark in my Naval career, but suffice it to say that boot camp at Farragut, Idaho, was still fresh in my memory and the ride across the Pacific in the smelly old SS *Eugene Skinner* continued to be the crowning insult of my eighteen years on this earth.

But as I was about to say, the Comseron outdoor theater, where a different film was run every night, was just one of perhaps a dozen such places on New Caledonia; and, of course, attached to each was a messhall or messtent, where any U. S. serviceman was welcome. Then add to this the lovely coral beach at MOB-Five Naval Hospital, where it was possible to see almost-naked Naval nurses on any given afternoon, and you have something very close to every serviceman's dream of good duty.

But, alas, all I could think of was going north! Where the fighting was.

For a time I had Tent Nine up on the hill to myself; but since all around me were other tents with from three to four occupants each, I never experienced loneliness. Indeed, I considered it a rare luxury to have the place to myself and took full advantage of the situation. I tossed my clothes and books on the other cots, used up all the nails on the center post for my mirror, towel, ditty bag, and binoculars and worried not at all what ended up on the floor.

Then one day in the late winter of 1943, according to the calendar (In that area of the world it was mid-summer), two old salts showed up at Comseron, smelling of spent cigarettes and an indefinable something that reminded me of the cesspool on the edge of town. Which was called, among other things, Halsey's Receiving Station and Navy RS-31.

I had just returned from below the hill with a batch of new outgoing mail when Admiral Weter whipped around the corner in his white Jeep and came to a sudden stop in front of the headquarters building. Instead of getting out of his vehicle and assisting the two men, he turned in his seat and said to me:

"Hey, Red, you still here? Thought you shipped out north."

"Don't I wish," I said, falling in behind the new arrivals.

They had not said a word until I spoke. Now, the swarthy one set his seabag down on the cobblestones and turned to me. "Did I hear right? You want to leave this place?"

The day Weter had delivered me from the Receiving Station I had made the mistake of telling him that I had no intention of remaining on the island of New Caledonia for the duration, that my one ambition in life was to go north and fight the Japs.

At his point Comdr. Farris, my C. O., appeared at the main door, causing the three of us to come to attention and salute. Admiral Weter was suddenly quite busy getting the Jeep in motion.

The swarthy one said, "Sharkey, Mortimer J. Sonarman, First, Sir."

Comdr. Farris chuckled, "I think you mean Second Class." But without waiting for a reply, he turned to the skinny, pale one.

"Smith, Sir. Loren W. Radarman, First."

Sharkey and Smith had never seen each other before landing at the Receiving Station. But both had lost their ships in the Coral Sea (Both ships had been tincans) and the Navy, without malice of intent or forethought, had billeted them in the same barracks building, one above the other. And, despite their obvious differences in looks and temperament, they had become good friends right away. Standing alongside each other they were Mutt and Jeff or, perhaps more accurately, a Laurel and Hardy. Sharkey was built like a short Russian peasant and had skin the color of old leather. His eyes were deep-set and jet black and shaded by heavy black eyebrows. Smith, on the other hand, was tall and angular and looked like he was getting ready to faint. He had pale, watery blue eyes that tended to bounce excitedly when he disagreed with you.

They were wearing old faded dungarees, not undress whites, which is what they were supposed to be wearing in transient. This announced them as old salts. They had just come down from up north where all the fighting was taking place, and being anxious to find out anything I could about that, I followed them inside and was standing there observing the scene when Comdr. Farris told them they would be bunking in Tent Nine.

"Hall, why don't you take them up and get them settled?" he said with a smile. He had taken a liking to me right away, probably because the former messenger had been such a pain in the butt for him. Anyway, before I knew what was happening, the stocky one turned his seabag over to me and the three of us went up the hill to the tents. They talked nonstop to each other but said not a word about the fighting up north. At this time, I was convinced they had been long-time shipmates.

The only thing I got out of them about up north was that each had lost close buddies when their ships went down. They didn't want to talk about it, what it was like up north, being a crewmember aboard a destroyer, or giving the Japs a little of their own medicine. About all either one of them would say was, "Forget it, kid. When you've found Heaven you don't go lookin' for Hell."

I watched them put clean sheets and pillowcases on their mattresses and pillows; and when we were all seated on our respective cots, I asked, "Where's Iron Bottom Bay?" I was looking at Smith, the more serious one, but it was Sharkey who answered:

"Who said anything about that hell hole?" he complained. He brought out a package of Chesterfields and tapped one across the back of his hand. Smith nodded and he tapped out another.

"Mr. Farris, remember? He said, 'Hall, take these two veterans from Iron Bottom Bay and get them squared away.'"

"What do they call you, kid?" asked Smith, not looking at me.

"Nothing, mostly. Red, once in awhile. But I don't much like that. In boot camp they called me Hall."

Sharkey shook his head doubtfully, blowing twin streams of smoke into the middle of the tent. To Smith he said, "He's no Hall. What do you think?"

Smith nodded and motioned for another cigarette. "Maybe Stud."

"Or how about Dynamite? I once knew a horse named Dynamite."

"Dynamite it will be."

"I don't like that one either," I said. "How about my real name?"

"What, Hall?" snorted Sharkey. "That's no name for somebody like you. It sounds like something inside a house. You're the outdoor type."

"Why don't you want to be called Red?" asked Smith.

Nobody said anything for awhile. Finally, I said, "It's about time for chow."

"What're we waitin' for?" asked Sharkey, lighting up another cigarette. "What kind of chow they got here, Dynamite?"

"I don't think he likes that handle," mused Smith. "Let's call him Horse."

"What kind of chow they got here, Horse?"

"Let's go see," I said, disgusted.

I led the way back down the winding path past the Recreation Room to the compound. It was a dirt path had been worn smooth by the occupants of Tent City, which was scattered over the highest point in the area. Finally reaching the level compound, we paused to look at the cobblestone area behind the main building where two Jeeps were parked.

"They have movies here?" asked Sharkey, irrelevantly. He had evidently noticed the large movie screen and a cluster of folding chairs on the west side of the old stucco-and-tile administration building.

"Every night. The best on the island."

"Who said?" challenged Sharkey. "That something you made up, or is that PR the brass is dishing out?"

Without another word, I turned and walked down past the main building, cut left around the Motor Pool, and found the end of the chow line. Shortly, they broke through the leafy thicket that surrounded the big mess tent and fell in behind me.

"Man, when you decide you're hungry, you don't wait for no one," said Sharkey. "What's an officer doin' in this line?"

A bareheaded officer wearing no markings was angling in toward the head of the line. Instead of joining the line, however, he ducked past the enlisted men and disappeared through the wide door.

"That answer your question?" asked Smith. To me he asked, "Do they eat with us?"

"Hall aint talkin' no mo," complained Sharkey. "I guess we stepped on his toes back there."

"Do you two have nicknames?" I asked at this point.

They stared at each other, fighting to keep straight faces. The swarthy one said, "I swear, Smitty, we forgot to introduce ourselves. Sorry 'bout that, kid. My name is Mortimer J. Sharkey. Call me Mort and I'll personally inflict bodily injury to you."

The other one said, "My mother called me Loren, but if you promise not to call me that—"

"Changing the subject," butted in Sharkey, "What'n hell does this outfit do?"

"It's Admiral Halsey's meat-and-potatoes outfit," I said. "Whatever he wants done. Mostly communications, I think."

Sharkey said, "Oh ho ho ho!" and began pounding Smith on the shoulder and laughing. "Hear that? 'Meat-and-potatoes' outfit. This kid's got a talent for colorful language!"

"Where in the world did you pick up an expression like that?" asked Smith.

Sharkey put his hand on my shoulder, "It's very good, but you didn't make it up."

"That's what everybody up here on the hill calls it."

"Okay," nodded Smith, "so what exactly do we do? I'm a radar operator. Does this place have radar equipment?"

"Yeah!" howled Sharkey, "and I'm a sonarman! Where's the sound gear's located?"

"I don't know," I said. "Thus far I haven't seen anything around here but typewriters. Do you fellows type?"

They just stared at me.

"My guess is you'll be up there in Communications, typing stuff," I said.

Both were shaking their heads. Sharkey was the first to speak:

"I don't think I can do that kind of work."

"My guess is you will type up decoded messages so I can deliver them down below the hill."

"You're a messenger boy," said Sharkey, faking a proud look.

"Yes, but I don't plan to be one for very long. I'm transferring to a ship that's headed north the first chance I get."

"No," said Sharkey. "That you don't want to do. Put such a thought out of your mind. Going north is not what you want to do." He glanced at the radarman, "Huh?"

"No way, Hosay."

Eventually, we went through the line and let the messcooks pile our trays high with steaming hot food. Neither of my new friends said a word until we were seated at a messtable.

"I reckon we've found Good Duty, huh, Smitty?" said Sharkey, soberly. "Goddamn, when was the last time you sat down before a spread like this?"

Later, on the way back to our tent, Smith, in response to an earlier question I had asked about duty on a destroyer, poked me and said, "Well, I'll tell you, kid, about life on a tincan. I like a whole lot better standin' one fuckin' watch a day and doin' nothin' but starin' at a typewriter. I do not like starin' for four goddamned hours runnin' at a fuckin' green window. I want no more midwatches and *no* more rollin' decks!"

"And," said Sharkey with exaggerated emphasis, "I want no more shit situations where you stand in line smellin' officers' chow and then find yourself havin' to eat something a dog wouldn't have no part of."

"We just had officers' chow," agreed Smith. "I've never in all the time I've been in the Navy, had officers' chow."

Back at the tent, they broke out cigarettes and settled on their bunks to pump me. I went outide and circled the tent, rolling up the lower three feet on the front and back sides to catch the breeze from the harbor; and when I went back inside and began to fuss with my mosquito netting, they were ready for me.

"Do we eat like that everyday?" asked Sharkey. "What's breakfast like?"

I laid it on thick and did some bragging about the other places around Noumea where Armed Forces personnel could eat. "And at none of these places do you even have to have a chow chit."

"Jesus Christ," said Sharkey. "Imagine that. Let us hope we can keep this duty for the duration, Smitty."

"You're joking," I said. "Wouldn't you really rather be on a ship heading north, helping out with the War Effort?"

"Hell no!" shouted Sharkey. "You nuts?" After a moment, he added, "You're shittin' me, right?"

"You mean you don't want to go back and kick the shit out of the Japs?"

They got up as one, tossed their cigarettes on the floor, went into crouches, and began to creep in on me. I took a step backward, trying to ignore them. "The war is not going to last forever. First thing we know, it'll all be over and—"

Suddenly, they were on top of me, with Sharkey at my throat and Smith trying to hold my feet. Down came my carefully constructed mosquito net, then the cot collapsed at one corner, and finally out onto the skimpy grass of the hillside we went, rolling and thrashing.

"Let us put an end to this kind of shit!" choked out Sharkey, red in the face. "Hold his goddamn feet, Smith!"

While a growing number of noncoms gathered to offer advice to me, I managed to get Sharkey on his back and sit on his chest. Smith tried to struggle away from me, but I pulled him in on top of Sharkey.

Suddenly, all struggling ceased.

"All right, all right!" screamed Sharkey. "Let us up! You big dumb kid! We just wanted to—!"

    *   *   *

"Show us one of your night spots, Hall," said Sharkey one afternoon. "You do know what I mean, don't you?"

The three of us had gone through the chow line together and Sharkey had chosen a table close to the officers, hoping to pick up some scuttlebutt. It turned out that they were chitchatting about nothing of importance; so we filed out upon the little cobblestone yard that separated the mess tent from the main building.

"There are no nightspots in Noumea, as far as I know," I said, gazing off toward the harbor. "But I could take you down to the end of the *Rue de la Pais* and show you Ile Nou Island."

"What the hell's that?" asked Sharkey.

"That's where the penal colony used to be, where the Navy Repair Base and a NATS outfit are now," I said, sounding like a long-time resident of the island. "A lot of little ships tie up there for repairs."

"What kind of 'little ships'?" frowned Sharkey. "For Christ's sake, you're not interested in going north on a yippy boat, are you?"

"All kinds of little ships, PT boats, subchasers, minesweepers—"

"Christamighty!" spat Sharkey. "Why would we want to see such a sight as that?"

"Doesn't sound like much to me," agreed Smith, looking sad. "How about MOB-Five Beach? Where the nurses are."

"Can't," I said quickly. "It'll be dark before long, and the enlisted swimming beach will be closed. Besides, you wouldn't be allowed to get near the nurses."

"I didn't say I wanted to go swimmin'," grinned Sharkey, with a wink in Smitty's direction. "Where there's a nurse there's got to be a way."

"They're off-limit to us," I said. "How about going down to the Red Cross tent? There's always a woman or two around there."

After shaking his head resolutely, followed by a prolonged spitting out of bits and pieces of a cigarette butt, Sharkey glanced at Smitty and said, "Might as well, huh?"

"Maybe after we walk off our suppers we could get a do-nut and a cup of coffee," I suggested.

"Hell and damnation," said Sharkey.

"Free do-nuts?" asked Smitty, yawning.

"That's what they call them, but they'll cost you ten cents each. It's a donation."

"That figures," said Sharkey. "A donation to help those less fortunate than us. But if it costs ten cents to get to talk to a living, breathing female, I say let's invest heavily."

"I haven't even seen a white woman for close to a year," said Smith. "Do they still have teats and butts?"

This was obviously aimed at me.

"The ones here on the island do," I assured him. "And heads and legs and—"

"I hear tell there's a house of ill repute here in Noumea," said Sharkey. "Know anything about that?"

Without hesitating I said, "I never heard of any such house. Of 'ill repute'?"

"That figures," said Sharkey, disgusted. "How long you been on this island?"

"About a month. And since the day after I got here I've been trying to get a transfer to a ship heading north."

We had drifted to the end of the cobblestone in front of the Comseron building, and at that point we turned right onto a street that dropped quickly down toward the center of town. Through the trees that lined either side of the street we could see the lights of Noumea coming on.

"This smells like Chink City," commented Sharkey. "What does laundry cost here, Hall?"

"I do my own," I said. We were walking past wide, flat-roofed residences, and in front of each was a large sign in Chinese. "I've often wondered what all that writing is."

"Hell!" laughed Sharkey. "You don't have to know what they say to know what's inside! Get a whiff of that!"

The Red Cross Tent was on the edge of the Square; and its top, which we could see long before we got there, was higher than the gazebo in the center of the Square, where the French band played on Sunday afternoons.

"I've never been down here at night," I explained, "except to pass through on my way back from the French class I'm taking."

"What French class?" asked Sharkey. "Don't tell me—"

"Twice a week. My teacher's the island Governor's daughter. She's eighteen and so beautiful it makes you hurt inside."

"The hell you say!" exclaimed Smitty. "And you had the balls to sign up for her class?"

Both of them had come to an abrupt stop and were staring at me as though I had done something earthshaking.

"Right now she's teaching irregular verbs."

"Goddamn!" burst out Sharkey. "How do we get into her class?"

"You can't. They've already started, and she won't take any more students. I guess she'll teach another class, but that won't be for another six or eight weeks."

"That figures," said Sharkey. "But maybe you could introduce me to her so I could check on takin' the class later."

"I don't much think so," I said.

By now we were actually hearing stateside music, which had to be coming from the Red Cross tent. It must have startled Sharkey and Smith because for a time neither of them had anything to say. As we neared the Square, a lively song fresh from home started up. It was a crazy thing.

"'Mairzy doats and dozey doats an' little lamsey divy!'" I sang, trying to stay with the music.

"What'n hell kind of song is that?" demanded Sharkey. "It don't make no sense at all!"

"'Kids'lly divy, too, wouldn't you?'"

Sharkey was shaking his head in disgust, but Smith slapped me on the shoulder playfully.

"It's the latest hit from the States," I informed them, "and if you hope to get any woman's attention on this island you'll have to learn the words to it. The Governor's daughter, now, loves it."

"You horse's ass!" spat Sharkey. "You think you're pretty smart, don't you? There aint no way I will learn that stupid song!"

"Actually," I said, now deadly serious, "the words are easy: 'Mares eat oats and does eat oats and little lambs eat ivy. Kids will eat ivy, too, wouldn't you."

"It's the dumbest thing I ever heard," complained Sharkey.

"It'll grow on you," I assured him, thoroughly enjoying his discomfiture.

At the door of the tent a very pretty young woman in a tight-fitting Red Cross uniform stopped Sharkey with a stiff finger in the chest. "Sorry, uniforms only. But that young man can come in!" To me she said, "What's your name, sailor?"

I told her, finding it hard not to laugh.

"Well, you come right in and make yourself at home. Try a cup of our fresh coffee down there at the end of the room. Would you like to listen to some Stateside music? We've got some records I'm just sure you'll love."

I was about to take her up on the offer when Sharkey caught me by an arm.

"Listen, buddy boy, you knew all along we had to be in uniform! And you let us walk a mile—"

"And going back it'll all be up hill," sighed Smith.

"This is a spit-and-polish town," I said. "You can't go to the head in dungarees around here."

From the Red Cross Tent we headed across the Square, at one point pausing in front of Admiral Halsey's Comsopac Fleet Headquarters.

"Where can we git some liquor?" asked Sharkey, gawking at the two-storey stucco-and-tile building. "I've heard tell a man can git drunk on two shots of the butterfly rum in this town."

Disgusted, I started off down the street. Over my shoulder I said, "I've heard it'll make you go blind, if it doesn't kill you first."

"Nobody asked you for a lecture on its effects," called out Sharkey. "Just tell us where it's located."

"Yeah," sighed Smith, "nobody lives forever."

"I'd rather die in a good cause, like fighting for my country," I said, pausing and waiting for them to catch up. "If you die that way—"

"Shit," complained Sharkey, "I wish you'd grow up. Sometimes you sound just like my little ten-year-old brother."

"If you don't cut out the shit, boy," put in Smith, "we'll leave you back at home next time."

I knew he was just kidding, but I stopped in my tracks and announced, "Listen, if you fellows don't want me along, I'll go on back right now. I'll not be someplace I'm not wanted."

"Forget it," said Sharkey. "We was just kiddin'. Where can we git some butterfly rum?"

I pointed toward a well-lighted two-story building directly head of us. "They sell a little of just about anything you want in there."

"Maybe they sell some you-know-what!" chuckled Smith. "How about askin' for us, Hall?"

"I don't know what you're talking about," I said, seriously thinking of returning to Comseron. After a time, I added, "I guess they sell more souvenirs in there than anyplace else in town. Stuff made out of shells and straw."

"Do they sell girls?" demanded Sharkey.

"Nobody sells *girls*!"

"Tell us, Hall, are you a virgin?" asked Sharkey. He reached up and grabbed me by the shoulders. "Don't lie about it, now. Have you ever been with a woman?" He tried to shake me, but I just stood there, solid on my feet.

When he dropped his hands, I grabbed him by the throat and slowly began to tighten my grip. Into his left ear I said just loud enough for him to hear, "None of your business, mate!"

"Okay, okay," whined Sharkey, "let up, boy!"

I released my hold and Sharkey slowly lowered himself to the cobble-stone sidewalk, faking extreme pain.

"I grew up on a farm a long way from girls," I began. Then in a lighter tone, "I did have a memorable time with my first cousin, Omey, one time. In an apple tree. Would she count?"

"What about her!" coughed Sharkey. "My God, what strength you have in them hands of yours!"

"Did you go to bed with this cousin?" asked Smith.

"Not really. We were up in an apple tree."

"'In an apple tree'!" burst out Smith. "Come on!"

"She was up in the top of this big apple tree, and when I passed below her she began pelting me with apples, daring me to climb up and stop her. Well, when I started up that tree, I saw she didn't have anything on under her dress. I began laughing and that caused her to fall out of the tree on top of me." I knew I must be blushing by this time because I could feel the heat rising in my face.

"She fell on you?" exclaimed Sharkey. "Then what did you do?"

"She was a pretty big girl, and first thing I knew I was lying on my back and she was sitting on my stomach."

"So? So? For Christ's sake!" cried Sharkey.

"Well, I tried to get up, but she wouldn't let me."

"My god!" exclaimed Sharkey. "You just laid there?"

"I said she was sitting right on top of me! And she was so heavy I couldn't do anything. She unbuttoned my trousers—"

"Well, I'll be goddamned," sighed Sharkey. To Smith, he moaned, "The kid was raped. Did you ever hear such a story before? In Chicago, if you git a pussy up a tree without skivvies—"

At this point, interrupting himself, the radarman yelled, "Hellfire, man, give us some details!"

"She played around with me for a time, then got up and ran off. I never could catch her. She was bigger than me, you know."

"That figures," said Sharkey, disgusted. "You was about ten and she was about—"

"You're close. I was twelve and she was fourteen."

"Goddamn." Sharkey's face was tragic to look upon. "And nothin' since, I'd say."

For a time we stood, wordless, and stared at the brightly-lighted store before us. Then Sharkey put his hand on my shoulder. "Now, Hall, old buddy, I want you to go into that place and ask if they sell cunt. Don't be bashful. Come right out and ask if they sell cunt. Smith and me'll wait right here for you."

"That'll be the day," I said with a determined shake of my head. Then I turned abruptly and headed back across the Square toward Comseron.

2

Navy Logic

One afternoon before evening chow the three of us settled in our tent, with them sitting on their cots smoking and me stretched out on mine with a writing pad and a pencil. Even with the sides of our tent rolled high, it was extremely hot inside, so hot I got up and carefully gathered all the mosquito netting on each side of my cot and stored it on top. Silently, my tentmates chain-smoked, flipping their ashes across the dirt floor. Then, instead of returning to my note pad, I sat down on my cot and tossed out:

"I wonder what's going on up north. Guadalcanal was quite a skirmish, I guess."

"Is that what you think it was?" demanded Sharkey, flipping his cigarette into the center of the tent in disgust. "A goddamned 'skirmish'?"

"Yeah," agreed Smith, looking tragic.

"Have either one of you seen any *kamikazes*?"

"Where in hell did you hear about that?" demanded Sharkey. "Look, what do you want to go up north for? What's it gonna git you, goin' up there and bein' shot at? For damn sure, you don't want to see no *kamikazes*."

He began to talk about the good duty we had on New Caledonia, eventually contrasting it with the hell up north. Smith had gotten rid of his tenth cigarette and was flat out on his back, with his hands behind his head. It was still too early for the mosquitoes, but he had pulled the netting down around his cot, as if he thought that would shut out the thought of what it was like up north.

I hated to hear Sharkey run down the war, but I had a lot of respect for him and Smith. When it came to what was going on up in the Solomons and on north in the New Guinea area, they knew what they were talking about. And as much as I hated to admit it, they probably deserved a rest on peaceful New Caledonia.

"You blind or somethin'?" Sharkey was saying. "Here on New Caledonia you've got just about everything a man could want in life, except maybe women. But if you go north the only women you'll see will be as black as the ace of spades with bones in their ears. You've got six or eight outdoor theaters here and at least that number of eating places plus the Red Cross Recreation Tent with free donuts and coffee and them little Frenchy joints down there around the Square with butterfly rum, and don't forget MOB-5 Beach and the nurses."

"The donuts are a dime apiece, and the nurses are off-limits," I said, off-handedly.

Sharkey leaped up and threw his cigarette out through the tent opening. "Well, hell, I know they're off-limits! I meant *to look at*. What do you git to look at up north? Water, water, water—and maybe a fuckin' deserted atoll with a few miserable coconut palms on it. At least out at MOB-5 you can look at well-built nurses."

Smith, still lying on his back, had begun to clean and trim his toenails. It was a job he took care of religiously, three times a day, immediately before each chow. "This is sure a hell of a lot better'n being shot at by the Japs."

"If I'd wanted to sit out the war—" I began.

"You some kind of grandstander?" snapped Sharkey.

"You're the hero, not me," I said. "I wish I'd had some of the action you've had."

"Shit! You don't know what you're talkin' about! I dang near bought the farm and you set there and talk about how nice it'd be to go through the same thing! I don't think I ever saw anybody as stubborn and ignorant as you are!"

That afternoon I took it upon myself to go to the laundry for all three of us. This was a concrete annex to the recreation hut and included the showers and the head. I gathered up all of the skivvies and socks strung out about the tent, most of which were Sharkey's. and stuffed them inside pillowcases, feeling rather good about the favor I was doing my buddies. Later, going all out, I rolled their socks boot camp style and folded the shorts and shirts so that their names were facing outward.

I completed this good deed by stacking the clothes in neat piles on the pillows; then, intending to write some in my notebook, I stretched out on my cot and fell quickly into a deep sleep. Sometime later I woke myself up coughing. Sharkey was leaning over me blowing smoke into my face!

"My god, kid! What have you been up to? Look at what this nut has done, Smitty!"

By this time I was wide awake and staring at him. I did not like the tone of his voice.

"Why'd you go to all that fuckin' trouble?" he complained. With that he grabbed the pile of carefully folded whites on his pillow and tossed it into his open seabag, which hadn't been completely unpacked since his arrival. "You beat all! God, I feel like I'm back home with my old woman!"

I said nothing at all and after a great deal of fussing about his cot, Sharkey said in a quieter tone, "Look, kid, I'm sorry for shoutin' at you. Thanks for the laundry job."

The following Monday afternoon when my two tentmates came in from work, they were talking about a softball game and beer party the Com Office was planning. According to scuttlebutt it was an annual affair and nobody had better miss out on it because the brass was behind it.

"Hell, Commander Farris said it was like a country retreat," purred Smith. "With a club house and a big grassy area for baseball and beautiful shade trees right down to the beach."

Sharkey put his short, chubby arm over my shoulders. "I need some skivvies, ole buddy, and I'll bet a sawbuck you know where Ship's Stores is on this island."

"There's one down near the docks," I said, "but I've never been to it. And there's one out at the Receiving Station."

"Forget it," said Smith. "He's in la-la land again."

"Yeah," said Sharkey, "I guess you're right."

"What do you mean?" I asked. "I've never been to Ship's Stores. All my stuff's still new."

"Hell, I just thought—" whined Sharkey, pathetically.

I suddenly blurted out something that had been on my mind for sometime: "Tell you what, Sharkey, you promise to help me get off this island and I'll find Ship's Stores and buy you all the skivvies you want, with my own money."

Sharkey looked at Smith, "Aint it pathetic?"

"Let's help the thankless whelp," said Smith, sounding terribly disappointed. "He deserves to be up north gettin' his ass shot off."

"Okay," sighed Sharkey. To me he said quite formally, "Any kind of ship at all, right?"

"It doesn't really matter!" I yelped, suddenly alive. "I'll settle for a row boat, if I have to."

"All right. First off, you've got to fuck up."

I stared at him. "What! That wouldn't get me a ship! More than likely I'd end up in the brig out at the Receiving Station!"

"Well, you might at that," said Sharkey, "but you've got to understand something here and now. About Navy logic, right?" He looked at Smith for confirmation. Then he stuck his nose into my face. "Huh? Navy logic doesn't work like any other kind of logic in the world. Step One, in a case like this, is fucking up royally. Our job—" (He pointed first at himself and then at Smith) "—'ll be to figure out *how royal* and exactly what you'll have to do to bring it off."

"Right," said Smith. "Explain Navy logic to the boy, Shark."

"All right." Suddenly, Sharkey's voice became that of a very old wise man. "This will not be easy for you. Are you up to it?"

By now I was on the edge of my cot. "I would do just about anything if—!"

"We know, we know," comforted Sharkey. "But you've been using common ordinary logic all this time. That doesn't work in the Modern Navy. Now, listen up. In this outfit today you've got to figure out not necessarily the opposite of common logic but what *would be* the opposite of what the Navy brass thinks you really want to do and/or are qualified to do. Understand?"

Smith was shaking his head doubtfully.

"You lost me completely," I admitted, frowning.

"All right, let me give you an example," said Sharkey. "Let's say you have a special talent as a cook and you like to cook more than anything else in the world. Common logic says you ought to be in the galley cookin' up all kinds of things. Right? Well, Navy logic says that because you are good at this and want to do it for a living you should be a grease monkey or a boatswain's mate or something that would get you as far away from the galley as possible. The logic here is that it is not good to give enlisted men what they want even if they're good at it, because if you do they'll become complacent and/or proud and maybe troublesome. To keep down shit every enlisted man must be put in slots for which they have no aptitude and no interest. If an officer thinks you do not want something in the worst way, he is likely to give it to you. Conversely, if an officer thinks you want something, he is more than likely to see to it that you do not get it. He does this to keep down insurrection and mutiny."

For time the radarman busied himself with rolling a cigarette and taking out a kitchen match and zipping it along his right leg a number of times. Then, staring me in the face with great sincerity, he added. "He does it in the name of *morale*. His own." Then, without taking his eyes off me, he lighted the cigarette and puffed smoke in my face.

"That's rather accurate," agreed Smith, nodding. "So you have to make the Navy brass think you want what you don't want and/or that you are most contented in what you are doin' and never want to change. That is, if you really want to get a transfer. Shark and I plan to complain a lot about this assignment here at Comseron."

"Right," said Sharkey. "And, to git the brass's attention, you have to fuck up. It has to be a real heinous crime in their eyes, not murder or anything like that, but something spelled out in Naval Regulations that brings into question your fitness to be called a Navy swab. And once you've done this, then you do your damnedest to make the brass think you'll do anything in the world to stay put right here on this island. You're contrite and you're scared to death of being sent north."

"Make them think you'd rather die than go north," said Smith. "That way they'll make sure that's where you'll go. You have to give them a hint about where not to send you."

"Now," said Sharkey, "are we ready for Step One?"

"I don't know if I can do this," I said, shaking my head. "I've got a very good service record—"

Sharkey held up his hand, scowling. "Now, there, see? You don't have a record at all. Nobody knows you're alive in the Navy, outside of Smitty and me. And maybe the Commander, who seems to like you in an unnaval way. Do you think the big brass knows you're alive?"

"And," said Smith, "how could you have a good record when you've never done a single thing since you enlisted? You have a blank record."

"Well, they transferred me here so they ought to know I exist."

"No, no, no!" argued Sharkey, patting me on the shoulder. "They don't pay any attention to particulars like *who* is going *where*. They look only at a swab's rating and whether the swab has fucked up or not.

Names don't mean anything to them at all. They're far more interested in your number than they are your name."

"You're really just a serial number and a rating," said Smith, nodding.

Sharkey broke in, "Actually, in your case, they're not even interested in your rating. This outfit needed a raw-assed second class seaman to carry the mail, and some yeoman came up with your service record. Do you want to go north, or are you just pretendin' you want to go north? Maybe to impress somebody back home?"

"I think he thinks he's sincere," cautioned Smith, pretending to erase what Sharkey had just said. "But it may be a subconscious thing that's happening here. All this talk may be to assuage his own self-esteem."

I was staring first at one and the other of these two old salts, and I could feel a great deal of heat in my face. "I swear to God I want to go north!"

"Well, all right," said Sharkey, sounding relieved. "Listen up then. I think I've got it. The nurses out at MOB-Five Beach. What would happen if an enlisted man decided to go swimmin' with them? Went out, crawled under the rope that separates them from the rest of the world and went swimmin' with them?"

"An enlisted man?" asked Smith, cupping his chin in deep meditation. "Hmmm. Good question."

I said, matter-of-factly, "He would be busted and sent to Mare Island for life! He'd be dishonorably discharged, and he'd never get to see his folks again."

"No, you're wrong," said Sharkey. "None of this would happen to him. It might if he tried something like this back in the States and it was peacetime, but out here, with the war on up north? Not a chance. You see, our here in New Caledonia there's something worse than all of those things you mentioned that the brass can do to an enlisted man that has screwed up royally."

"And what is worse than Mare Island and a D. D., in the brass's arsenal of punishment our here?" asked Smith, rhetorically. "Tell him, Shark."

Sharkey's big peasant face was right in mine now. Our noses were practically touching.

"Do you know what the brass thinks every enlisted man thinks is a hell on Earth, worse even than Mare Island, dishonorable discharge, and death?"

I waited, knowing he was going to tell me whether I wanted to hear it or not.

Sharkey was almost shouting now, "Ever' officer in the U. S. Navy is *gung ho kill the Japs*, but they all think enlisted men are scared shitless and ever'one of them wants to go back to the States as soon as possible! Nobody could convince them a patriotic boy like you even exists!"

"You could talk all day and they would never believe that you really want to go north," said Smith. "And if they did believe you, you would surely never get to go there."

"Then why are they keepin' me here?" I demanded.

"Very simple," countered Smith. "As far as the brass is concerned, you don't even exist. They don't even know you want or don't want anything. You've never done anything wrong."

"He's the kind of clean-faced kid they like to keep around," said Sharkey, throwing up his hands in disgust. "Let me spell it out for you, mate. If you go out to MOB-Five Beach and go swimmin' with the nurses, you'll antagonize the brass so much they'll send you north on the very next ship. It's just about the only crime that would get you there from this island, but sure as hell that one would. You see, the brass does not want enlisted men to get close to the women. Women are their property. That's in Naval Regulations. Enlisted men must act like little boys, not men. It makes the brass nervous as hell when they don't act like little boys. They want us to remain in our segregated, celibate world.

"If you should kill one of these Melanesian natives or maybe a Frenchman, they would give you ten days in the brig. Now, if you killed an Army dogface or a girene or even another sailor—I'm talking about enlisted personnel—you'd probably get Mare Island and a D. D. But if you spend an afternoon with the ladies out at MOB-Five Beach, you'll be sent north on some kind of ship. North to hell."

"He's right," said Smith, with finality. "Or you could kill a Navy officer." He began erasing that quickly. "Forget I said that. The punishment for such a crime would be instant death and dismemberment. You want to get on a ship?"

"If you go out swim with the nurses, I guarantee you you'll go north," nodded Sharkey. "Right, Smitty?" To me he raised his big bushy eyebrows and said, "What is it goin' to be?"

"The nurse thing," I said, feeling very sick at my stomach. "If you're sure it'll get me a ship."

Looking quite pleased with themselves, my tentmates lighted up fresh cigarettes and sat back on their cots.

*   *   *

Rear Admiral L. J. Johnson was quiet possessive about his little service squadron on the hill, an assignment which had dropped out of Naval heaven (via Bull Halsey) like an inheritance from a relative he never knew he had. He felt a particular affection for each of the quonset huts down on the *Rue de L'Amour*, having seen to the details of their location and construction himself, and even for the mess tent and the small village of enlisted men's tents on the hillside above his headquarters building. It was his wartime hobby; and, if he played his cards right, it just might lead to something really big, like another star and the quarterdeck of one of the new battlewagons rolling out of the shipyards back home.

His own residence was on the second floor of the picturesque old stucco building that had once been a first-rate civilian home. It was actually three rooms and a bath on the back end of the house, and the roominess and old-world accommodations reminded him of a Victorian dwelling he had once lived in as an undergraduate student at the University of Chicago.

In the early evenings, after the hustle and bustle of his little family doing their various jobs in the rest of the house, he would relax in his quarters with a tall fruity, vodka concoction, which he would make himself, and, until two minutes before the movie was to roll (It couldn't roll with his presence), entertain fellow staff officers from both Comsopac and Comseronsopac and the nurses from MOB-Five Hospital. On these occasions he dressed informally in white linen trousers (military style), a colorful short-sleeve silk shirt, and white canvas shoes. And his diction, on these occasions, would became decidedly Southern and accommodating.

The movie theater was, in his opinion, at the top of the long list of his accomplishments; and it had become, through his own delegated efforts, a strong drawing card for him in his relentless pursuit of the attention of the higher brass down at Comsopac. Indeed, it drew officers of all ranks from the various branches of the Armed Services, as well as the cream of the local civilian population. And occasionally it landed for him a really big duck from Cincpac, in Honolulu.

Admiral Halsey had never actually attended one of his movies, but there was always the distinct possibility that it could happen. He had fantasized about such an honor being bestowed upon him, beginning with a telephone call from Flag Allowance. "Luther, this is Cameron, down the street from you. Think you could cordon off about fifty seats tonight for the Admiral and his entourage?" There would be a tightening of security as the day advanced, and by sixteen hundred hours the whole compound would be fenced off and placed under the guard of the Admiral's spit-and-polish body guard, the First Platoon of the First Marine Division.

He would, of course, be asked to sit down front with the Admiral and his staff. And it was altogether likely that he would be asked to say a few words about his service squadron. Perhaps he would be asked to introduce the movie. On his own he might stand before the National Anthem and say a few words to the men of his command, something about giving it their all, pride in the outfit, that sort of thing.

His conviction that he was destined for greater things kept him ever alert to the little nuances of his command, the pieces that made up the big puzzle. And it was this alertness to detail that eventually led him to become aware of my existence, and, incidentally, that of Sharkey and Smith.

"Tell me something about your new messenger boy," he said one day to Comdr. B. L. Farris, his Chief of Communications. "How's he working out, Bert?"

"Well, he's not lazy and he's not as incompetent as Braden, the kid he replaced. Why do you ask?"

"Okay," nodded the Admiral, "that's two things he's not. How's he behavin'?"

The commander's eyebrows went up. "Well, interesting you should ask. We moved two tincan sailors in with him awhile back, a second class sonarman by the name of Sharkey and a first class radarman by the name of Smith. Both lost their ships up around the Solomons; and if I'm not badly mistaken, they had something to do with the mess this boy's presently in."

"'Mess'? What mess?"

"Well, it seems he went out to the beach at the U. S. Navy Mobile Hospital Number Five one afternoon recently and ducked under the line that separates the enlisted beach from the officers' and spent the entire afternoon fraternizing with the nurses. They even gave him a lift back into town, delivered him right up here to our door like it was perfectly natural for him to be—"

"My God," said the admiral, frowning. "'Fraternized', you say? An enlisted man? When did this happen, recently you say?"

"Yes, sir. I was going to include it in my weekly summary later this morning. He will have to be disciplined, of course. We can't have enlisted mixin' with—"

"Well, hellfire and damnation, I guess not."

"I think he ought to be recycled. Maybe we could give him to Cincpac."

"You think this Smith and the other one talked him into it?"

"Yes, I do. I think it might've started out as a dare, on that other one's part. Sharkey, the radarman. But one thing I'm certain of is that they put him up to it."

"Is he a half-wit?"

"Not at all. Maybe a bit naive, but he's got good potential, I think. And he thinks the world of these knuckleheaded tentmates of his. I'm convinced if they told him to go swimming with the nurses he'd do it. He probably wasn't even aware that—"

"Well," mused the admiral, "you handle it. Get him out of here. And keep a close eye on Smith and Jones. The first time you get something concrete on them, mail them north on whatever's available."

3

Ace

The tincan went down ass first. And with it all of Ace McCormick's worldly goods, including a letter from Dolly that said in four pages what he already knew the instant he saw the "Dear Ace" beginning. He watched her go down and once the chewed-up fantail got under water she looked clean and sleek, like she always did. Not a barnacle on her. All the trouble was back around the stern, he figured.

Anyway, he was by himself in the middle of a lot of rubble and so didn't need the bundlesome Mae West he'd hung onto right up till the moment he got ready to jump. Then he couldn't find the fucker and had to jump without it.

After the old *Bryan* went down and everything got quiet, he heard moaning off in the distance and began dog-paddling toward the sound. Finally, he saw a helmet bobbing amidst some gooney birds, who must've thought they had found supper. It turned out to be Willoughby, from the black gang and he was alternately spitting out water and cursing the fickle finger of fate.

Ace recognized the voice of the grease monkey but for some reason couldn't concentrate on what he was saying. That's when he realized he was in pretty bad shape himself. He was bleeding in several places around the neck and shoulders, and apparently his right leg was broken just above the ankle.

But the funny thing was he hadn't felt any pain at all.

Willoughby, beginning to blubber like an idiot, wallowed around in his lifejacket and yelled, "That you, McCormick? You all right?" Things were becoming pretty hazy about then, but Ace remembered later telling him he felt fine but that everything looked blurred. The last thing he remembered saying was, "Goddamn clouds!"

Then he woke up on a firm white bed and Snow White was bending over him with a needle at the ready position. At least it looked like Snow White to him, appearing as she did out of the mists and clouds of nowhere. Later, he learned that he was in a Navy hospital on the island of New Caledonia. Outside his window was a big sign that said: UNITED STATES NAVAL MOBILE HOSPITAL NUMBER FIVE, Noumea, New Caledonia.

It took some time but Comsopac finally got the paperwork together on him and moved him out to the big smelly Receiving Station, where he limped around pathetically for weeks, pretending until the end to be too stove up to go on work details.

He wasn't paying much attention to the slow passage of time, but one day somebody said it was October and he said, "What year?" And he wasn't kidding. It was around the middle of July, 1943, when the *Bryan* took that direct hit on the stern and went down, and he was thinking that maybe if he'd skipped four months he just might have skipped a year and four months.

But he hadn't. It was still 1943.

The summary court martial proceedings caught up with him during the fourth week of his convalescence at the receiving station, about the time he had forgotten all about the shit he had been in on the *Bryan*. In fact, by then he'd begun to think maybe the Navy had either lost his records or decided just to let bygones be bygones. But he should have known better than that.

The officer he had laid out, instead of going down with the ship with the others, was there in person, smart-assed as ever and anxious to relate the details and standby for the sentencing; but when all Ace got was a reduction in rank, two weeks in the brig, and restriction to the compound for a month, it took some of the starch out of his prissiness.

To his girene lawyer, Ace said, "I guess he wanted me shot."

"He got most of what he wanted, your Chief's rating," said the lawyer with a grin.

The restriction was even dropped a day or so later, since Ace had already spent the better part of five months convalescing and goldbricking. But he was still waiting for the other shoe to fall. It was his opinion that in the U. S. Navy you don't strike an officer and walk away from it unbloodied. It might take awhile, but the brass would surely come up with a more fitting punishment for him than the loss of his CPO rating.

To the Marine lieutenant, who was feeling good about the outcome of the trial, he said, "I guess beltin' that officer was a real snafu."

The lieutenant nodded. "But one thing in your favor was losing your ship. That hurt the prosecution."

On Saturdays and Sundays at the Receiving Station those that hadn't fucked up during the week were given liberty. His first liberty Ace went lookin' for a cat house he'd been hearing about that was supposed to be located down around the docks in Noumea. According to one veteran of that house of tarnished reputation it was not far from the Square on a street named the *Rue de Rimbaud*. But being unfamiliar with the street names in this Jewel of the Lower Pacific, Ace dropped into a little bar on the Square and invested in a tall, lukewarm-warm glass of joy juice and looked around for somebody to ask directions.

The bartender was a Melanesian woman who spoke just enough English to take his money, but in a booth on the front wall a white-haired Chief Gunner's Mate was whispering sweet nothings to a young white girl in a Red Cross uniform.

He tapped the Chief Petty Officer on the shoulder, "Sorry to cut in like this, Chief, but—"

"Then don't. Can't you see we're busy?"

"Just thought maybe you could direct me to an establishment called the Pink House."

"You must be new in town," sighed the Chief, glancing hastily at the girl. "Go down *Rue de la Pais.*" He pointed a thumb toward the window at his right shoulder. "Three blocks and take a left on Rimbaud. You can't miss it. Just look for a long line of dogfaces and swabjockies in front of a big ugly red building."

Ace finished his drink at the bar and went out on the sidewalk and stood facing the Square. Without putting any thought into it, he rolled a Bull Durham cigarette (using only one hand), holding the draw-string between his teeth. His new undress whites, fresh from the Receiving Station's Ship's Stores, were tight on the left side of the crotch, a danger- ous reminder that all the saltpeter of the old *Bryan* had left his system. He glanced up the street to his right, contemplated the big sign in front of a two-story stucco-and-tile office building: "COMSOPAC, Flag Allowance, Admiral William F. Halsey, C. O." Then he lighted his cigarette and stood for a time enjoying its deep-down goodness and thinking about what was down on Rimbaud Street.

The Pink House was the first thing he had heard about New Caledonia. It was, he had been told, the most famous building between Honolulu and Sidney, a thing of legend and song, the home away from home of thousands of old Navy salts. The U. S. Navy, Army, Marines, and the armies of New Zealand and Australia had found it only since Pearl Harbor; but merchant sailors from around the world had known about it for many years, maybe as far back as the island's discovery by Captain Cook.

In good time he proceeded down *Rue de la Pais*, found *Rimbaud* and took a left. And there it was, at the end of a long line of khaki and undress whites. He had no idea what time it was, but from the bare backs of many of the soldiers and sailors, it had to be close to noon.

To the casual tourist the Pink House was quite an uninspiring exam- ple of late seventeenth century French-Oriental architecture. Looking at it from a detached viewpoint, which was the only way Ace looked at anything, it was hardly more than a plain old two-story stucco built like an apple crate, without one touch of human warmth about it. If there had ever been a shutter or a window box or a piece of gingerbread about it, no evidence of it remained. And although it may have been pink at one time, it was now a dirty, washed-out brown.

Around the Pink House, however, other structures (such as the recently painted white-stucco and red-tiled "U. S. Navy Ship's Stores, Noumea, New Caledonia") were well-maintained and quite respectable in appearance.

Ace saw the line of servicemen long before he caught his first glimpse of the building itself. At that point he had stopped and checked to make certain he had the required ten bucks. Then he fell in behind the last man, a smartly-dressed Aussie serviceman.

While he was sizing up the situation and calculating his E. T. A., based upon distance (to the entrance) and speed (of the line), I rounded a street corner a block away and instantly concluded that I had indeed found the Ship's Store line. Everyone in sight was a serviceman; so where else could the line be going?

Just to be on the safe side, I asked the man on the end line if this was the Ship's Store line.

Ace had not had a good laugh since San Pedro. For a time he studied my face, convinced that I was joking but cautious. He did not laugh immediately because, one, I just might turn out to be a smart-ass kid trying to pull his leg, in which case it wasn't all that funny; and, two, if I really was looking for the Ship's Stores line, here was a situation that needed some encouragement. His answer was, "What else kind of line could it be?" Then, testing the waters, he added, "It's been a long time for me. How about you?"

"Oh, not too long," I said. "Maybe a couple of months."

"Yeah, sure," he nodded. "Do you mind if I asked how old you are?" He stopped and looked around at the Aussie, who laughed.

"He's wearin' a uniform, mate, so I guess he's old enough!"

"I'm eighteen," I said, wondering what was going on. "I've been in the Navy ever since last June." Then I told him my name and outfit and stuck out my hand.

Ace's long, bony hand snaked out. "McCormick, Cess Pool Thirty-one." After a time, he said, "Tell me, kid, how many times have you been in one of these places before?" He looked at the Aussie and the two of them burst out laughing.

I could not figure out what so funny, but I had decided this McCormick was quite harmless; so I said, "Several times, back in the States. I went to the one at Farragut a lot and once to that big one at Shoemaker."

Ace stared, his grin frozen on his face.

"You've been a lot of them, haven't you?"

Ace shook his head slowly, "Well, this is a first for me, but I've been in a lot just like it."

When we were nearing the end of the line, he said, looking wise and winking at the Aussie, "Well, watch out for the pickpockets. They'll steal you blind."

"Sure, you too. I always buy more stuff than I can afford."

At that point I caught sight of a faded and dilapidated sign over the door. It made no sense to me at all. I turned to McCormick and discovered that he was bent at the waist unlacing his shoes!

"What does that mean?" I blurted out, dumfounded. "Why should we take off our shoes? I'm not buying anything for the feet today."

At this McCormick burst out laughing. "You are jokin', right?" When I just gawked at him, he added, "You do know about local customs here, don't you?"

"'Local customs'? They don't allow you to go inside with your shoes on?"

"You got it, kid."

"Ah!" I said, hesitating. "That must be the Oriental influence down here in New Caledonia. Is this place run by the Chinese or somethin'?" I leaned forward, trying to see what was going on in the darkened interior of the place.

By this time McCormick was inside, holding his shoes in the crook of his right arm. He glanced at the Aussie, who nodded, grinning broadly. "I understand the head honcho here is a very big lady from Shanghai."

This wisecrack turned out to be surprisingly close to the mark, because just inside the door, we encountered an enormous, smiling Chinese woman, who was there to make sure everybody was shoeless. When she saw the startled look on my face, her smile broadened and she bounced out of her chair to welcome me.

"Come een, jung sailor, come een! Dere's end of line!" She pointed toward a bench on the wall to her left.

"Do I git the royal treatment, too?" asked McCormick with a laugh.

"You sit by nice jung man and behave, sailor," she scolded, faking a backhanded slap in his direction.

I could barely make out the bench at first; but shortly, as my eyes slowly adjusted, I began to stare in astonishment at the men at the head of the bench, who had undressed completely and wrapped their clothes around their shoes!

"Look, mate, the kid's blushin'!" McCormick said to the Aussie.

"What's going on here!" I burst out, leaping to my feet and staring about in amazement. "What are these men doing with all their clothes off?"

Unable to restrain himself, McCormick called out, "They're probably being fitted for tailor-made skivvies!"

At that moment, just as I was ready to bolt, a very fat black woman, wearing only a pair of sandals, pushed a door inward from the back wall and bellowed, "Next!" At that moment her eyes settled upon me. "Oh, wow wow wow!" She began to giggle and bounce!

Without so much as a glance in Ace's direction, I bolted from that den of inequity, down the room past the head honcho, who was laughing hysterically, and headlong into the impatient line just outside the door.

Ace followed me to the door and scanned the street, but I had already vanished. He turned and stared at the shiny black shoes on the bench, which seemed about to dash off, too. He undressed, placing the shoes on his pile of undress whites; then for the hell of it, he decided to hang onto them, with the idea that one day he pay me a visit at Comseron, just to see the look on my face and find out what kind of a story I told my buddies there.

         *   *   *

Perhaps a week after the Pink House incident, Ace received his long-expected orders. He had been hoping for a berth on one of the big boys of Halsey's fleet, perhaps a cruiser or a carrier; but after what had gone under the bridge he was willing to settle for another tincan. Maybe he would get one of the newer class cans that had been built since Pearl.

What he got was a shock that left him pale and speechless.

A pasty-faced, overweight yeoman at the Receiving Station Personnel Office, looking like a cat hovering over a wounded canary, couldn't wait to give him the news. He handed Ace a very fat manila envelope; and after remarking that Flag was working on his service records, delivered these encouraging words, "I don't know what it is, Mate, but my guess is it's about the size of a yippy boat."

Ace took the orders and glanced past the opening words, which he knew by heart.

"You seem particularly jolly about this transfer, Fatty."

"You struck an officer, right?" snapped the other. "I'm surprised they didn't hang you from the yardarm." He snickered and added, "I'll bet this *SC-995* hasn't even got one of those things."

"I'm a tincan man," Ace groaned, turning to leave.

"Not anymore you're not."

Although he had no idea what the *SC* stood for, he knew very well what it did not stand for. He stuffed the orders inside his shirt and headed back for the barracks. At the big bulletin board in front of the messhall he met Chief Garnes and Baldini, two old salty boatswain's mates, headed for the Pentagon.

"Now, here's a man that got screwed like me," said Baldini, happily. "Got it in the butt."

Garnes, looking like something out of a recruiting poster, put out his hand to stop Ace. "Got your orders? Where they sendin' you?"

"To hell."

Baldini laughed explosively.

"That's no sea-going ship," said Garnes, staring at the orders. "The *SC* must stand for small craft."

"Hell," chuckled Baldini, "they've screwed you royally, Mate."

"You know what happened," mused Garnes. "Somebody at Flag is out to get you. What'n hell did you do to land in something like that?"

"Hit an officer."

Baldini was visibly pleased. "I'm sure as hell glad they don't have something like that on me."

"Yeah," nodded Garnes, "all they got on you is deserting your battle station during that raid on Pearl. That and refusin' to obey a direct order in a general quarers condition."

"Well," said Ace, "I've got all day to report aboard so I guess I'll go down in Noumea and find something wet."

"Let me see your orders again," said Garnes with raised eyebrows. He reached inside Ace's shirt and removed the brown envelope. "In all the time I've been in this outfit, I have never seen a set of orders that would allow me time to get drunk. He unfolded the orders and studied them. "'Report immediately to the Commanding Officer of the SC995'. Just what I thought." He handed the orders to Baldini. "How do you interpret them?"

Baldini glanced at the top page and handed the orders back to Ace. "By the time you git your seabag to the front gate there'll be a Jeep waitin'. It'll take fifteen minutes to git you to the docks in Noumea and maybe another thirty minutes to reach your destination. LCVP's make that run to the Ile Nou Naval Supply Base ever' thirty minutes. So I'd say if you report one minute past noon chow you'll find yourself on report."

"Well, sure as hell I'll be on report then," nodded Ace. And with that he walked off, singing quietly, "I've got a Dolly with a hole in her stockin', her toes keep a rockin', her knees keep a knockin'."

"Poor, devil," said Garnes.

"Yeah," agreed Baldini. "Well, I'll tell you one thing. If they try to give me something like that—"

"Oh? What would you do, refuse to go?"

"I would go over the goddamn' hill. I'd go back in the hills—"

"The hell you would!" Garnes laughed at the thought, adding, "The *kanakis* would have you for supper the first night."

*   *   *

At thirteen hundred hours the following day Ace was transported by the Comsopac Duty Jeep from the Comsopac brig on Balzac Street to the docks at the foot of the *Rue de la Pais*. There, under the leveled gaze of a lieutenant wearing an SP armband, he caught a waiting LCVP to Ile Nou Island and got off at the NATS landing. There he stood for a minute holding his head with both hands as the small dock bobbled about. A very pretty Army nurse, amused at his appearance and garbled attempts at cursing, directed him to where the Supply Base had been the last time she had seen it. It was, of course, in plain view of where they were standing.

"Have you been in some kind of—fisticuffs?" she asked.

Ace nodded tentatively. "I guess you could call it that. Best I can remember—"

"Well, good luck, sailor."

Ace nodded and began to inch his way across the narrow walkway to dry land, dragging his new seabag and fifty pounds of new Naval

Regulation issues behind him. He did not want to look at an SC, much less board one of them. But there they were, bouncing up and down at their moorings. It was a beautifully calm day, and the surface of the harbor was glassy smooth. So why were those matchsticks at the dock leaping and pitching like that?

He was dressed in new soiled and wrinkled undress whites, minus the neckerchief. And the socks. He felt of his head again and was mildly surprised that his cap was still there. On the little hilltop above the smallcraft mooring he stopped and worked on it for a time, trying to get the brim back up and looking more or less salty. But in the end he gave up and jammed it down over his head. What the hell difference did it make what his fucking cap looked like? He would be spending the next ten days in the brig anyway.

"I've got a dolly," he moaned unhappily, taking the last few steps down to the dock. "Help me, Dolly, for I have sinned."

There were two wooden boats moored side-by-side at the point where the path from NATS ended. He stood unsteadily and read the numbers on each bow. "One three one eight. One oh six six." Then he moved down the dock, dragging his heavy seabag behind him. After what seemed a very long time he stopped and stared at two wooden boats moored side-by-side.

"Goddamn, I could've sworn—"

He blinked for a time and with a supreme effort read off the numbers on the bow of the nearest one: "Six six six." He grimaced, shaking his head: "I'm off that butterfly rum." The numbers on the second boat looked vaguely familiar: "Seven eleven." To a seagull walking on the dock he observed with a scowl: "Seven come eleven on a rusty dime. And her knees keep a knockin' and her toes keep a rockin.'"

He dragged his bag on down the dock, trying to be more alert. Only one boat remained, he realized; so where were the numbers? The paint on the hull of this one, what was left of it, was peeling badly; and there were definitely no numbers on the bow. He faced the boat, staring at the wreckage on deck. This was a derelict!

"Oh, Jesus H. Christ! I have died and gone to hell."

Amidst piles of garbage so thick no part of the deck was visible were rolls of cable and bare wire, unlabeled wooden and cardboard boxes, rotten and broken timbers, and one scantily-dressed swab staring at him. There was no Union Jack on the mast and no Old Glory on the fantail; but he saluted in the direction where they were supposed to be and, carrying his gear high on his chest now, crossed the two-by-twelve gangplank and began picking his way through the rubble, aiming for what had to be the pilothouse.

"You the quartermaster?"

Ace stopped, looking slowly about for the source of the words. Atop a large spool of coaxial cable sat a smiling, chubby-faced swab with wavy, pampered hair.

"This the *S Ceeeee-995*?"

Ace was not a stutterer, never had been, but for some reason he had real difficulty turning loose of the *C*. Without waiting for a reply, he made his way to the small laticed deck amidships, which was not quite as cluttered as the rest of topside.

"I'm Tracy, the gunner's mate," said the swab, following him. "Finally, we're getting a crew. Yesterday, we got a signalman and a motormack."

"Do tell. Where do I sleep?"

"Not in there," said Tracy with a laugh. "Follow me."

*   *   *

It was the damnedest thing he had ever seen. In some ways, Ace was convinced, the *Subchaser 995* was more civilian than the banana boat he had begun his career on as a sailor, back when Heck was a pup. There was no sign of the Navy aboard the ship at all. The two young ninety-day-wonders, Ensigns Howorth and Darling, spent most of their time at the Supply Base Officers' Club and on the Officers' Beach at MOB-Five Naval Hospital; and when they were aboard they dressed so informally there was no need of saluting or sirring.

Vanderveen and Leafdale and Kwaitkowski, along with Bill Tracy, the skeleton crew that had brought the 995 from the States, set the example for the newcomers. They slept late each morning, skipping chow; and, had it not been for the noon whistle at the Ile Nou Naval Supply Base, they would surely have missed noon chow. Finally roused, they would make their way noisily over the little hill past NATS and up the long cement walk to the enormous messhall, formerly the main dormitory and administration building of the French prison.

The only sign of a commitment to a routine aboard the ship was the inevitable evening bull session on the fantail. Everyone financially incapable of liberty in Noumea would begin to drift aft about sundown; and unless the scuttlebutt happened to be extremely positive about the "show" up on the hill (at Tent City), the stories and lies and wishful thinking would continue until after midnight. Once in a blue moon the movie would be a new, recent release directly from the States or, even rarer, a stage show sponsored by the USO; on such occasons only Ace and Vanderveen, the big, jolly motormack would remain aboard.

One evening Ace was in a talkative mood. Previously, he had sat cross-legged in his favorite spot, on the K-gun rack, and listened to Tracy and Vanderveen tell their wild stories about East Lansing, Michigan, and Troy, New York. But on this occasion he jumped in with a remark about the Pink House. Everyone had heard about this fabled place, but not one among them had actually been there.

"Well, one day here'while back I decided to check out this place. The line stretched around the corner out of sight, but this Aussie and me settled in, determined to stick it out. All of a sudden here came a kid in starched undress whites and fell in with us. I swear he couldn't've been more'n fifteen or sixteen, and when he asked if this was the Ship's Store line, me and this Aussie 'bout died laughing. I figured I'd string him along as far as I could, just to see how he would take it when he found out what he was really lined up for."

"He must've been a half-wit!" said Tracy, laughing. "Not to have noticed the Aussie."

"Aw, he was just a babe," countered Ace. "He wasn't thinking about a thing but pickin'up some skivvies for a friend. I know for sure he had no idea a place like the Pink House even existed."

"So how far did he git before he found out?" demanded Tracy.

"Right up to the time the Madam said, 'Next' and grabbed for him!"

When the laughing died down, Ace added, "And I've got his shoes to prove how far he got!"

*   *   *

It was from Tracy mostly that Ace learned about how the little one-hundred-and-ten-foot subchaser and her four sisters had been built back before World War I to chase rumrunners along the New England coast. During the Great War they had been used as "anti-submarine" patrol craft, thus picking up the name"submarine chasers." Mothballed for years, these and others like them had suddenly been re-commissioned in 1942 and 1943 to serve as escort and patrol craft in the Pacific. These five at Ile Nou had been specifically earmarked for General MacArthur's island-hopping operation, although Tracy or no one else apparently could explain what their specific duties would be.

The five little wooden ships (Ace insisted on calling them *boats*) had left New London, Connecticut, about the time he was being fished out of the Coral Sea. They had made their way down the East Coast, some-times reaching speeds up to twelve knots, crossed the Gulf of Mexico on a beeline for the Canal. Finally, from Balboa Harbor they had launched forth, like tiny splinters lined up end-to-end, on the six-thousand-mile crossing of the mighty Pacific Ocean, ending up at the Ile Nou docks.

Ace was curious about every detail of the story, how the four enlisted men and a junior grade lieutenant had brought the 995 across, living on K-rations and rainwater, always clinging to something, having to strap themselves into their bunks at night. None of them had believed the 995, or indeed any of the subchasers, would make it to New Caledonia. These slow little ships had been designed to run up and down the Atlantic seaboard, staying always in easy reach of a sheltered cove, not cross the treacherous, misnamed Pacific. What were the chances they would not run into a storm, given the distance and the time it would take them to reach their destination? Any kind of a storm, they were convinced, would send all five of them down.

"So, you were lucky," Ace admitted, impressed.

"We reached the Pacific just in time for the monsoons," bragged Tracy. "From the Marquesas on the only thing that kept us from starving to death was the fear of sinking. Fifteen-foot waves, forty-mile winds. We didn't have time to think about food and fresh water or anything else. Ask Cookie, he'll tell you. There aint nothing that can sink this—"

"How about a twenty-two bullet?"

4

The Splendid Five

Comdr. Farris stared at me above a great pile of radiograms and folded rolls of teletype paper.

"What got into you, Hall? I can't believe you went out there by yourself and went swimming with the nurses."

I had never seen this kindly and generally cheerful man look so sad. That he thought a lot of me I had no doubt, and standing there in front of him I felt like a bastard child who had disgraced his sainted father.

"Did Sharkey and Smith put you up to that?"

"Oh, no, Sir. I did it on my own."

"Why?"

For a time I just stood there like a knot on a log, thinking about what I should not tell him. I wanted to tell him how much I wanted to go north and fight the Japanese, but I did not want to get Sharkey and Smith into trouble.

"I thought it might get me a transfer, Sir. To a ship heading north."

"Well, how in the world did you come to the conclusion that—?"

For a time we stared at each other, and I could feel the heat rising up my neck and into my hair. He raised both hands and shook his head.

"So you want a transfer. Why, in Heaven's name, didn't you just come to me and ask for one? What kind of a ship do you want?"

"Any kind, Sir, as long as it's going north."

"Aren't you interested in radio? Haven't I seen you carrying around a ham handbook?"

I could feel my blood pressure rising.

"Yes, Sir. I qualified for radio school at boot camp, but something happened and I didn't get to go."

"Would you like to go to radio school? There's a fleet radio school out at the Receiving Station. It's an eighteen-week training session that's divided into two nine-week courses. The end result is a third class petty officer's rating, if you can cut the mustard. The charter class is halfway through, and a new class is forming. I could see about getting you into that."

I was in a daze. Braced for a court martial, I had just been handed a great opportunity. If I could cut the mustard, and I had no doubt that I could, I would have a ticket north. Radio operators were badly needed in the war effort.

That very day word reached me that my orders had been cut. I was going to the Receiving Station, and this time I would be Ship's Company, as all residents of that cesspool were called who weren't transients. I packed my seabag, shook hands with Sharkey and Smith (who could not understand why I wasn't on my way north already), and went down to the Motor Pool. There I found Admiral Weter waiting for me, asleep with his salty golfball cap pulled down over his eyes, but nevertheless waiting.

"Man, I heard about thet MOB-Five thing," he said, looking contrite, but faking. "Why yuh not in jail?"

"The case was thrown out. Lack of evidence. Take me to the Receiving Station."

"Shit, man, they th'owin' 'way the key on yuh! It shore a wondah tho they didn't send yuh up no'th."

"Hey, I wonder that, too. And one of these days that's where I'm going. Come on, Admiral, let's get underway."

All the way down through Noumea and the two miles out into the country to RS-31 Admiral Weter said over and over, "I shore hope not, boss. I shore hope not." Finally, this became a chant, picked up some tempo and rhythm, and blossomed into the chorus of a song.

The radio school turned out to be two large tents, one for radio fundamentals (called Theory) and typing and the other for Morse Code (called Practice) and passing the Third Class examination. When it became known to the CPO in charge of Theory that I knew the typewriter keyboard and had had a course in Radio Fundamentals at Kerman Union High School, back in California, I was immediately dispatched to Practice and informed that I was a bona fide member of the Charter Class.

Two months later I took the examination with the first class, passed it, and received my new petty officer's rating and a transfer.

"Hall, you lucky sonofabitch," said Chief Garnes, the CPO in charge of Tent Two (Practice). "Out of fifteen bright boys you're the only one NXZ wanted. I swear, when I first set eyes on you on the old *Eugene Skinner* I never thought you had a chance in this world. You've turned out a lot better than I ever thought you would."

My orders read: "Report without delay to the C. O., NXZ Base Radio, Comsopac."

The prospect of working at Admiral Halsey's headquarters radio station was both exciting and scary. I realized that it was a pat on the back, being selected for that job, but at the same time did this not mean that I would have an even harder time getting a transfer to a ship? I thought of Sharkey's lecture on Navy logic and how to get a transfer, concluding that perhaps if I did not do a good job at NXZ I would have a better chance. This line of thinking was interrupted by a little voice in the top of my head that asked pointedly: "Did you not learn anything at all from the mess Sharkey got you into?"

The following morning a Comsopac Jeep showed up for me at the main gate at the Receiving Station. I tossed my seabag in the back and got in without a word. The driver paid me no attention at all, and when he stopped in front of a big square building next-door to Comsopac headquarters, I got out and went inside.

Here it was the first of March, 1944, and I was farther away from getting a ship than I had ever been.

After piling my gear on an empty bunk in the Comsopac barracks, I went in search of the C. O. This took me eventually downstairs to the radio station, which was noisy, reeked of cigarette smoke and electrical shorts, and surrounded by offices. One of these belonged to the C. O., Comdr. Thompson.

"Glad to have you aboard, Hall. Commander Farris said some good things about you recently. I want you to check with Chief McElhaney as soon as possible. He knows you're on deck, and he'll fill you in on the routine here, what you can and can't do."

It was McElhaney that found me, at evening chow, and after listing some things that I should know about the station and the routine, he informed me that I would begin with the mid-watch. My job for the time being would be running errands for the watches, keeping the coffee cups filled, keeping the coffee pot going, keeping track of the "in" and "out" baskets.

"Stay away from the split-phone watches, but keep an eye on them. Do whatever they want when they want it. Understand? They're what we're all about."

In time I was subbing for some of the watches, getting my feet wet; and, unbeknowance to me, I was being watched closely by both McElhaney and Comdr. Thompson (and their spies). I was in awe of the split-phone watches, especially the one that handled incoming and outgoing traffic with Honolulu and San Francisco. At first, it was incredible to me that any-one could keep up with the volume of high-speed incoming mail, get it down with a typewriter without an error, and roger for it at the same time something was coming in from another circuit.

By early May it was still impressive but not incredible, and I was occasionally being called to substitute during coffee breaks. The split-phone watches had to take breaks, were the only watches to do so; and this was one of the first embarrassing lessons I learned after beginning there as a bus boy.

All of it, incoming and outgoing, was in Morse Code sent with a "bug" (a semi-automatic key); and it was a real adrenaline flow to be on one end of an operational priority message zinging along at thirty words a minute!

About the time I decided that I could hold down the Cincpac-Frisco watch, I was summoned by Comdr. Thompson and given the opportunity to volunteer for that very watch, from four-to-eight a. m. As far as I was concerned, this was the best watch of them all, for it would free me for the entire day and early evening, and it would allow me to spend my afternoons at MOB-Five Beach with Sharkey and Smith.

An added bonus, I was to learn, was being able to watch the First Platoon of the First Marines do their classic snap-and-click Sixteen-Count Manual of Arms march in front of the Comsopac Building and hear the brilliant French band perform at the gazebo in the Square. As a bus boy I had learned that by stacking crates one on top of the other against the forward wall I could fashion a grandstand from which I could witness through the high basement windows the comings and going on the Square. Now, this daily *international* performance began just as I was getting off for the day.

How better to start off the day than to experience such a spectacle, which was concluded with a grand rendering of *La Marseilles*, performed by an authentic French orchestra?

*   *   *

Four of the five little wooden ships at the Naval Supply Base looked like yachts. Their hulls and bridges had recently received fresh coats of pale gray paint, and their decks had been cleared of all the debris and clutter caused by the base repairmen. Their conversion to LCC's, which,

I learned, stood for Landing Craft, Communications, had been accomplished; and all of the brass and woodwork in the pilothouses and bridges had been completed.

The fifth ship, moored by itself at the end of the dock, appeared to be destined for scuttling. I had become quite well acquainted with the radiomen on the converted ones, having visited their radio shacks a number of times; but after being told more than once that the ugly duckling down the dock would not be going north, I had avoided it.

For sometime I had begun to look upon the little ships as my last chance to go north before it was too late. Each had a complement of three radiomen; and although all of the slots had been filled, I was optimist enough to believe that one day one of those twelve radiomen would be transferred, for some reason or other. So day after day, week after week, I made the trip from Noumea and checked aboard each ship, like a mortician looking for a casualty.

Then one day, having decided that I was wasting my time (Scuttlebutt had it that the "Splinter Fleet" was preparing to head north any day), I drifted down to the derelict for a last look. Standing in the pilothouse doorway was a tall Nordic type in khaki. It was obvious to me that he was an officer; but when I crossed the gangplank, he smiled and waved, like a regular person. Which was both a surprise and an encouragement.

Another surprise was the mountain of coaxial cables, new timbers, and buckets of paint that blocked my way to the pilothouse.

"Are you looking for someone?" called the officer.

"I'm a radio operator at the Base Radio Station, in Noumea, but I would like to find a ship."

He stared me, obviously amused.

"I really would like to—be a radioman aboard a ship heading north."

"Oh? You want to go north? Can you do anything to a radio besides turn it on and off? Any tech background?"

Without batting an eye, I blurted, "That's actually what I do best, work on radios. I went to the fleet radio school because—"

"Come on down to the wardroom and let's talk. Maybe we can work something out."

The half-truth that I had told him was already bothering me, but I followed him down to the wardroom and listened to a lengthy explication of the needs and realities of the *SC-995*. He had recently been assigned the job of getting the ship ready for sea, and although there were three radio operators aboard the ship, one of them was probably going to be rotated back to the States. What he really needed, though, was a radio tech, somebody that could repair the big TDE transmitter and all the other junk that had been gathering dust for years down in the radio shack.

"But I could never steal you away from Halsey's base radio. Any chance you could transfer over to Ile Nou as a tech? I know the Operations man here."

I left convinced that the poor old *995* would never make it out of the harbor, much less go north into the War Zone; and even if by some miracle it did I would not be on it. It was ridiculous for me to think I could get a transfer from Base Radio; and it seemed ludicrous that Ile Nou Supply Base, even if it had a vacancy to fill, would be willing to fill it with a radio operator!

Nevertheless, that very afternoon I paid a visit to Radio Repair on the Ile Nou Base. It was practically on my way to NATS landing; so what did I have to lose.

"You say you know something about radios," said the old CPO in charge of the place. He was obviously not interested in what I had to say. "Why do you want to transfer to Ile Nou?" Before I could reply, he looked at me with raised eyebrows and demanded: 'Where'd you say you're stationed?"

I told him, already leaving. He was shaking with laughter.

"Tell you what, Red. I've got six good men in my repair staff. Up in tent city there's a CPO friend of mine madder'n hell at me because for over a year he hasn't been able to listen to his short-wave radio. You go up there and fix it for him and I'll do my damnedest to talk McElhaney into parting with you. Deal?"

"What are the chances you could influence Chief McElhaney to influence Commander Thompson?"

The old chief laughed happily and slapped the workbench in front of him so hard things leaped into the air. "Hell, I don't know! I think Mack gets about what he wants from the Commander, and I think I have some pull with Mack. But who's to tell? What are the chances you could fix that radio? We've rebuilt it three times from scratch, and it still won't make a sound."

"Could I borrow a VOM meter, soldering iron, and a pair of sidecutters? Where is this radio?"

The thing was I had nothing to lose. What was a stroll up the hill to Tent City?

I found the tent without trouble, went inside and laid some of my basic tools out on the only cot in the place, and looked around for the radio. It turned out to be a little evil-looking desktop thing with two dozen knobs. Nothing happened when I turned the volume control knob fully clockwise, reversed it all the way, heard it click off. I followed the AC cord to a tent stanchion and removed the plug from the receptacle. It fitted very loosely in the old socket; so I spread the contacts apart, turned it over, and reinserted it into the socket.

Suddenly, the tent exploded with noise! I fell back away from the plug-in, leaped up, and ran to the volume control! I had forgotten a basic rule of radio repair: Turn the set off before attaching the AC line plug to a power source.

From the doorway a man in tie-dyed skivvies said, "You got my radio fixed?" There was a mixture of disbelief and joy in his face. "You really got my radio fixed?"

I adjusted the tuning knob to an AFS station before replying.

"No problem at all. Would you mind giving Chief Winegarten a call and telling him I'll return his tools tomorrow sometime?"

"By God, I'll tell 'im more'n that!"

Not that afternoon but the next I waited in line to see Comdr. Thompson, nervous beyond words. Requesting anything from an officer, I had decided, was a very risky business. It could color my entire Naval career. I sat there twiddling my fingers while the clock of fate ticked on.

"What is it, Hall?"

The commander was standing in the door to his office with his glasses down on his nose. There were still two swabs ahead of me, but I got up and when the officer turned and disappeared into his office I followed him.

"The Chief told me you're requesting a transfer. Why?"

I was ready for this question and immediately began to blurt out how stressful it had been for me the past month. The commander let me talk, on and on, and I got into things like how much I liked to work on radios and, finally, how I felt about sitting out the war on some island.

Finally, he lifted a hand for me to stop.

"So you feel that what you're doing is 'sitting out the war'?"

"Yes, Sir. And I think if I can get a transfer to Ile Nou, the skipper of the *SC-995* can work a swap for me."

"My God! You have put a lot of thought into this! Wouldn't it be better and quicker just to request a transfer to that subchaser?"

*   *   *

When I finally made it to the beach, it was crowded with Comseron and Comsopac swabs, most of whom were out near the platform; but Sharkey's and Smith's heads were not among those. And as far as I could see down the beach there was no Mutt and Jeff duo. A

Melanesian teenager with a large orange spot in his barrel-size head of hair came running toward me, waving a flyer. I shook my head at the sheet of paper and handed him a fifty centavo bill. Then he tried to pretend I had given him a forty-five centavo tip. I wadded my change in my blouse pocket and headed for one of the little telephone booth dressing rooms.

When I emerged, Sharkey and Smith were getting out of a Jeep up near trees above the beach.

"I finally got a transfer to a ship," I said right off, before Sharkey could get started. "And I didn't have to fuck up." With that I headed down toward the water.

"Hold on there!" shouted Sharkey. "You got a transfer? Where to, Tokyo Bay?"

I stopped, turned around, and let them have it, laying it on thick about what a neat little ship the *SC-995* was, how many radios the Supply Base was installing in the, what a great guy the skipper of the ship was. And when I finally let up for a second, out of breath, Sharkey jumped in:

"He's brainwashed, Smitty. Be damned if he aint. He's going up against the Imperial Jap Navy in a John boat and he thinks the Navy's doin' him a favor!" He continued on toward the water, still talking. "I'm just glad it's not me. Now, look at this! A beach as white as the insides of a coconut and right over there on the other side of that hemp rope is a gaggle of young soft stuff that's as pretty as anything you could find in the States."

We waded out toward the float on our side of the rope, horsing around; but I for one was very careful about where I put any weight down. All I needed at this late date was an infection from a piece of sharp coral.

The float was a twelve-by-twelve platform held up by fifty-gallon drums. We waited our turn and climbed up at one corner, getting splashed badly by an overweight yeoman from Comseron Personnel.

"How'd you get that transfer?" demanded Sharkey, eventually, a question I had expected.

"I just asked for it. You know, Shark, you've got the wrong idea about the officers and the Navy. In fact, I think you've got everything about this outfit bassackwards."

"Yeah, an' we're hearin' this from someone that's been in the outfit all of six months. Git off my case, kid! I aint got anything backwards. Tell me one thing I've told you wrong. If it hadn't been for me and Smitty here, you'd still be carrying mail at Comseron."

The platform became quiet suddenly, and I looked around to find that we were the only ones on it. I stood up and dived and when I looked back, my two friends were stretched out on their stomachs. I treaded water, too antsy to relax and enjoy like them. My mind was on the weighty business of transferring to a ship. I had every detail of it worked out in my mind, from the tossing of my seabag into the back of a Jeep to the walk across the gangplank. I would finally be a radio operator aboard a ship headed north. It was a very big dream finally coming true.

At this point, with my feet at last planted firmly on the ship (I had been there many times already), my mind would leap ahead to that moment when I would come face-to-face with the enemy. How would I behave, with my life on the line?

Then the inevitable questions about the why of it all. Why was I bound and determined to risk my life? Why had I been unable to accept what everyone else seemed to think was so great?

I swam to shallow water, touched bottom, and walked out upon the beach. Swabs were stretched out on towels, some of them reading paperback books but most just soaking up the sun, their faces hidden by their golfball caps. Far down the beach, away from MOB-Five Hospital and the park-like compound around it, I could make out half a dozen naked black figures. Melanesian youths probably, skinny dipping.

They probably had no idea a great war was going on in their Pacific.

*   *   *

From NATS, where a PBY was loading for take-off, I carried my eighty-five-pound seabag nonstop over the little hill and down the considerable slope to the beginning of the Ile Nou docks. On my right were two damaged PT-boats and a yippy boat, all apparently deserted. It was nearing ten hundred hours, still rather comfortable topside on the little ships.

After a once-over of the four sharp-looking subchasers and a brief exchange with a swab on the bow of the *SC-1318*, I hoisted my seabag, settled it on my left shoulder, and continued down the dock. I became aware that two swabs, one tall and skinny and the other stocky, were watching me from the bow of the *995*. At the stern of the second pair of subchasers I paused and waved at them. They just stared me, the one with his mouth open and the other grinning like a possum shitting peach seeds.

At the bow of the *995* I set the bag down, waiting for one of them to say something.

"You comin' aboard?" the tall one asked, still gawking.

I nodded, "I'm Hall, Radioman Third Class."

The short one without a neck laughed. I did not like his exaggerated grin. It made him look as if he smelled something bad. He nodded toward 'midships: "Don't tell us, tell Fletcher. Down there at the gangplank." Then he turned and said something to the tall one, who looked familiar to me, and burst out laughing; but the other just continued to stare at me, with his shoulders lifted high.

In a flash, I remembered, painfully. He was the joker that had let me believe I was in the line at Ship's Store. Why he had done that made no sense to me.

"Hey, kid," he finally said, taking a step toward me. "Remember me? McCormick. The Pink House. This is Tracy."

I said nothing in return and was proceeding toward the gangplank when the stocky swab burst out laughing and yelled, "Do you mean this is the—"

Fletcher, whom I had met briefly, was standing at the flared hatch opening that led to the engineroom, talking to someone below. When I paused at the gangplank, uncertain whether to salute the fantail or not, he looked at me and waved.

"Come on aboard, Hall. I've been expecting you."

I crossed the gangplank and set the seabag down, my mind still in a whirl over seeing McCormick on the bow.

"Let's go find you a bunk in the fo'c's'le. Have you met our quartermaster?"

"I'm afraid so. And Tracy, too." I was thinking , what a lousy way to start off on an ocean voyage. And as the thin, immaculate Fletcher started toward the bow, I could not help adding: "Are there any others like them aboard this ship?"

I had hardly got this out of my mouth when we were facing these two. Fletcher, sensing that something was out of joint, merely nodded and continued on. McCormick, however, stepped in front of me.

"Listen, I'm sorry I pulled that stunt on you at the Pink House."

"Let's forget it," I said, between gritted teeth. I wanted to show him just how I felt.

"So this is Pinky," said Tracy, pushing his way in front of me. "You really thought that was the Ship's Stores line?"

"Okay, Tracy," said McCormick, "let it go. He had no way of—"

"Pinky! Pinky, baby! You plannin' on goin' north with us? Won't you be lonesome for your mother? I'll bet you wish you was back home right now!"

I tried to use my seabag as a battering ram to get past the two, but Tracy started jabbing me in the chest. Instinctively, my free right hand went toward where his throat was supposed to be. He ducked quickly and squared off.

"Oh, you want somethin', Pinky Boy?"

At this point McCormick, backed up by Fletcher, shoved Tracy to one side and held him until I could pass. I had never wanted to hit someone so much in my life; but this was no way to start off. Somehow, I told myself, I was going to have to get along with this pug ugly.

In the forward crew's quarters Fletcher introduced me to Tabor, the signalman, and Milleson, a motormack; and in the lull that followed he told them about my encounter with Tracy, who, he said, was a member of the original crew and the ship's gunner's mate. He made no reference to the Pink House incident.

"That Tracy is one bad egg," said Milleson. "He tried to pick a fight with me the day I came aboard, and if Vanderveen hadn't got between us he would've got his way. And according to Van he averages about one fight a day with someone on one of the other subchasers."

Tabor shrugged, "Best thing is to pay him no mind."

Fletcher was anxious for me to meet the other two radio operators aboard, Jines and DiAugustino, both Second Class. I followed him up the narrow metal ladder, braced for another encounter with Tracy. But I had by this time decided that I would avoid a fight with him no matter what he did.

In the radio shack, which was a small space below the pilothouse, just aft of the wardroom, I met the two radiomen, who were staring into the innards of a monster transmitter, the TDE. Harold D. Jines, tall and broad-shouldered, with an easy grin, volunteered to go get coffee; and while he was gone Tony DiAugustino, dark and handsome, admitted that he had just learned that he was being transferred!

"How did this come about?" asked Fletcher. "I'm expecting my orders any day."

"Well, I don't rightly know. The first day I came aboard I put in for a transfer to the base radio station; and when the Skipper came aboard and I told him I wanted no part of going north in this thing, he said he would see what he could do."

"That leaves the ship short one sparks," said Fletcher, with a frown. "I sure as hell hope that doesn't get in the way of my rotation to the

States." After a pause, he added: "I don't think two men can handle sixteen transceivers plus the Navy frequencies."

Jines returned with the coffee, on a tray, and for the next two hours I listened while Fletcher and Jines talked. First, about my radio duties and the routine aboard the ship. The ship's radio call was *Splendid Five*, Jines said with a grin. All of the subchasers had the word *splendid* in it. The *1318* was *Splendid Eight*, for example. Eventually, they got around to the weighty matter of what still had to be done on the ship before it would be ready for the "shakedown cruise" and the trip north.

"I doubt seriously that this ship will go north," said Fletcher. "Despite the go-ahead from Flag. Ask Vanderveen about the engines. If all they needed was an overhaul, that would not stop us. But according to him, one of them is past repairing. And my guess is that Flag Allowance does not know that. We can't go north on one engine."

5

Baldini

On October 11, 1944, Commander Jackson, Chief Operations Officer at Flag Allowance, in Noumea, paid an unscheduled visit to the Ile Nou Naval Supply Base. He was carrying in his briefcase Flag's accumulation of information about the five subchasers at the Ile Nou dock, including requisitions and damage reports from the trip across the Pacific, and the preliminary findings of a three-man inspection team concerning what needed to be done before they could be sent north.

His first stop was the Base Operations Office, where he listened to reports from three department heads, each of whom had overseen a part of the work that had been done on the subchasers.

At the conclusion of the reports, he said to the Base Commander, Lt. Comdr. Herschel P. Thomas: "We've been hanging fire on this thing primarily because of other priorities but also because of this fifth subchaser. I came over here to assess the situation for myself, but from these reports it would seem that there's no doubt left about that *995* boat."

The commander laughed. "None at all. We looked all over this island for another engine for that one, even sent requisitions to Pearl and Frisco. And even if we'd found one, I doubt seriously that the *995* would've ever made it out of the harbor. Hell, Jack, that thing's a friggin' disaster! The bilges are full of cracks, and I'd bet you fifty bucks she'd sink if somebody was foolish enough to shoot off one of those K-guns on her stern."

The commander stood up and nodded at the C. O., then glanced about at the others. "Keep your seats, gentlemen." Gathering up the reports on the desk, he said, "I guess I'll go down and take a look for myself."

"You'll get seasick if you're not careful!" laughed the Base C. O. "Sittin' at the dock, those little wooden rascals roll and toss to beat the band, and every time an LCVP goes past there it's something to watch."

At this bit of raillery everyone in the room laughed, and the Commander said, "I'm aware they're not fit for man or beast, but every single one of them is needed up north. We're giving these things to MacArthur. Gentlemen."

Once the door was closed behind Commander, the Base C. O. grinned mischievously. "Wait till he tries to stand up on one of them."

A few minutes later the appearance of commander and his staff on the small craft dock brought a standstill to all activity. Dock workers and deckhands alike stood at attention while the brass balanced themselves across the gangplank to the immaculate deck of the *SC1318*, where the commander was immediately escorted to the bridge.

"I thought a sub was crowded," he joked, returning the skipper's salute. "What's your complement again, London? Twenty men?"

The young lieutenant grinned and nodded, "Twenty-one, sir. And three officers."

The commander shook his head in amazement. "Where do they all sleep?" Without waiting for a reply, he added, "Let's look at the accommodations for these men."

London led the group from the bridge to the fo'c's'le, and everyone took turns looking into the darkened quarters. But no one suggested descending to the deck below. The commander waited until everyone had had his look.

"The billets. Stacked how high?"

"Three, except on the point of the bow."

"And where's the head?"

"In the point of the bow. It has a shower."

"And how about fresh water? What's your storage capacity?"

Mr. London shook his head sadly. "I'm afraid storage space is something we just don't have much of, for water or food. Away from the dock we use sea water for showers."

All of the officers groaned.

The tour continued, passed through the pilothouse, dropped down to the radio shack and wardroom, and came to an end in the after crews quarters, where the cook and his messcook served the visitors coffee and cookies.

When the commander was ready to move on, he shook hands with London and said, "Well, sir, we appreciate your hospitality. Compliments to your cook. Now, we must see the other boats."

Topside, at 'midships, he paused and caught the skipper's eye. "All these boats have about the same arrangements, London?"

"Yes, Sir. We're a little better off in some respects, but all five of the ships are built alike."

"Then that ought to speed up things a bit."

And it did. With each ship the inspection picked up speed. Finally, the commander and his officers made it back to the dock and stood looking at the last one, the ugly duckling.

Ensigns Howorth and Darling were waiting stiff-backed on the bridge, which had recently been covered with a skirt of new canvas. They were dressed in khaki, brand-new regulation caps, and shiny black shoes; and while the high-ranking officers were still fifty feet up the dock, they saluted and froze.

At the gangplank, the commander, who had not bothered to return the salute, waved and shouted, "I think we'll just take a look from here!"

Mr. Howorth was the first to relax. He slowly lowered his hand and smiled. Then he waved and moved to the ladder and descended to the quarterdeck. Mr. Darling, paler than usual, lowered his hand but continued to stand at attention.

"Perhaps you two could join us on the dock!" called the commander impatiently. "We know what your boat is like."

Mr. Howorth bounded across the gangplank, neglecting to salute the fantail. All of the officers on the dock stared first at him and then at the stern of the ship, where the Union Jack should have been.

"Ensign Howorth, Suh. Lawrence W."

"Are you the ranking officer aboard?" asked the Commander, incredulous.

"Yes, suh. The Captain's ovah on the island. And beggin' your pardon, suh, we're not at all like the other boats. Ships."

"In what way?" demanded the commander.

"In almost all ways, suh. I guess this is a' older model—"

"Hell, I doubt that! They're all as old as Methuselah!"

Mr. Darling crossed the quarterdeck and finally made it to the dock, where he immediately resumed his salute. The commander continued to interrogate Mr. Howorth, ignoring him completely.

"What is your opinion of this boat's chances of being ready to go north with the others, Howorth?"

The ensign shook his head doubtfully, "I reckon I hadn't ought to comment on that, Suh. I'm a bit prejudiced."

"Ensign, where you from?"

"Rawlee, suh."

"That in this country?" Commander cleared his throat and glancing around at his officers. Then he turned back to Howorth. "Why can't you comment? You've got eyes, you're the senior officer aboard, nobody's here to stop you."

"Yes, suh. Well, I guess I would say no, suh."

The commander turned to Ensign Darling, "Well, what do you think?"

Darling swallowed and smiled sadly. "I think it will sink as soon as we untie it from the dock, sir. We have to keep the bilge pumps going all the time, day and night."

The commander nodded, turned and began to pace up and down on the dock. Finally, he said, to no one in particular, "I wonder what we ought to do about this one." He approached the stern, where most of the men were slumped about looking at him. "Hell, it wouldn't do any good to dry-dock it, even if we had a dry-dock handy. Maybe we ought to scuttle the sonofabitch."

Darling, who had not heard any of this, moved up behind the commander, anxious to get his attention. His right hand was back in place above his eyebrow, even while he was moving about the dock. The commander, turning suddenly, bumped into him!

"Goddamn, why don't you look where you're goin'?"

"Yes, Sir! I beg your pardon, Sir!"

"Well, what's on your mind? Be quick about it."

Darling's voice, already a bit high, rose quickly as he spoke. "I've never seen anything like this—subchaser. Sir! It is not actually a naval vessel. That is, one that crosses oceans and—uh—goes against the enemy—the Japanese. I mean. It is decidedly not a man-of-war! It isn't like anything I ever saw before, even in Naval literature! When I volunteered for service, Sir, I—!"

The commander had by this time turned and was striding up the dock. The ensign hurried after him.

"Surely, Sir, we won't be expected to go north in this boat!"

The officers and crews of the other subchasers had gathered on the respective sterns to view the spectacle at the end of the dock.

Ignoring Darling's plea, the commander called back over his shoulder, "Well, thank you. We'll make a determination about what we're going to do with this boat. Give your captain my regards. That'll be all. Good day, gentlemen!"

As the brass cleared the dock, with not so much as a glance backward, Ace McCormick met Ensign Howorth at the gangplank. "Sir, there's nothing wrong with this ship but its engines."

"Should I call the Commandah back so you can inform him of that fact?" asked Howorth with the hint of a smile.

As the two officers worked their way back toward the wardroom, the following conversation was overheard by Ace and others:

Darling was overheard to say, "The Navy's got more sense than to send good officers and men into war in a thing like this."

Howorth countered with, "Git yo'self undah control, Mye'n. If wuss comes to wuss, we'll write to our congressmen."

Mr. Darling, sounding weary, said, "I've been wondering what in the world I'll tell my girlfriend I did during the war." After a pause, he asked, "Have you sent a picture of this thing home?"

"Ah reckon not."

"I've got a picture of me in front of a destroyer."

"I hope it's not one of them the Japs has sunk."

*   *   *

Out of the bedlam and wreckage of Pearl Harbor, with balding head lowered like an angry bull, there had appeared on the docks of Noumea an ex-Chief Boatswain's Mate by the name of Benito Caesaro Baldini. Two terribly cruel things had happened to this old salt almost simultaneously: His beloved light cruiser, the *USS Portland*, had gone down during the Japanese attack on Pearl, and his coveted Chief's stripes had been taken away from him ('for failing to carry out a direct order by a commissioned officer').

To all who would listen and who had not seen his service records, Baldini swore vehemently that there was no connection between the two tragedies, certainly no cause-and-effect relationship. He had lost his stripes merely because a green-behind-the-ears ninety-day wonder had taken a dislike for him and reported a lie.

Around enlisted men this old boatswain's mate was incapable of sustaining another subject for more than two minutes. Using the flimsiest of transitions he would launch into one or the other of his sad stories, how he had been wrongfully brought down from that loftiest of perches, what an ideal life he had had as Deck Chief of the *Portland*, and his present lowly circumstances.

When everyone else he knew was being promoted and sent on to greatness against the mighty Japanese Navy, he was getting shit thrown at him from a fancy Dan deck officer straight out of an Ivy League 90-day-wonder V-12 Program. He had come up the hard way, without benefit of formal education or training in Amy Vanderbilt etiquette; but he was Navy through and through and proud as hell of it. Yes, the officer had been aboard the *Portland*, and, yes, it was this sad excuse for a human being that had falsely accused him of refusing to obey a command during the bombing of Pearl.

Baldini did not question the way the Navy did things. It had been good to him during his sixteen years of active service, had indeed been both his home and his savior (from the squalor and chaos of a big family in a New York City ghetto). So after a frustrating stint at the receiving station, that ugly shithole of the South Pacific, and was handed orders to report to the Commanding Officer of the *SC-995*, he dutifully hitched a ride to Ile Nou Island Naval Repair Base and checked in at the base headquarters, refusing to believe that his beloved Navy had decided to stick him on one of the little boats tied up at the docks there. He reported to the officer at the front desk, a lieutenant, that he had seen nothing in the area that could be called a ship.

His orders had given Ile Nou Island as the location of his ship, he said; but except for some NATS gooney birds on leashes and a bunch of small stuff on one side of the island, there was nothing. Perhaps his ship had already departed for the War Zone.

"Oh," said the lieutenant, grinning, having not so much as glanced at the proffered orders, "that would be one of the subchasers over at the docks. Straight down the walkway from the front door. You can't miss it. The number'll be on the bow."

"Subchaser?" growled Baldini, turning and speaking in a subdued tone. "What the hell is that, sir, begging your pardon? A fuckin' small craft?" But the lieutenant was busy and pretended not to hear him.

He retrieved his seabag beside the front steps of the building and, with a heavy sigh, struck out toward the little row of masts that were just visible to him over a low hill. "Well, whatever it is it's a U. S. Naval vessel, and at least I'll be back on a deck again," he rationalized aloud. It was a comforting thought, for he loved being at sea on a good ship, away from the complications and smells of shore duty. And he loved dearly being in charge of a rolling deck.

Baldini, with his old battered seabag slung over one shoulder, moved down the walk that led straight as a two-by-four to NATS, from the front door of famous old prison barracks, now under a ninety-nine-year lease by the U. S. Government. He knew the entire history of the French political prison that had at one time been the principal industry of this little island, but at the moment he was not interested. What he wanted to know was, What the hell was a *subchaser*?

He went all the way to the end of the walk, a considerable distance out of his way, and then cut left toward the matchsticks that were peeping over the hill at him. From there he took the well-traveled dirt path to a spot close to the top of that hill, where he paused to catch his breath. From that somewhat elevated position, he could see, to his right, the big pregnant NATS PBY's floating contentedly at their moorings. He sighed, pathetically, feeling sorry for himself. The small craft were still off to the left, and he had no inclination to continue toward them.

The first floating objects he saw as he neared the top of the hill were two PT-boats moored to an old piece of dock, and behind them a sorry-looking yippy boat, with a ridiculously high bridge. Then as he circled farther and farther around to his left, he caught sight of first two and then four brilliantly white wooden boats, tied side-by-side in pairs. other small craft came into sight. The question was, What were they? Each had large numbers on its bow, evidently, but he could see only the first two. Thank god neither of them had *995* on it.

Then it became obvious that what he was looking at were *subchasers!* Sick at his stomach, he stumbled down to the long dock to which the things were moored. He passed the first two, clutching his orders, and read aloud the numbers on the bows of the second two. Neither of them was the *995*. What was left? he moved down the dock, aware that there was one more matchstick.

"Aw, naw, God!" he protested. "What have I done to deserve this?"

Before him, finally, was a fifth subchaser, so dilapidated and ugly it took his breath away. There was no number on the bow, that side of it which he could see, but he knew without a shadow of doubt that it was the *995!*

But as he stood there, not breathing, instead of openly blaming the Navy for this *snafu*, Baldini began cursing the little narrow-butted god of the sea (He had no idea what his name was) that he felt certain was behind all of his ill luck of recent months.

In the end, he concluded, "God damn it, I can't do this!" he fumed, looking sadly up at the sky. "No self-respectin' bosun—!"

*   *   *

When Baldini showed up on the Subchaser *995* that blistering hot afternoon in early September, 1944, he was dressed in brand-new (but already sweat-stained) dungarees and an old Chief's khaki cap. One look at him and it was clear to the old hands aboard the subchaser that Comsopac had finally reached the bottom of the barrel.

"Where's the C. O.?" Baldini demanded, standing defiantly on the dock, well away from the gangplank. It was already one hundred degrees in the shade, but his dungaree shirt was buttoned both at the collar and the cuffs.

"You reportin' aboard?" asked the gangway watch, who happened to be Pop Law, an old man of thirty-two due to be rotated to the States any day. He had come in as one of the four deckhands that were to do the new deck chief's bidding. Baldini's deep-set beady eyes, heavy black eyebrows, and sloping brow did not impress Pop in the least. If it had been Admiral Bull Halsey himself, he might have shown some respect; but no one who knew him would have given odds on it.

"What the goddamn hell you think I'm here for?" blasted Baldini.

"I don't know and I don't give a fuck, mate."

Baldini was startled into silence at the blatant insolence of the sorry-looking little seaman. All he could do was open and close his mouth and hop up and down a bit. When he finally had his voice back, he delivered a ten-minute oration, about himself, which included information about his former assignment aboard the USS *Portland*, his prowess in all things relating to deckwork, his intention to make this garbage scow a shining example of a Naval vessel, and his lifelong dedication to the eradication of goldbricking in the United States Navy.

He was interrupted by the arrival on deck of Ensign Howorth, the now tanned and always affable gentleman from Raleigh, North Carolina, who looked to be about twenty-one and who wore no visible sign by which Baldini could have guessed he was an officer. He was, as usual, bare to the waist but otherwise dressed in faded dungaree cut-offs and old white tennis shoes.

"You reportin' aboa'd?" asked the ensign casually, with a smile.

"Goddamn!" shouted the boatswain's mate. "This is a fuckin' believe-it-or not! You the gangway watch, too?"

"I think he's reportin' aboard, Mister Howorth," said Pop Law, "but if he keeps yappin' he's gonna miss chow."

Baldini was instantly all ears, for he had heard the magic word *mister* affixed to the name of the naked young man in front of him. He wanted no part of an entanglement with the brass at this stage of his career.

"We've been expectin' you, Boats," said Mr. Howorth. "You 'bout missed noon chow." He continued to look at Baldini quizzically, as he spoke to the gangway watch. "Pop, show 'im where to stash his gear. He'll be back with the Department Heads I reckon, so tell Cookie to set one more plate for dinnah."

Baldini's mouth, open the entire time, began to flap, "Uh, Sir, did you say 'Department Heads'? If it's all the same with you, I'd just as soon bunk with the men."

"Why, I like thaet," said Mr. Howorth, nodding affably.

* * *

Baldini had decided once and for all that the world had gone absolutely crazy. He had seen a lot of shit in his day, but this took the cake! What the goddamn hell was goin' on back in Washington, sendin' shave tails like this out to give orders to seasoned veterans twice their age! This wet-behind-the-ears kid ought to be back in Alabama or Georgia, wherever he came from!

"Show him where the fo'c's'le is, Pop," Mr. Howorth added and headed for the bridge.

"Well, Boats," sighed Pop, looking at Baldini, "you'll live to regret that bit of stupidity."

The four recently converted LCC's, which still looked very much like wooden subchasers, now spruced up with colorful pennants flapping from their yardarms, were preparing for a turn about the harbor, a kind of preliminary to the all-important shakedown cruise. There was much scurrying about on the little ships, and the boatswain's mates seemed to be vying with each other to see which could shout the loudest.

Most of the crew of the *995* had drifted forward and were lined up along the port and starboard lifelines to watch the proceedings. The deckhands and other noncoms were conspicuously missing from this assemblage, because they were hiding from Baldini.

This worthy, armed with the rather vague order to make things ship-shape on the *995*, came lunging up the deck from the stern. He had been having a last cup of breakfast coffee with Leafdale and time had gotten away from him. Like a tank out of control, he bowled his way past the left-arm rates, stuck his long, pointed head deep into the fo'c's'le hatch and began to shout. The flared hatch-opening served to amplify greatly his lengthy oration, attracting attention all the way to the *1318*.

Within five minutes he had covered his 'big-ship' background, his love of the Navy, and his hatred of goldbricking and fuckin' up. He threw in for good measure that he did not consider this matchstick of a ship nor anyone on it a real sailor. It was a piece of shit that should be manned by shallow-water sailors, and no real big-ship sailor should ever be seen aboard such a scow. He ended with, "Now, fall out on the double!"

When he removed his head from the hatch opening, he found himself facing a big blob of a swab he had not seen before, a very wide, heavy-looking kid in grease-smeared dungarees.

"So, what's the goddamned point?" demanded the young man, who was a good six inches shorter than him but also a good twelve wide. "You some kind of a' officer-type?"

It was the second time in one day Baldini had encountered this kind of crap, and while his mouth was still flapping soundlessly, Pop Law came through the hatch, dragging a dirty seabag. He was dressed in dirty whites and smoking a cigarette. It should have been obvious to Baldini that he was ready for bear.

"Well, I'll be goddamned!" said Baldini. "Git rid of that butt, sailor!"

"Go to hell," said Pop, moving toward the boatswain's mate. "You know, men like you don't do very well in civilian life. You've got to have rank and regulations to get you what you want. In civilian life you would have to rely on your wits and intelligence." He glanced around and said to his applauding audience, "Well, fellows, I guess I'll see you back in the States. Good luck with *this*," he nodded backward toward Baldini. Then he turned and headed for the gangplank, where he did not bother to salute either the fantail or the O. O. D., as he bounced his seabag across to the dock.

"Now, there goes a lucky sonofabitch!" groaned Big John Leavy, the big blob who had spoken so irreverently to the boatswain's mate a moment before. "What I wouldn't give to be in his shoes."

Leavy, who had grown up on the back streets of Brooklyn, had weighed into the Navy at just over one hundred and ninety pounds. But after a long and dangerous youth searching unsuccessfully for food, he had in less than a year put down enough of the nutritious Navy chow to bring him to around two hundred and fifty pounds. And he was still growing in all directions.

"What's your name, Fatso?" demanded Baldini.

The big, unhappy sailor looked around at everything but the boatswain's mate, frowning ambiguously. A cloud of confusion and embarrassment began to work its way up his enormous pimpled neck.

"I said, scum bag, what's your name?"

"Leavy. What's yours?"

"Well, Fatso, I'll tell you—and these other fuckers along with you! I happen to be Baldini, the goddamned boatswain's mate of this ship! And you cocksuckers are goin' to turn to right now and git this ship sea-worthy! You hear me?" He stood back to let two more swabs through the hatch. "All of you, turn to on the double!"

With that he whirled and glared at the men along the lifelines. His eyes settled on Jines, who had just become the new Sparks on the ship. He walked over and tapped the big Iowa farm kid on the shoulder:

"I want ever'body turning to on the deck, and that includes the kid you've got in the radio shack. Mister Howorth's okayed it." He waved the sheet of paper he was carrying in Jines' face. Then he turned to

Tracy, who was standing next to Jines, and said, "And that goes for that so-called striker of yours, the one with a French name."

"Fuck you, Baldini," laughed Wild Bill. "Roucloux stays on the guns. I've got work to do same as you."

"Same goes here," said Jines. "I need Hall in the shack."

At thirteen hundred hours that same day, having just given up on Kwaitkowski's first attempt at cooking a chow since the ship had arrived from the East Coast, practically all of the Department Heads were gathered at the messtable in the after crew's quarters drinking coffee. Baldini, having eaten earlier with the deckhands and the other forecastle noncoms, came lumbering down the metal ladder like a man weighing five hundred pounds. Without preliminary he made a place for himself at the table and introduced himself.

"I don't have to tell you we've got a slop bucket here. And in case it hasn't occurred to you, it's my job to put this slop bucket in shape, and I intend to do it. I would like to have your cooperation, but you need to know that I have the backing of the officers to do what it takes. You'll save yourself some real problems if you throw in with me."

The old salts of the ship appeared to be in a state of shock. Ace McCormick later described the scene to me, saying that Baldini looked and sounded like something that had dropped unannounced and unwanted out of the sky, and he remembered thinking that this hairy simian creature was both an abomination and a bird of ill omen.

Pills was the first to speak: "Where the hell did you come from? You're not talking to a bunch of deckhands, you know."

Bill Tracy had begun to roll his eyeballs and snicker. "Unbelievable, don't you think, fellas?" To the boatswain's mate he said, "Stay out of my business. Leave Roucloux alone."

Kwaitkowski was suddenly standing next to the island that blocked the view of the galley, and there was no humor in his voice when he spoke: "You got away with using Eddie Jake on deck today, Boats. But if you ever do that again, you will surely die of malnutrition or food poisoning once we go to sea. I need my messcook more than you do."

"Well, hell!" blasted Baldini, getting up from the table. "I guess I'll just have to pull rank on you bastards. I am the ranking enlisted man aboard this ship, you know! Cross me and you will be in deep shit."

*   *   *

Across the harbor and the city, on a break from their duties in the Communications Office at Comseron, Sharkey and Smith chain-smoked in Tent Number 9 and talked about me.

Sharkey suddenly stood up, lifted the field glasses off the nail on the center post, and turned to Smith. "What do you suppose he saw with these? I don't think he missed one afternoon takin' these things up on the hill."

"Couldn't have been much," mused Smitty. "There aint anything around here to see from there, except the harbor and the top of the Red Cross Tent. I'd say he was gazing out at sea hoping a man-o'-war would show up and take him lands away. Does he ever think of anything else?"

"But he's a red-blooded boy," said Sharkey, "and I for one think he was going up there to look at something besides ships. I think I'll go up and take a look around. You comin'?"

"Might as well. It's too hot to sleep in here."

Sharkey led the way, circling around behind the tents and picking up the little path that cut to the right through the low, stunted trees. Before they had gone fifty yards, Sharkey was bending over, huffing. At the crest, they got their first glimpse of the red tile roofs of Noumea, a patchwork quilt stretching out below them toward the harbor.

"I guess he got his ship at last," sighed Smith. "You know, I think the Commander suspects us of something. The way he looks at us gives me the heeby-jeebies."

"What could he suspect us of?" objected Sharkey. "We haven't done a damned thing. Besides, he's too interested in the nurses to pay any attention to us."

"If what you say about Navy logic is true, do you think we ought to act a little unhappy at times, complain a bit? We wouldn't want him or the lieutenant to think we're too happy with our job."

"Naw, we'll be all right as long as we don't rock the boat. The Navy never pays you any attention till you rock the boat or put in for a transfer. Besides, we happen to be pretty high on the Admiral's list after gettin' our ships knocked out from under us."

"Well, I just hope Comdr. Farris knows that," said Smith.

Sharkey had been surveying the scenery below them with the binoculars. Suddenly, his whole body stiffened and he began to adjust the glasses frantically.

"What?" demanded Smith. "Have you spotted something?"

Sharkey did not reply. He and the glasses appeared to be frozen. Then he sighed, "Oh, Christ in Heaven! You will not believe what I am lookin' at!"

"Well, hell, give!" Smith had moved beside Sharkey and was trying to follow the line of the glasses. "Is that somebody sunbathin?"

"I may be hallucinatin'!" moaned the incredulous Sharkey.

Smith wrestled the glasses away from his stocky friend and began wildly adjusting them to his weaker eyes. Like a starving man, the sonarman commenced to jump up and down and urge him to get on with it. Finally, he could stand it no longer, "Hey, you're pointin' that thing in the wrong direction! Look, down there, at the Governor's backyard! See the girl on the towel? She's stark-ass naked!"

"Yeah, yeah!" exclaimed Smith, "The girl on the big towel!"

"Wha'd you think I was lookin' at, the birdbath?" howled Sharkey, trying to retrieve the glasses.

"That must be the girl Hall took French lessons from!" said Smith, beginning to breath hard. "And all he had to say about her was that she was quite good-lookin'! My God, look at them bubbles, Smitty, and, oh me oh my Miss Molly, look at how she flares out at the bottom! Git back, for Pete's sake!"

The yard below them was completely encircled by a very high rock wall; and the girl was lying on her back with her arms and legs spread wide apart. Except for a pair of narrow sunglasses, she was completely nude.

"If you don't stop hopping around like that, you're gonna cause her to git up and move inside the house," said Smith. "My god, a person would think you've never seen a young, beautiful, naked female!"

Sharkey, once again in charge of the glasses, took a handkerchief from his dungarees, and began to dab at his eyes. Then, without a word, he gave up the glasses.

"She's a looker," sighed Smith, "maybe the best I've ever seen."

"Shit," sneered Sharkey, snatching the glasses back. He adjusted them methodically this time, and when he had them pointed in the right direction and focused, he said calmly, "She's built like a brick shithouse, and the way she's layin' it looks like she's cocked and ready for someone. Oh, oh, she's turnin' over. Oh, lovely lovely lovely melons, flat little belly, well-developed butt—"

"Somebody's comin'," said Smith.

"Looks like she's about eighteen, maybe nineteen. And I'd guess she's five—"

"Hey, Shark, I hear somebody comin' up the hill!"

"Man," said Sharkey, unconcerned, "that's prime beef." Then, Smith's words having finally soaked in, he quickly lowered the glasses and turned around. "Wha'd you say?"

At that moment an officer's cap popped into sight around a bush, followed by the amused face of Lt. Monahan. "There you are! I've been lookin' for you two!" He was breathing heavily, and one hand was supporting his belly. "What're you looking at?"

"Nothin' at all, Sir. We was just headin' back down," said Sharkey, offering the glasses to Smith. "Come, on Smitty." He took a step down the hill toward the compound, having failed to rid himself of the glasses.

"Hold on a minute," said the lieutenant. "Let me borrow those." He held out his hand for the glasses.

"There's not a thing to look at," said Sharkey. "Huh, Smitty?"

"Not a thing," hastened Smith. "Miles and miles of nothin'."

"Yeah, well, I happen to know better," said the officer, taking the glasses and walking to the highest point. "Hmmm, just what I thought. Pretty, pretty girl and naughty, naughty boys. Know what this means?"

"What could it mean, Sir?" asked Sharkey quickly. "We was—"

"Gazing upon the nude body of our Governor's fine young daughter," snickered Lt. Monahan. "International incident maybe. Who knows, perhaps France will ask for the death penalty for this most embarrassing breech of decency."

Smith tried to chuckle, "You're funnin' us, Sir."

Lt. Monahan, who had never cared much for the Navy's policy of modley-coddling enlisted men who had lost their ships, bawled out, "Hell, no, I'm not funnin' you, you lousy peckerwoods! I'm placing you on report! Now, go to your tent and stay there till I tell you you can leave it!"

Sharkey, hatless, started to salute but stopped and glanced across at Smith. "Yes, Sir."

"We was just tryin' to spot Hall's ship," said Smith. "I personally didn't see anything."

"Me neither," said Sharkey. "And that's the truth, Sir."

"You two slugs never told the truth in your lives," said the lieutenant, calmly. "But if that's your defense, I'll see that it's entered in the record."

*   *   *

The following day, two sad-looking swabs mustered on the cobblestone quarterdeck in front of Comseronsopac headquarters. They were on time and, in keeping with Comdr. Farris's specific orders, they brought along all of their earthly belongings.

"Does it appear to you that we are about to quit this place?" asked Smith, his face deadpan.

"It would appear," sighed Sharkey. "And just when I was gettin' to like it."

Having lost their liberty duds in the Coral Sea, they had on this occasion dressed in their best dungarees, another minor point in their favor. But when Lt. Monahan caught sight of them through his upstairs window, he snarled at the yeoman behind him:

"The wiseackers, what they're gettin' is just what they deserve!"

A yeoman called out cheerfully, "I guess you want some orders, sir."

"You know the ones." Lt. Monahan said harshly. "But I've forgotten the name of the scow we're sendin' them to."

"Something I never heard of before," chortled the yeoman. "Something called an *SC.*"

Lt. Monahan nodded, thoughtfully, taking the two envelopes and turning toward the stairs. "I hope it takes them right into Tokyo Bay." When he reached the quarterdeck, the two enlisted men were at attention on the cobblestone front yard. Sharkey's belly was out noticeably.

"You'll lose some of that where you're goin'," said the officer, glaring at them. He had not returned their salute.

Neither of the men spoke.

"Why aren't you in uniform?" Monahan demanded. He walked up to Sharkey and stuck his nose within inches of the enlisted man's. "You cannot go anyplace in dungarees."

"We can't?" burst out Sharkey happily. The scowl on Monahan's face made him add, "Uh, Sir, our undress uniforms went down with our ships in the Battle of the Coral Sea. Does that mean we're not goin' to be transferred?"

The lieutenant threw up his hands in disgust. "That was how long ago? Do you intend to spend the entire war dressed like this?" He turned and looked toward the building, as if he expected help. Then he turned back and snarled, "On your way out of here I want you to go by Ship's Stores and pick up undress whites. You show up at your new duty station in dungarees and they'll throw the book at you!"

"I thought that was what you're doin' to us now, Sir," said Sharkey.

The lieutenant wheeled, his head down between his shoulders. Sharkey quickly added, "Yessir, and thank you, Sir!"

Smith, upon receiving his orders and reading the first line, said, "Could I ask a question, Sir?" He pointed and held the paper out for the lieutenant to look.

Monahan, at the end of his patience, ignored Smith, handed Sharkey his envelope. "You two are very fortunate, you know, getting out of this with not even a Captain's Mast on your record. Maybe this assignment will straighten you out a bit."

"Uh, we've already been straightened out," Sharkey assured him. "Have you had a ship shot out from under you recently, Sir?"

Monahan cleared his throat noisily: "That little accident up north won't save your ass this time, sailor. You see, gazing at the Governor's lovely *unclothed* daughter, without permission, wiped out all the points you had."

"But, Sir, beggin' your pardon, sir, I don't think there's any tangible proof we actually saw that young lady."

"I'm an eye witness that says you did. Both of you. And I guess an officer's word is about as tangible as the occasion calls for."

The Duty Jeep was ready to pull out, and as Sharkey climbed into the seat beside the driver and glanced back toward the lovely old residential building, he said quietly, "I hope that fucker gets what's comin' to him. Maybe they'll transfer his ass up north."

"Don't you think that's where we're headin'?" groaned Smith. "Maybe this thing called the 'SC-995' is so small it won't be able to make it up north."

"Whatever it is and wherever it's goin'," growled Sharkey, "it aint gonna be good. We're bein' shanghaied, if I'm not badly mistaken." He turned to the driver, "Hey, Admiral, where you takin' us?"

After glancing at Sharkey's orders, the young black man said, "All the way down to the docks!"

"Well, what're we gonna do there?"

"Hell, I don't know. Wait around for a boat, I guess. It says 'Ile Nou Island'. Wait for a' LCVP to take you there."

Smith, taking out his orders and looking at them for the tenth time, cleared his throat. "Maybe we're goin' to one of them little yippy boats that putt-putt around harbors and look cute. Somebody's gettin' that duty."

"Nope, it aint that," said the driver. "They aint 'signin' men to them things no more. What's your ship called ag'in?"

Both Smith and Sharkey groaned, "*The SC-995*."

"Hell, man, that's one of them suicidal crafts they're outfittin' fo' up north."

Sharkey cried, "Cut out the shit! You don't know what it is!"

"Wha'd you boys do to git such lousy duty, rape the Commandant's wife?"

"The Commandant's wife is in Flint, Michigan," snapped Sharkey. "We put in for sea duty."

"Yeah, sure you did. You preferred the sea to *El Paradiso*, right? That's like choosin' Death Valley over the Pango Pango. You couldn't wait to get away from the good chow and nightly movies and all the liberty you can handle."

"Don't enumerate," said Sharkey. "We thought we might get a wagon or a heavy cruiser or something like that. I guess we thought wrong."

"Well, about as wrong as wrong can be!" laughed Weter.

After they had passed through the laundry district and was circling the Square, Sharkey, speaking in his very best conciliatory tone, said to Weter, "Say, Admiral, speaking of telescopes, have you ever gone up on the hill behind Comseron?"

"There's quite a view from up there," admitted Smith.

"I'm not interested in the view from up there," said Weter. "There aint a thing on this entire island I want to see."

"Oh, but I beg to differ," said Sharkey. "Do you know that the Governor's daughter sometimes lies naked right down below the top of Comseron Hill, not more than a hundred yards from where you sleep?"

"What hill?" squealed Weter, swerving the Jeep into the curb.

"Watch out!" shouted Smith. "Be careful, man!"

"The hill behind Comseron," said Sharkey. "On the other side from where your tent is."

"You guys're shittin' me!"

"Nope. It's the gospel truth," Sharkey urged. "Right, Smith?"

"Right on the money."

"Well, I don't think that lovely piece would lie naked right out in the open, for all to see," said Admiral Weter, unconvincingly.

"She's inside a yard that's sheltered from all sides by a twelve-foot wall, for Christ's sake!" argued Sharkey.

"An' up there you can see over that wall?" said Weter, staring at them wide-eyed.

"Right on," nodded Sharkey. "Seein' that lovely creature baskin' in the sun, turning her lovely butt every which way, spreading out her lovely melons for the sun to do its duty—"

"Oh, god damn, man! What do you want for them glasses?"

*　　　　　　*　　　　　　*

Later, while waiting for a barge to transport them to Ile Nou and their new home, Smith asked Sharkey, "Do you think he's dumb enough to fall for that?"

"Fall for what? Hell, we told him the truth. And we made twenty-five bucks out of the deal. For property we didn't even own."

"Yeah, that's right, we did tell him the truth. But if he's not a complete idiot he'll put two and two together and come up with the reason we're headin' north."

"He's from Louisiana," said Sharkey, as if that settled the issue. "And he's too contented with Comseron for his own good. I think it's time for him to change his duty station."

Shortly after thirteen hundred hours on that brilliant but unusually hot day in the first week of October, 1944, which was just the beginning of summer in New Caledonia, the two old tincan sailors managed to hitch a ride across Noumea Harbor and drag their brand new seabags to the top of the little hill that looked down upon the five subchasers.

Sharkey began looking about for some kind of shade in which to sit, abandoning his bag and other gear in the sun. Finally giving that up, he slumped with a groan onto a little knoll and stared belligerently at the scene below them. Smith managed to position one end of his seabag in the shade of a sickly bush and, making a chinrest with his hands, fell to gazing off toward the big-bellied gooney birds at the Naval Air Transportation Service.

"The fickle finger of fate has been pointed at us," said Sharkey. "I think we have hit the bottom of the proverbial bucket."

"Yeah. And I seem to remember hearin' you take on about things bein' about as bad as they could get when we was out at the Receiving Station. At least there we knew we wouldn't have to stand no watches or be eaten by sharks. Want me to quote it back to you word for word?"

"Well, hell, until then that was as bad as things had ever got for me. I didn't even know about shit like this."

"Let us not judge too hastily, Shark, old buddy. Maybe Lt.Monahan made a mistake. Maybe this'll turn out to be the best duty in the service."

"Quit lookin' at the gooney birds over at NATS and look down there. That's were we're goin', for Chrissake!"

Smith turned and studied the little subchasers. The four pretty ones appeared to be deserted, but on the ugly one at the end of the dock there was an amazing amount of activity, despite the heat and humidity.

"I just hope *SC-995* don't stand for that one at the far end of the dock," commented Sharkey, raising a limp hand and pointing. "Maybe it stands for one of them new dudes. Can you believe sailors of the United States Navy would be scurrying about in this heat with nobody pointin' a gun at 'em?"

"Well, I'm not about to find out what anything stands for until this heat wave diminishes," said the other. "Maybe about chow time."

6

Sharkey and Smith

The scene below them, viewed at that angle and distance and without prejudice or bias, would surely have inspired Monet to paint a masterpiece; but Mortimer L. Sharkey and Loren B. Smith saw only five little wooden suicide boats on their way to disaster in the General MacArthur Island-Hopping Campaign. With them on the sorriest one of the bunch.

It was becoming uncomfortably warm there on that bare little hill overlooking the Ile Nou Naval Supply Base docks, but they knew that on the exposed decks of the subchasers it had to be much worse.

Smith was the first to notice that a man wearing baggy dungarees had left the derelict and was bee-lining it up the hill toward them. He was wearing a long-sleeve shirt buttoned at the wrists, and pulled down over his eyes was a salty old chief's cap. "Pay attention," he said calmly to Sharkey, leaning and punching the dozing sonarman. "Here comes trouble."

"Shit, that looks like a CPO," mused Smith. "Did he come off one of them lousy boats?"

"The ugly one at the end of the dock."

The closer the man got the more he resembled a very large chimpanzee. His head sloped from the top of his bald head, his arms were much too long for his body, and he had entirely too much hair over his ears.

"Look at that sucker," said Sharkey. "I'd hate to run into that in a dark alley."

Baldini had spotted the two goldbricks the minute they settled down on their seabags. He noticed that once they were comfortable beneath a small tree on the hillside, they amused themselves by tossing small rocks in the general direction of the *995*. It was obvious to him that they were transcients, and he happened to know that the other boats had full complements.

He prided himself on being a keen observer of deadbeats and gold-bricks in golfball caps. These two were planning to get out of half a day's work, but he would be damned if it was going to happen. Finally unable to take it any longer, he barreled his way out to the dock and began the ascent. When he was still some distance from them, he called out, "Hey, you there! You supposed to be on the *995?*"

Sharkey put his hands to his ears and turned the palms toward Baldini, "Who wants to know?"

"I do, goddamnit! Git your asses down there and sign aboard!"

"You sound kinda like a Chief Bosun!" called out Sharkey. "But you don't smell like one and you're dressed like a fuckin' deckhand!"

Smith was lying back on his seabag, with his eyes closed. "Hey, Shark, would you call me when I make Chief?"

"Let's see your orders!" demanded Baldini, coming to a halt over them.

"Not unless you're the C. O. of the *SC-995*," said Sharkey, taking out his papers and looking at them. "What's your name, sailor?"

Smith commented casually, "We haven't decided when we're reportin' aboard, or even if. You use to be a Chief, or what?"

"As far as you're concerned, I still am," snarled Baldini. "Hand over your orders."

"I guess not," said Smith, opening his eyes and looking at the ground at his feet. "We'll hand them to our C. O., when we report aboard. And it's a lead pipe cinch you aint him."

Baldini began to wipe sweat from his brow with his arms. Then he stared at them hard for a time, his small black eyes snapping from one of them to the other. "You think you're mighty damn smart, don't you? Well, I've dealt with shit like you before." And with that he turned and headed back down the hill toward the dock. "I'll just see what the Wardroom thinks about this!"

"What wardroom?" asked Smith, blinking.

They watched the angry boatswain's mate plough down the hill, disregarding the path and making a cloud of dust.

"Now, that," said Sharkey, "is scary as hell. I didn't know the Navy was harboring zoo creatures these days."

"Yeah," moaned Smith, "an' to think we've got to live with that hairy bastard. What do you guess, he's a busted chief?"

"No doubt about it. And them things can be worse'n a wounded bull elephant." Sharkey lay back on his bag and closed his eyes.

"Don't you think he looks a little like that messcook at Comseron that ole Hall beat the shit out of? You know, the one with the bushy eyebrows and hair growing out of his ears?"

"A little. But I had in mind an orangutan I once dated in Cleveland. There's no doubt about his kinship to that species. Long slopin' brow, little narrow black eyes, heavy black eyebrows, a mouthful of long, yellow teeth."

On Baldini's way through the pilothouse, Ace McCormick stopped him with, "I don't think you'd better disturb them right now. They're recuperatin' from that trip to Noumea last night."

"Mind your own goddamned business."

It irked Baldini that this long drink of water was always meddling in other people's affairs. He was like a nosy old woman squirreled away here in his pilothouse, peering through the portholes at everything that moved on the ship.

Baldini was not a big man physically, but he gave the impression that he was. And when he went up or down a ladder, it sounded like a Notre

Dame fullback. The whole ship knew when he moved from one deck to the other.

He lunged down the ladder into the radio shack, catching the corner of Jines' swivel chair as he went by and sending it crashing into the radio desk. Without so much as a glance backward at the possible damage he might have done, he went to the wardroom door and began rapping. From inside came a loud groan, then the door opened wide.

"Yeah, what is it now, Boats?"

"There's two new men, Sir, up on the hill and they won't come down."

"What 'two new men'?" came another voice from behind the door. "How do you know they belong to us? Have you seen their orders?"

Baldini cleared his voice. "They're settin' up there in the shade lookin' down at us. I know they're ourn."

"Leave them alone. They're free agents until they sign aboard."

"Their orders say—"

"Baldini!"

"They're just stallin' till evenin' chow, Sir. I know it."

It was Ensign Howorth talking this time, no doubt about it: "Baldini, I want you to go set in the shade someplace and cool off. Yoah soaking wet with sweat, 'cause I c'n smell yuh thoo thet doah. I think the sun's gettin' to you. Go on now. I don't want to see yoah face down heah ag'in this afternoon."

*   *   *

When I caught sight of my two old salty friends dragging their brand-new seabags down the dock, I ran out of the pilothouse, waving and yelling. Baldini was right behind me making noises in his throat.

"Now, this cannot be," said Sharkey casually when he reached the gangplank. "The world is not this small. Smith, do you agree?"

"It looks like our boy all right," said Smith. "Be danged if I don't think 'tis! How'n hell are you, Hall?"

They dropped their seabags next to the engineroom hatch and shook hands with me, making a big fuss. Then they began on me, about how dirty I was, saying that I was scroungier than they had ever seen me before.

"How's old Comseronsopac?" I finally got out. "What caused you two to leave? I thought you really liked that place! Did you get homesick for the sea?"

"Wait wait wait!" shouted Sharkey, raising his hands and waving them. "One thing at a time. We decided it was too risky to let you go north without a chaperone."

"Aw, come on!" I laughed. "Listen, I'm really glad to see you! The three of us will be there in the pilothouse together!"

"My God, that little outhouse?" cried Sharkey, who turned and stared as if he had just noticed the ship had a pilothouse. "Smitty, do you think we can handle bein' that close to this unclean kid?"

"Wait till you see all the stuff we've got to work with!" I bragged. "You think just because this's a little ship—!"

Sharkey put his hand on my arm. "Now, now, boy. Smitty, I don't think I've ever seen Hall this discombobbled before." He tried to mess up my hair. "What have they done, made a pirate out of you?"

He was referring to the way I was dressed. All I had on were soiled dungaree trousers cut off at the knees. I think this was the first time they had ever seen me in public without a shirt.

"I had to work on deck today." After a pause, during which they just grinned at me, I whispered, nodding over my shoulder, "We've got a new Boats." Baldini was right there beside us, listening.

"You mean noncommissioned officers of the U. S. Navy have to work on deck?" howled Sharkey in alarm. "That's against Naval Regulations. Any asshole knows that!"

"Uh, Shark!" I cautioned, speaking quietly and moving my head slightly toward Baldini. "That's what Ace and Jines and everybody else says. By the way, where do you get a copy of this document I keep hearing about? I don't think some people aboard this ship has ever seen it. At least they don't act like they have."

"Yeah, and I know somebody aboard this mighty Naval vessel that's more than likely never heard of the Geneva Convention," growled Sharkey, turning his eyes over in Baldini's direction. "Something from darkest Africa, I reckon." He was not trying to keep his voice down. "With long arms and a face that would scare hell out of King Kong."

"Better not let him hear you say that," I warned just above a whisper. "He's having a hard time adjusting to the ship. But what does Navy Regs say about left-arm rates?"

"Well, it expressly forbids the man with such a thing from doin' any physical work. We're like white collar workers in civilian life."

"Baldini hasn't heard about that," I assured him. "What he says is that he is the ranking enlisted man aboard, which makes him a kind of Fourth Officer."

"The hell you say. Well, it's about time somebody clued him in on a few things. And, Hall, I myself will convey that message to him first chance I git."

"He's right there behind you," I mumbled through stiff lips.

"What's that big fellow in the apron sayin'?" asked Sharkey, ignoring what I had said. "I am certain he's mouthin' 'chow down.'"

"Port section eats first," I said. "Let's go find out which section you and Smitty are in. Our yeoman is down below." I turned to leave.

Carpenter, the yeoman striker, came out of the pilothouse at just this time, no doubt heading for chow. I grabbed him and nodded toward my two friends:

"Sharkey there is a sonarman and Smith is a radarman. Will they be Department Heads?"

Carpenter, who reminded me of a cheerleader back at Kerman Union High, smiled at me and shook his head. "They'll be part of the Bridge Gang, under Ace. Port Section. Find 'em a bunk in the fo'c's'le."

I nodded, "Port Section, up in the fo'c's'le." I faced Sharkey and Smith. "I sleep in the fo'c's'le, with the lowlies."

"Then that's where I'll sleep," nodded Sharkey. "Smith, now, may want to bunk with the old salts."

"It gets very bad up there," said Carpenter. "That's what Tracy told me. Much worse than the after quarters."

"He's an old fo'c's'le man," I said, nodding toward Sharkey. "Besides, he deserves to be up there. Baldini and Leavy and the other deckhands sleep there, not to mention the grease monkeys."

"I know I won't like it," admitted Sharkey, sounding like a spoiled young thing. He had picked up on my attitude toward Carpenter. Then he added quickly, as if to wipe the inference: "I don't like the sound of *fo'c's'le*, and as for Baldini, well, enough said. But if that's where ole Hall bunks, I reckon I can take it."

*   *   *

After chow, the three of us worked our way forward, and at the fo'c's'le hatch Sharkey stopped and pointed into the darkness below, wrinkling his nose. "There's been a bad mistake made down there. Smith, git a whiff of that!" He dropped his seabag through the hatchway. "I don't know who or what made it, but I'm sure as hell I don't belong down there." Well after the heavy bag had landed on the deck below, he called out, "Heads up!"

"I think the mistake is not in the fo'c's'le alone," said Smth. "Maybe we ought to go talk to the Skipper about our presence on this ship." After a pause, he added: "It's not like the Navy to admit a mistake, but at least we could try."

I knew they were just kidding but at this point, leading the way down in the crew's quarters, I began trying to convince them that things really weren't all that bad. "You liked the chow, didn't you? I think it's great the three of us are going north together."

At the foot of the ladder, I looked up. Sharkey had put his foot through the hatch opening and, holding to the cover with both hands, began to descend on his heels, facing away from the ladder. I shouted at him to go back on deck and try descending with his face toward the ladder.

Once he was safely down, he turned to me as if he had had no trouble at all getting down: "Now with all due regard for your obsession to go and single-handedly end the war, my boy, please try to look at this thing from our viewpoint. Smith and me do not need any more north, and what's more we've lost a great deal of our earlier cravin' for the sea and the delights therefrom. Right, Smitty?"

Smith said nothing until he was on the deck beside us.

"Is it always this dark in here? Where are the port'les?"

There were no portholes, of course, and the only light in the quarters besides what little made it down from the hatchway was a single lightbulb that dangled from a cord. And it had gone out the day I came aboard. After a time, I had learned, it was possible to make one's way about down there.

"My God!" exclaimed Sharkey. "Can't say I ever run into anything quite so pronounced as the smell down here. It's got death and decay in it, but there's something else. Mule puke?"

Smith continued to stand at the bottom of the ladder and peer around at the chaos, nodding tragically. "Old socks, unwashed bodies, mildewed sweat. Do you suppose it could be attributable to one person? Say Baldini?"

"No, I don't think so," said Sharkey. "More'n likely it's a communal thing. Hall, have you actually *slept* down here?"

"Sure!" I laughed. "You get used to the smell. What you don't get used to at night is the *noise*."

"What kind of noise?" asked Sharkey.

"Well," I teased, drawing the word out. "I guess you'll find out."

"I don't want to find out," said Sharkey, grabbing me by the throat and pretending he was going to choke the information out of me.

I removed his hands quite easily and said, "I'll give you a hint. You know what you sound like after you eat a lot of garlic and get drunk on wine and then try to sleep it off?"

"Oh, God!" said Smitty.

"Why, I never heard a thing on such occasions," said Sharkey. "I don't even dream when I'm in that state."

"The Boats and Leavy are even worse than that," I said proudly. "Boats snorts and snaps all night long and Leavy groans and sounds like a storm coming up that gets fiercer and fiercer."

"Smith, let's jump overboard and swim away."

We stood looking about at the compartment, what we could see of it. Stacked metal bunks, three high, covered the starboard and port bulkheads. They were suspended from the overhead by chains; and lowered, as they were now, they took up most of the room in the compartment. In the after end was a tiny head with a stool and a shower.

I pointed out Tabor's bunk, on the starboard forward end of the compartment, highest up. This had been his nest and his sanctuary ever since Groton and New London, and during this time he had done a remarkable job of personalizing it. He had installed a curtain and another hanging light (which I was certain worked) and covered the bulkhead with pictures of shapely, black-eyed girls with no clothes on.

"Who the hell is Tabor?" exclaimed Sharkey, incredulous.

"A Blackfoot Indian," I said. "From Oklahoma, where I came from."

"What this place needs is a Captain's Inspection," said Smith. "But I doubt that an officer could stand to come down in here. Does anybody ever use the laundry aboard this ship?"

"We have no laundry," I said. "We use buckets and when we go to sea we'll play it out on lines in the ship's wake."

Sharkey poked Smith: "Can you guess which one of the bunks is ole Hall's?"

"No problem," said Smith, grinning and pointing toward the middle bunk on the port side next to the ladder. It had a clean, smooth mattress cover and a very clean and fluffed pillow. "This is probably the only bunk in here that would pass an inspection."

"You haven't seen behind Tabor's curtain yet," I said quickly. "When he's up there in the daytime, you can see that everything's in order. He keeps his bunk every bit as clean as mine, and nobody dares get close to it. Leavy's always leaning on mine, and he sweats a lot."

Sharkey unrolled a mattress on one of the bunks, flattened it, and stretched out with a sigh, with his hands cupped behind his head. Smith selected another empty bunk just forward of it and did the same thing.

"Tell us something about the crew, Hall. What kind of a lot have we cast ourselves in with?" Sharkey closed his eyes and got comfortable, preparing to contemplate my reply.

"Oh, I don't know," I said with a laugh, leaning against my bunk. "Most of them have been busted, I guess, from what Ace says."

"Who's this Ace fellow?"

"He's a tincan sailor, like you two, and lost his ship same as you did. And he's the quartermaster aboard the ship, which makes him your boss, I guess." It suddenly dawned on me that I had no idea what his rank was. "He spends all of his time in the pilothouse polishing brass or something, and he never raises his voice. You have to listen close to figure out what he's saying sometimes. Oh, yes, he's always singing or humming the same song, about a gal that's got a hole in her stockin'."

"Sounds like he's gone Asiatic," said Sharkey. "Right, Smitty?"

"No doubt about it. How about the other radiomen aboard this boat? God, tell us you're the only one they could find."

"'Aboard this *boat*'?" I asked, putting my face in his and glaring.

"Okay, *ship*," conceded Smith, faking chagrin. "Answer my question."

"Just Jines and me, since Fletcher's being rotated back to the States and DiAugustino got a transfer."

"How'd he get a transfer?" Sharkey tried to sit up in the bunk and bumped his head on the metal framework. "He actually got a transfer?"

"He told the Skipper he didn't want to go north."

"Oh?" cried Sharkey, leaping out of the bunk. "Was that all he did?"

After we had stared at each other for a time, I said, "You and Smith and I are going north, Sharkey. I really like having you guys on the ship."

"Like hell we are. I'm going to the Skipper in the morning and explain that I hate like hell goin' north. And don't you doubt it for a minute."

"It won't do you any good."

"Why not? You just said—!"

"We're heading north any day now, and he could never replace you and Smitty in time. You would just get his dander up, and he is one officer you had better not do that to."

"Well, hell, that figures." He crawled back into the bunk and settled down. "Any other odd ducks on the ship?"

"Well, there's William Tracy, better known as Wild Bill."

"What's queer about him?"

"He's a practical joker that likes to fist-fight. He has sent two to the hospital since I came aboard, and he teases me every chance he gets."

"Yeah, well, if he goes around puttin' people in the hospital, he's more than a joker," said Smith. "What's his rating?"

"First Class Gunner's Mate, I think. A Department Head."

"You put up with this, Hall?" asked Sharkey. "Why don't you give him a little what you gave Bowker?"

I didn't say anything right away because I was remembering the thing with the messcook at Comseron. Finally, I said, "I lost my temper. It was the third time he had done that, you know, and when he called me yellow that was just too much."

"Well," sighed Smith, "I bet old Bowker never pulled that stunt on anybody else. By the way, Comseron got rid of him as soon as he came back from the hospital. Maybe he ended up on one of these subchasers."

"I've made up my mind I'm not going to fight anybody aboard this ship," I said. "We've all got to get along if we're going north."

*　　　　　*　　　　　*

Immediately below the Skipper was the open flag box. Into this he dropped his cap with a flourish, revealing a great mass of blond hair. Then with another flourish he removed his tie and dropped on top of his cap. "I'm not much on ties and such," he grinned. "Grew up on a boat about this size. It had sails on it and could outrun a speedboat when the wind was just right."

I was standing below him on the little quarterdeck with most of the crew, and up on the bridge with him were the two ensigns. This, I had informed Sharkey and Smith a few minutes before, was to be Lt.(jg) Hiller's first muster since coming aboard the ship.

"Let me say, first of all, I'm glad to be aboard the *Subchaser 995!* Actually, I mean that. Oh, I've been on bigger boats, and I know from your service records many of you have, too. But this beats the heck out of a land base, anytime. I like the wind in my face, and I like to get the raw feel of the ocean when it's acting up a bit. In this old boy we will live every minute of our stay aboard her."

This brought a laugh from most of those around me, but there were also a few groans.

He went on to say that he was sorry it had taken him so long to reach the ship, and that he knew there was a lot to do to put it in shape for the journey north. With a miracle or two we should be able to make it. He had it on good authority that the other subchasers were just about ready to go, but that same authority had informed him that we would be given one week to catch up.

Now he leaned over the bridge skirt and spoke just loud enough for us to hear (There was an audience of swabs watching and listening on the sterns of the *SC-419* and the *SC-664*): "Just about everyone, from the brass at Flag Allowance to our fellow subchaser sailors right up ahead of us here on this dock, is convinced we will not be taking the trip north. They think we don't have what it takes to put this ship in shape in the time that we have, and what's more they probably think we would rather sit out the duration of the war right here in Noumea Harbor!" His voice had risen considerably.

I glanced around, met the eyes of a number of my shipmates, and knew something extraordinary was happening to that bunch of misfits and goldbrickers. I wanted to shout and, turning to see how old Shark was taking it, was amazed at what I saw. He was grinning and nodding like a half-wit. Smitty nudged me and nodded, and I felt a lump rising in my throat.

The Skipper had straightened up and was speaking quietly to Ensigns Howorth and Darling, who were nodding and smiling. Turning back to us, he raised a hand for silence:

"All right, let's do it. Round the clock, four-on, four-off. Baldini, take the Port Section and begin the work on the hull. I want it scraped down to the raw timbers, red-leaded, and painted; and since the wood on this thing is about as old as our grandfathers, I want two coats of red-lead and about six of that baby blue stuff Supply sent over. We'll look a little different from the rest, but that won't be anything new. Right? Then git to it, men!"

*   *   *

None of us had ever been asked to do physical work around the clock before; and by the end of the first day we were exhausted, our hands were covered with blisters, and the end was definitely not in sight. One thing, however, sustained us, kept us going: Our three officers worked right along beside us!

The old salts in the crew were incredulous. *Stunned* might be a better word. At any rate the rest of us were so impressed by their reaction that we worked all the harder, and voluntarily gave up our god-given right to bitch and gripe. Even Sharkey, who was a world class goldbricker, worked like a Trojan and not once did I hear him come down on officers or Navy chow or lousy duty.

During the two days of scraping and the three days of red-leading and painting, the Ile Nou Supply Base moved in, cluttering up our main deck with rolls of coaxial cables and electrical wiring, mounds of crates and boxes, and enough lumber to build an entire subchaser. They completely occupied the pilothouse, where they installed sixteen U. S. Army transceivers, and the bridge, from which they installed cables and antennae to the top of the mast and from there to the point of the bow and the extreme stern. And while they were at it, they placed a very impressive radar dome on our masthead and gave us a new sound head.

And they did all of this and were gone before we had used up all of our baby blue paint.

Baldini, of course, spent most of th daylight hours cursing and reviling the noisy, nasty, careless seabees from the base. On a number of occasions he was near death from the messing and gauming on his deck; and once, for almost an hour, he was so distraught he could not make any noise with his mouth. The Skipper took this opportunity to pull him aside and warn him that the repair people were actually doing us a favor. Without them we would not be able to help General Macarthur out with his island-hopping, which was the rumored reason we were going north.

*   *   *

On the eve of our departure from New Caledonia on the long-awaited shakedown, Kwaitkowski was standing at the railing on the fantail of the *995* trying to decide when it would be appropriate and legal to throw his collection of potato peelings and empty food cans over the side. He had never been aboard a ship as small as this one, and so he didn't know whether it was all right with the officers to get rid of garbage while still inside a harbor or not. For all he knew there just might be a regulation against it. Then he thought of the only other alternative, and without further hesitation he leaned over the railing and turned the bucket upside down.

He straightened up, facing across the stern into the setting sun. In the hazy distance he could just make out the harbor exit and the whitecaps on the sea beyond. He stood there for a moment, breathing in the damp, cool air. It was most refreshing after the dead air of the galley. On his right, just out of sight, was the Ile Nou Repair Base, and on his left Leprosy Island, indistinguishable at this distance from the forested green hills of the eastern edge of the harbor.

Baldini, Kwaitkowski had noticed, was going up and down the ship carrying on about what a sailor he was, how much sea duty he had under his belt, how he guessed now the softies aboard this ship would find out just what going to sea was all about. He wondered if were possible this "big-ship man" was trying to convince himself?

Eddie Jake, wearing a dirty white apron, appeared in the hatchway complaining about the number of times he had been forced to climb that narrow metal ladder. And once again as banged his head on the hatch cover.

"Have you ever been seasick, Eddie?"

"About twenty-two times," said the big Texan, rubbing his head. "That's how many days it took us to git here from the States."

"Well, you're going to have a lot of company in about thirty minutes to an hour, if I'm not badly wrong."

The messcook took up a position beside the K-gun rack, swaying with the motion of the ship. "We're gonna roll pretty bad, I guess," he said.

Kwaitkowski nodded, smiling. "That's not the half of it. This thing will bounce like a cork the minute we leave the harbor; and if that doesn't do it, we'll feed them something that will. Look, we're already rolling and the surface of the harbor is as calm as a farm pond."

Eddie Jake nodded, already a shade paler than usual. "I was wonderin' about chow."

"What's to wonder?"

"You don't expect anybody to eat that stuff you're cookin' down there, do you? If the ship's rollin' and tossin', I mean."

Cookie smiled happily. "Like Baldini says, we will find out who the salts are on this boat. Those that eat my hearty supper and can keep it down any length of time at all will deserve the name *sailor*, and those that refuse to eat or end up feeding the fish will keep quiet in the future about their saltiness. You watch."

"Yeah, but fried pork chops and greasy gravy and watery potatoes? Did you—?"

"Tradition, kid, tradition. Someday, if you last long enough, you will understand." With that Kwaitkowski turned and headed for the galley.

7

Shakedown

It was, as Kwaitkowski had said to Eddie Jake, a choppy sea the instant the little ships cleared the harbor entrance; and to a subchaser a choppy sea means rolling, pitching, and bucking. By sundown it was considerably more than choppy, or so it seemed to Baldini. Even inside the harbor he had had to stay close to the lifelines while traveling up and down the deck. But once outside in the open sea, he found that quite often he had to hang on with both hands, especially when the bow plunged into a particularly ambitious wave. And twice within an hour his feet had popped out from under him on the slippery deck, a jolting and incomprehensible thing to him. In all his years at sea such a thing had never happened to him! Each time he had jumped to his feet and glanced quickly about.

Indeed, the waves were sometimes cresting at a height of eight and ten feet (which, on the *Portland* would have meant nothing). He noticed that the other subchasers, when they were pat the crest of a wave, could be seen for miles but a subchaser at the bottom of a valley could be seen by no one, not even the men aboard the nearest subchaser. He was aware that the old salts who had ridden these little mavericks all the way from the States were looking at each other and grinning maliciously. He suspected that they were saying to each other, "Let's see what that 'big-ship' prick has to say about real sea duty!"

A tower of strength and manliness at the dock, rock firm and Old Navy all the way, he began to feel a queasiness that he had never felt before. Could he, *Benito Caesaro Baldini*, be getting seasick? In the little mirror in the forward head he looked upon a face that resembled very much that of his late father on his deathbed. With the difference that his father had been white around the mouth, whereas he was a pale green.

The little trip to the fo'c's'le cost him dearly, for while he observed with rising terror the green-coloring in his face, he began to fear he would never make it topside to fresh air. In his moment of confusion there came into his mind the conviction that this just might be the end of him!

Once topside he could not be absolutely certain which side of the ship was *leeward*, so disoriented was he. Did it matter? He slid across the wet deck, caught the lifeline just in time, and hung his head and upper body over the side.

But the fish did not get a great deal of his noon chow on this occasion because back into his face it came, the warm undigested lumps mixed with the cold saltwater of the sea!

He was already soaked from head to foot. He felt it inside his clothes, but he did not care a hoot in hell. Other drenchings would eventually take it all away *and if that little narrow-butted god of the sea would only go away perhaps he would survive this goddamned thing after all!*

It was little comfort to him that everybody else was looking a bit out of it and having to cling to something all the time. He emptied himself completely, feeling his body shake like a leaf in a windstorm, and crawled to the pilothouse, where he managed with Herculean strength to lift himself and brace his butt against the port bulkhead. There, with weakening resolution, he waited for the stupidity in his head and stomach to disappear.

"Hey, Boats!"

From behind him, sounding totally out of place, came a revoltingly strong voice. He tried to turn around but once again his feet gave way and he fell.

"How's it goin'?"

He did not recognize the voice and did not care to crane his neck and look. Maybe the sonofabitch would go on about his business.

Then quite close came the unmistakable voice of none other than the practical joker on the ship:

"Hey, Boats, what was that you said about all that rugged duty you had aboard a cruiser? You still of that opinion?"

"Uhhhhhg!"

Tracy burst out laughing. "You interested in chow, Boats? I think I hear Eddie Jake yelling, 'Chow down!' just now."

*　　　　　*　　　　　*

The two newest members of the bridge gang worked their way hand-over-hand down the port lifeline, as the *995* began to roll dangerously from side to side. They had crawled out of the forward hatch and, after waiting for a starboard roll, had made it to the lifeline on the port side. Both of them were pale-faced and completely humorless, as they inched back toward 'midships.

Sharkey, out in front, began to moan pitifully.

What had surprised them both once they were topside was the apparent calmness of the sea around them. Why the ship was cutting up that way was a real mystery. The forward quarters had been a pounding, rolling hell; and the thing that had finally sent them topside was the conviction that the very next wave just might bash in the bow and send the ship down so fast they wouldn't be able to get out before it hit bottom.

"My God!" shouted Sharkey, as a port roll brought sea water up to the toe rail. "We're heelin' too far! I think this thing's going to capsize."

"I was wonderin' how Cookie manages chow, with all this rollin' goin' on!" came back Smith.

"I don't think I'll be able to eat the entire time I'm on this scow!" said Sharkey, through clenched teeth.

"Ditto on that!"

But Sharkey had never missed a meal in his life. Just about the only enjoyment he had ever gotten out of the Navy was eating a lot of free food, and the thought now of passing up what might turn out to be his last chowdown seemed the ultimate irony to him.

"Maybe we could drink a little orange juice or something," he said, projecting his voice above the wind and the loud engine exhausts.

"I'll watch you," said Smith, "but I don't think I'll be able to keep anything down. This fresh air—uhhhhk!"

"God damn!" shouted Sharkey. "If you're gonna puke, go over to the leeward side!"

"You go!" said Smith, hanging far out over the lifeline, into the wind. "I could never make it to the other side!" He held onto the lifeline weakly, weaving back and forth with the roll of the ship. At times it seemed that he would lose his grasp of the line when the ship started to roll back toward the starboard.

Ace McCormick had settled in at the helm and I was standing beside Martinez at the engine controls. We watched the two old salts making slow but steady progress toward us, and when they finally reached the pilothouse and made it to the back where the door was, Ace looked around and began to whistle his Dolly song. Martinez, who was paler than any Mexican I had ever seen, laughed.

"What's so goddamned funny?" Sharkey wanted to know. To me he demanded, "Why aint you on the helm?"

"Ace said he'd spell me so I could go get some chow with you guys. I saw you making your way down the bow and I knew that's where you were headed!"

My old buddies, looking like drowned rats, stared first at Ace and then at me in disgust. They were still bent at the waists like old broken men clinging to a lifeline, and in their faces was disbelief and pain.

"If you had come down the starboard side," I said, pointing, "you wouldn't have taken on so much water. That side's pretty high and dry most of the time."

"No shit," said Sharkey. "Well, git out of my way, I'm goin' to chow."

"I hear we're having pork chops!" I said enthusiastically, clapping Sharkey on the back. He was standing braced with legs apart, trying to fight the roll and leap of the ship.

"That's a damned lie," said Sharkey. "No cook in his right mind would serve pork chops in a mess like this."

"Not even a cook straight out of Hell would do a thing like that," agreed Smith.

"Actually, that's about my favorite food," I said, and meant it. "That and mashed potatoes and brown gravy."

Sharkey and Smith humped it outside quickly and leaned into the wind. I followed in time to hear them making loud choking and gurgling noises, exaggerated for my benefit, I thought at the time.

"You really ought to move over to the other side of the ship to do that, fellows!" I yelled. "For your own good."

Sharkey led off and when we finally reached the hatchway above the galley, we met Baldini coming up. He was holding a mouthful of food in his open mouth, and his face was so white his two-day stubble looked like burned over forest.

"What's wrong, Boats?" asked Sharkey, almost cheerfully. "You comin' up for some air?"

"Gmmuppp!" said Baldini, shoving us all aside and lunging for the starboard lifeline.

"First time I ever saw him when he wasn't blowin' his horn," said Sharkey. He turned and yelled, "Hey, Boats, what was that you said about the sheep bein' separated from the goats on this trip?"

*   *   *

It turned out to be an altogether bad night for most of the crew of the *995*. All three of the officers, who spent the night on the bridge being soaked by the saltwater spray from the bow, were later reported in a weakly, sub-human condition, though no one actually witnessed them feeding the fish. Those who might have done the witnessing were, for the most part, in no position to brag about what they might have seen. But among the crew there were nine of us, if you count Carpenter, who either rode out the night with no noticeable effects or were somehow able to sleep out the storm.

Tabor, the Blackfoot Indian signalman, stood a twelve-hour watch on the bridge and was later given credit for single-handedly saving the ship from colliding with the *1066* after the radar went out; Ace, apparently not the least affected by the storm, stayed on the helm all night humming, whistling, and singing variations on "Buffalo Girls." It was rumored later that he had eaten what was left over of the pork chops.

I spent the night with Ace in the pilothouse, looking after the radar, sonar, radios, and engine controls, when I wasn't making emergency trips to the galley for "mud," as Ace called it. And I personally accounted for three of the pork chops myself.

Tracy, Leafdale, and Kwaitkowski, all members of the original crew, reportedly made it through all right. At least no one would say that they had been seen feeding the fish. And Vanderveen, the remaining member of the salts who had crossed the ocean on the *995*, evidently did not leave the engineroom; and since nothing alive should have survived that hell hole that entire night, he was given high marks.

Carpenter did not appear at evening or morning chows and was not seen topside the whole night, but somehow word got around that he was one of the few on the ship who had not fed the fish. It wasn't until some fourteen hours after the cruise ended back at the Ile Nou docks that he was discovered beneath a bottom bunk in the forward crews quarters in a stagnant pool of his own making.

Miraculously, everyone survived the night, despite the scuttlebutt to the contrary. About noon the following day the Skipper ordered me to do a head count, which I did to the best of my ability. I reported that although the crew seemed quite weak from a sleepless and foodless night, everyone was beginning to move about. I was proud to report that Cookie had spent most of the night in the hot, stuffy galley with no noticeable effects and wanted to know if the Skipper would like to order breakfast. No, the Skipper said sadly, he thought not.

Mr. Howorth had fared considerably better than Mr. Darling, his primary complaint being that he had lost a great deal of sleep and saw no hope of ever regaining any of it on this sea-going coffin. Mr. Darling was near death at nine hundred hours when the Captain ordered him topside to relieve Tabor on the bridge. In the fresh air he eventually began to recuperate; and by noon chow, when a large tray of food was delivered to him in the wardroom, he managed to get down a spoonful of candied yams.

About mid-afternoon the Skipper conducted his own tour of the ship and came upon Baldini doubled over the lifeline at 'midships. On the heel to starboard, the face of the boatswain's mate was within a foot of the water.

"Are you doing all right, Boats?" asked the Skipper, not unkindly.

The very feeble reply was, "I guess I've had better nights, Sir."

"It's just a matter of getting used to the ups-and-downs."

"Yeah, and the pitchin' and wallowin'—"

When Baldini's face finally came around, Mr. Hiller was shocked at what he saw: The countenance of a very old and disappointed mariner.

The boatswain's mate's eyes were bloodshot and his two-day beard had caught and retained a great deal of stuff from the galley.

"Hell, Sir, if you don't mind my sayin' it, this aint no place for a sailor of the United States Navy to be. This is what I call suicide. Are we expected to put up with this day after day?"

Despite himself, Mr. Hiller had to laugh. "Now, don't get discouraged, Boats. Last night was actually rather mild, if we are to believe Tracy, who made the trip from New London. Think what it will be like when we encounter some real weather."

"'Real weather, Sir?" cried Baldini. "My guess is we'll sink and nobody' will ever hear of us ag'in. Sir." This was delivered in such a quiet, plaintive voice Mr. Hiller could hardly make it out.

"Get hold of yourself, Boats. May I suggest that we air bedding this afternoon? And let's have the men clean out their quarters. Keep them busy doing something, right? How about a clean sweepdown, fore and aft?"

"Aye, Sir."

"Let's get to this right away because we may not have much time before the shakedown begins."

At this Baldini cried out, "I thought last night was the shakedown!"

"Oh, no. That was just the warm-up. The shakedown's today. We're going to test out every movable part of this ship; and then we'll run through half a dozen different drills, to find out about the crew. By tonight we'll know where our weaknesses are."

"My God," sighed Baldini. After a time, he turned and, keeping one hand on the lifeline, shuffled off, his tired old butt fairly drooping.

The Skipper's parting words were, "I hear the weather's supposed to turn mean tonight, Boats."

*   *   *

The shakedown cruise turned up a number of important problems in three of the subchasers, all in the enginerooms. This resulted in a weeks' delay of the E. T. D. for points north. As for the *SC-995*, there was one minor problem, something to do with the radar, which Smith had repaired on the way back in.

Mr. Hiller, hearing about the problems the other chasers had and fearing that someone might become curious about his own engineroom, reported that his engines would require serious maintenance and repairs. After receiving a summary of the shakedown cruise from Flag, Lt. London, whose ship had come through with no real problems, sent his condolences, along with an offer to do whatever he could. Was there any hope at all? he wondered. His yeoman would stick around for his reply.

The reply was brief: "Thanks, Jack, but I think we can handle the repairs."

The next day the messenger was back with this terse note: "The name is John. Not Jack."

*   *   *

The first morning following our return to Noumea Harbor, word was passed for all hands to muster on the quarterdeck. Baldini, still somewhat subdued, sent Leavy and Martinez to represent him.

Eventually, everyone except Ace and Cookie was lined up at the railing around the 'midships gundeck, a twelve-by-twelve area the Captain insisted on calling the quarterdeck.

Above us leaning over the bridge railing were Mr. Hiller and Mr. Darling.

"Well," Mr. Hiller began, his face deadpan. He looked around quickly, trying to remain serious. "Where's our Executive Officer?"

"Heah," drawled Ensign Howorth, who was sprawled out on the flag-box below. "You choked up 'bout somethin', Cap'n?"

We could tell that the Skipper was holding something back, but I for one had no idea what it could be. Now, he began to laugh so hard he had to hang onto the railing to keep from falling. We all quite naturally joined in, and some of the cut-ups in the crew began stamping their feet and clapping their hands.

"You did fine on the shakedown," he eventually got out. Then, grinning mischievously, he said, "And as far as this ship is concerned, I guess we're ready to take a little trip north. We didn't get to put our engines to a real test, but we now know they will be fine. I can now tell you that we are in better shape than the other subchasers, with the possible exception of the 1318, and we will make the trip north. Van has done a fantastic job on our engines, and he tells me that our bilge problem is no worse than any of the other ships. It might be a little chancy to lay a pattern of depth charges, but we'll worry about that when the time comes."

After Mr. Howorth talked for awhile about what he wanted done about getting ready for a long voyage, and Mr. Darling talked about our "sea routine" and our "duty stations" while at sea, we were dismissed. Sharkey, Smitty, and I strolled up to the bow.

"Hey, what turned over the Skipper's tickle box, Hall? Any ideas?"

"I've got an idea but maybe I ought to keep it to myself."

"Now, why would you want to do that?"

"Well, I think what the Skipper has bottled up inside him might not better get out until we leave the harbor. Maybe not until we're past the point of no return on the way to the Fijis."

"Now, Smitty, do you hear this boy talking? Don't it sound like he knows something and he's afraid we might spill the beans to some of them jerks on the other subchasers?"

"Well," I said with a laugh, "I don't really know anything. But one night before we left on the shakedown I couldn't sleep and was drifting around topside. I noticed that the hatch to the engineroom was closed but a light was on down there, and I heard a banging noise. About that time Van came down the dock and got between me and the hatch. I could tell he wanted to tell me something, but suddenly he asked me could I keep something to myself."

"And obviously you can't," said Sharkey, snickering.

"I told him I could and he said, 'Will you git lost and not ask any questions?', and I told him I would and he said, 'This is going to be the fastest goddamned subchaser that was ever built.'"

"That all? Hell, that wasn't nothin'! He's a motormack and they was overhaulin' the engines; so naturally he had to brag a little. The Skipper's just giddy because he finally came to the conclusion we're going on this little trek with the other subchasers."

"I'm sure that's it," I said, nodding. "Anyway, how about we get liberty and head over to MOB-Five Beach? You and Smitty can duck under that line and go swim with the nurses."

"Funny boy."

*   *   *

Within a day or two after our return to the Ile Nou dock, Baldini underwent a miraculous change. One moment he was hanging, forlorn and wasted, over the starboard lifeline at 'midships, his favorite spot on the ship, and the next he was barking commands at Leavy and Martinez, like his old self.

His Chief's cap had disappeared during that first night; and when a thorough search of the ship did not turn it up, he was quite certain one of the practical jokers had tossed it over the side. To Leavy, who continued to suffer from the cruise, and Martinez he made the promise, over and over, that the *995* would, under his watchful eye, become the pride of the *Splinter Fleet*.

Almost every time he made this boast, Leavy would whine, "Shit, Boats, can't we just survive for awhile? After what we've just been through? I oughta be in the hospital."

"I don' want to become the pride of nothing," observed Martinez. "What I would like to do is lie flat on my back for maybe a week without having to be strapped in."

"Git the lead out!" Baldini would then shout. "Goddamn goldbricks."

The humiliation that Baldini had suffered was in some respects worse than having to exchange the starched khakis of a CPO for the new, evil-smelling dungarees of a common deckhand. In a weak moment he confided to Leavy that he had a strong urge to kill something and the only thing that was keeping him from doing it was the conviction that he would one day become the Fourth Officer of the ship. And in the meantime he would show the suckers in the after crew's quarters what a real sailor was like, and he would make them eat crow till it choked them.

"Uh, Boats, I don't think they make boatswain's mates fourth officers," said Leavy, his bloodshot eyes and his big flabby, drooping face giving him the appearance of a sick Dachshund.

"What do you know?" said Baldini. "You pile of shit."

It made perfectly good sense to him, what Mr. Hiller had said in the wardroom the day they returned, that since he had at one time been a Chief Boatswain's Mate, perhaps in time he would be able to spell the officers on bridge watches, especially when the ship was on long convoy duty. Maybe, he confided to his deckhands, he would be asked to stand O. O. D. watches at sea. Technically, that would make him the Fourth Officer.

The thought of taking over the bridge of a naval vessel never failed to send a shot of adrenaline racing through the old boatswain's mate's veins. He would be in charge of the whole she-bang for entire four-hour watch periods. Tracy and McCormick and—all of the Department Heads, in fact—would have to take orders from him on such occasions! No doubt there would be times when all three of the officers would be crapped out in the wardroom, leaving him entirely in charge of the ship. At such times he would do as he damn well pleased, and it wouldn't do anybody any good to complain.

It was even conceivable, he confided to them (He was incapable of keeping anything to himself), that this sorry little ship could lead him to a field commission, something that he had never even dreamed of on the *Portland*. At least he would regain his former CPO rank, if the Skipper gave him a bridge watch.

As the days went by and the time approached for the *Splinter Fleet* to sail north, Baldini became louder and more belligerent, out of the hearing of the officers. Around them he was surprisingly mild-mannered and quiet-spoken. He rarely slept more than four hours a night, and he dearly loved to take a swing through the fo'c's'le during the early hours of the morning, whacking the metal bunk frames with his club and shouting, "Drop your cocks and grab your socks!" His attitude was that if he could be up and around so could everybody else.

Of course, he did not go near the after quarters at such times.

One morning word was passed from the wardroom that we were to receive new paint for the hull. Somebody had evidently complained to Flag that the 995 was *inappropriately painted*, because those two words appeared twice in the communique from that office.

Baldini was anxious to change our color, admitting that he was sick and tired of the other boatswain's mates pointing at his ship and making wisecracks about how we looked. Not only was our paint job off, so the criticism went, but we still had not received our Disney *logos* on the bridge. He had no interest in the Donald Duck thing, but he could sure as hell shut up the critics about the paint.

Immediately, while the new paint was in transit, Boats conscripted all the noncoms (most of the Port Section) and put them to scraping the hull. Which, of course, got rid of both the very attractive baby blue but the red lead as well. Inside of a day and a half we were back to ground zero, looking like a plucked goose, and the paint still had not arrived from the Supply Base.

When the new paint finally showed up, it was in five-gallon buckets labeled "Battleship Gray." Baldini went immediately to the wardroom and reported the goof up.

Mr. Hiller was in one of his playful moods: "Battleship Gray will do just fine. Slap it on, Boats."

Baldini began to fidget. One thing he did not want was another odd color that his fellow boatswain's mates could kid him about.

"But this is the last change we're going to make," went on the Skipper. "Who cares whether we look like the rest or not? Has the artist arrived from the Base?"

"Beggin' your pardon, Sir, but I don't know anything about a' artist from the base, or anywhere else."

"How do you think we're going to get a Walt Disney cartoon on our bridge skirt?"

"Oh! Well, Sir, I was sorta hopin' we would be able to avoid that."

"No, no! I've requested a Daffy Duck for our bridge. Don't you think that would be appropriate?"

"Yes, Sir, if you say so."

When Baldini made it back to the fantail where the paint had been stacked, Martinez was holding up a dripping bucket lid for Leavy and the other two deckhands to see. It was a hocky-colored yellow and Gilberto had dripped a complete circle about five feet in diameter on the deck!

"Hey, Boats," complained Martinez, "this don't look much like Battleship Gray to me."

"Put that lid back, you lame brained idiot! Look what you've done! Get a rag! And be quick about it!"

While Martinez sopped up the paint there on the fantail, Baldini went back to the wardroom, carrying the dripping lid by two fingers. He knocked on the door, dripping paint on the radio shack deck as he did so. Jines and I watched, hoping he would be stupid enough to enter the wardroom with the lid.

"What is it now?" asked Mr. Hiller, keeping the door almost closed. He glanced down at the lid.

"This is what the Base sent us, sir. Do you want me to put it on?"

"Check all of the cans and if it's all like that, go ahead."

"Beggin' your pardon, Sir, but if we put this stuff on they might not let us go along."

"Who won't let us go?"

"The other skippers, Sir. Mr. London."

"It's not up to him. Tell you what, if the rest of the paint is like this, tell your men to get some rest and start painting at dark tonight. By morning they ought to have a couple of coats on, if you keep after them."

"Uh."

"Do it, Baldini. You want to stand a bridge watch someday?"

                    *   *   *

Lt. John London, having retired for the night with the comforting knowledge that the Ugly Duckling was still as naked as a jay bird and therefore could not possibly venture out of the harbor, much less make the trip north, awoke at four-hundred hours to the news that something was located just a hundred yards off the port bow, something that had the silhouette of a subchaser. When he inquired whether it was moving or anchored or what, the reply was:

"It is stationary and has its running lights on."

"That you, Murphy?"

"Yes, Sir. I think it's the *995*. But that couldn't be, could it?"

"Shine a light on it and find out what it is," said London. "If it is the *995*, Bill Hiller must have worked his crew all night."

It was us, of course, and Mr. Hiller had decided that he would have a little fun. We had had a quiet reveille at three hundred hours; and as soon as the engineroom gave the okay, we had drifted out a bit to wait for the others.

Just as the eastern horizon began to soften a bit, out came the *SC-1066*, which had been tied outboard of the leader, the *1318,* blocking her view of us. The obstruction finally removed, the blinkerlight on the *Splendid Eight* opened up. Tabor translated aloud, "Stand aside. What color are you?"

Mr. Hiller laughed: "Tell him we're a canary yellow."

From the quarterdeck I read aloud to Jines what Tabor actually sent: "Hocky yellow." Back came: "Has Flag been informed?"

This brought another laugh from Mr. Hiller, who told Tabor to notify Mr. London that we had tried repeatedly to notify Flag but evidently everybody was asleep over there.

Tabor sent: "Not yet."

Eventually, after we promised to inform Flag as soon as possible about the paint, the *1318* headed out toward the center of the harbor and the other subchasers lined up at one-hundred-yard intervals, in this order: the *SC-1066,* the *SC-664,* the *SC-419,* and the SC-995. We were the brightest thing in the entire harbor, and on our proud bridge, centered and inside a round frame, was Bugs Bunny fishing from a surf board!

Soon we were on an easterly heading and the entire horizon was bright with the new day. Strung out in front of us, looking fragile and of little consequence, the other subchasers seemed to be moving in every direction except straight ahead. They reminded me of so many corks bouncing and rolling in the mighty Pacific Ocean.

A short time later (The crew had barely had time to settle into a sea routine, with part of the crew at their watch stations and the rest strapped in their bunks), from the bridge came a shout from Tabor, "Get the Skipper up here. I've spotted something that looks like a periscope."

"Good lord!" squawked Ace. "Hawkeye thinks he's spotted a sub!" He unfurled his leg from the ship's wheel and leaned toward the voicetube: "I'm not about to wake the Skipper and tell him that!"

"Tell him, Ace. There's a periscope off our port bow, about three hundred yards, traveling parallel with us."

"Can't be, or sonar would be pickin' it up!"

"Check sonar out, but go ahead and alert the Skipper!"

Ace wheeled around and shouted, "Smitty! You dead or somethin'?" When he received no reply from the curtained-off sonar closet, he turned to Milleson, who was on engine controls. "Check on him, will you?"

Milleson lunged across the room, opened the flap, and dived inside.glance inside. "Hey!" he yelled. "I hear it! I hear it! About three-five-zero! Can't figure the distance!"

"Ace! Git the Skipper up here on the double! There's no way of knowin' whether it's a bogey or a friendly!"

"We're too far south for it to be a bogey!" shouted Ace.

When Captain Hiller slammed up the ladder past me into the pilot-house, still half-dressed, he wanted to know if the other ships had confirmed the sighting. "Is Tabor absolutely certain that's what it is?" But before Ace could say anything he was out through the door and slamming up to the bridge.

"It's a friendly," Ace assured Milleson. "No Jap is down this far."

Sharkey, who had been napping on his folded arms, called out from his little radar closet:

"What's gonna happen if he doesn't identify himself?" asked Sharkey. "If he's a friendly he'll probably break radio silence. Maybe somebody'd better make sure we're on the Navy operatin' frequency."

"We're monitoring," I said from the ladder to the radio shack.

Through the voicetube the Skipper's voice was high-pitched and serious, "Left standard rudder, engines ahead two-thirds! Come to a heading of two-seven-zero, and let's see what these Chryslers will do."

"Oh, God," said Milleson, leaping across the room and grabbing the engine controls. "Look out below!"

"What's the matter?" asked Ace.

"Van's gonna blow his stack when he gets this command."

"Why, didn't he put the things together right?"

"It's his firm conviction that our new Chrysler engines are capable of tearin' this little nothin' barge all to pieces."

"Well, what'll happen if we start droppin' depth charges?"

"It will open the bilges," nodded Milleson, "and hasten along the inevitable."

We could see the *419* up ahead of us most of the time, but only occasionally could we see the others, as they crested a wave at the same time we did.

Through the voicetube came the order to sound General Quarters. A moment later we could hear the Captain yelling through his hand-held megaphone, "All hands on deck! Tracy, git your depth charges ready!"

"I'd swear he's plannin' to drop depth charges," worried Milleson. "He surely won't, now, will he? If he does this will go down as the shortest convoy in the history of the Navy!"

"He plans to do it," said Ace.

"Maybe Wild Bill will set the damned things to go off deep," said Milleson.

"More than likely they'll go off as soon as they hit the water, no matter what he sets them at," said Ace. "They're old as the hills."

Sharkey sidled up next to Ace, yawning and batting his eyes. "There's a pip on my radar over on our port side, about five hundred yards, runnin' parallel with us. And I'd swear the other subchasers are tryin' like hell to move away from it."

"Why do you say that?" asked Ace.

"Because they're scatterin' like a bunch of wild geese! We've been runnin' parallel with the thing now for sometime, I guess."

"Hmmm," mused Ace, "I wonder why you kept that information to yourself."

8

Fiji

Suva Harbor was a sizable chunk of ocean, sprawled out there ahead of us in the simmering heat and humidity. Compared to Noumea it was pale and ugly and enormous in size. And we must have looked like a tiny yellow pea drifting in amongst all those giant supply ships, tankers, and U. S. Army LST's.

We were considerably ahead of the other subchasers, because the Skipper had "tested out the Chryslers" for the past two days; and although we had no way of knowing just how fast we were traveling at any one time, we did know that no wooden craft made back before WWI was supposed to go that fast.

There was a smell about Suva that I had not experienced before, something dark and dank, smoldering, not burnt but getting that way. And even at sunup, which is when we entered the harbor, it was swelter-ing hot. We anchored not far from a white Australian frigate, which was about the size of a U. S. destroyer, immediately impressed by how white and noisy it was. Everything about it was white, down to the swabs in shorts and long socks. The noise was coming from loudspeakers mounted all over the ship, and most of it sounded like Stateside music.

The land surrounding the harbor spread out gradually toward low wooded hills, and beyond the town we could see a scattering of native huts, what Ace called *bures*, made entirely of bamboo and straw. From where we were anchored we could not see much that looked like the U. S. Navy, but we knew that somewhere near the center of the harbor down on the water's edge there was a supply base. And the word was that we needed to requisition water, diesel fuel, and food supplies as soon as possible.

What little I knew about our general situation was scary: We were part of the Navy on our way to being turned over to the Army, and our line of communication with anybody was complicated by the little feud that was going on between our Skipper and the skipper of the *SC-1318*. Everything in the Navy, I knew, had to be conducted along a chain of command. *Protocol* was another word that I kept hearing.

That first day in Suva Harbor we baked and listened to some lively big-band music until about two in the afternoon, when a cloud came over and dumped a lot of lukewarm water on us! Without warning out of a pale, almost silvery, sky came a dark little cloud right over us; and before anybody had time to run down and get soap and a towel, here came the rain! Half the crew missed it.

I was in the radio shack when Ace yelled, "It's raining!" and I tore up the ladder and fell out upon the quarterdeck. Crewmembers were yelling and carrying on, and some of them were sticking their hands in the air and bowing a giving thanks. I remember thinking that I sure hoped Baldini and Leavy were caught out in this.

For a time everybody was in high spirits, laughing and slapping each other on the butt and joking about Mother Nature doing favors for us. Then, as we dried off and the sweat popped out again, it was back to the old grind. We had learned on the way from New Caledonia that we could depend on about one shower a day, plus maybe two or three at night; and if the bridge watch didn't happen to be asleep when a cloud came over and would pipe the news down to the pilothouse, at least some of us in the bridge gang, as well as the officers, would enjoy a good shower.

There was some talk about making it a rule that the bridge watch had to keep track of all clouds and when one headed our way broadcast the news with the megaphone. The stronger advocates of this rule went so far as to suggest that dereliction of this duty should be punishable by a public flogging.

Our three officers dearly loved a downpour. Like the rest of us, they had abandoned long-sleeve shirts and full-length trousers and were dressing in shorts and T-shirts; and I am convinced that seeing them romping with the men had a strong stabilizing effect on the crew.

We had not known heat until we anchored in Suva. At sea, clipping along at twenty knots or so, there was always a breeze; and a breeze, cool or warm, is a far different thing from the stagnant, humid, heavy stillness of a sheltered harbor. It is true that Suva was large and open to the sea, but while we were there the wind did not move in it.

The subchaser, conceived and built on the upper East Coast before air conditioning, was an uncomfortable means of transportation in the South Pacific. There were no portholes in the bulkheads and no fans (overhead or otherwise); therefore, below the main deck a smell might linger for days and weeks, disappearing only when a stronger one came along to replace it.

By the second day in Suva we were becoming just a bit envious of the Aussie lads, not because of their lovely white home or the lively loud American music but because of the *bimini* that stretched from the frigate's 'midships to its stern. It was a wonder to behold there amidst the sprawl of ugly, uncomfortable, uninspiring LST's, LCI's, LVI's and other punishments Uncle Sam had sent over. Why hadn't somebody thought of installing awnings before? Perhaps they had, but lined up along our starboard lifeline with nothing at all worth looking at but that white ship with its white bimini, we were pretty sure they hadn't. It took an Aussie to do that, somebody who didn't give a dang for what had gone before.

We had heard that each and every Aussie was issued a bit grog daily. But what were we issued daily?

Scuttlebutt had it that we were supposed to be issued one beer and one softdrink *ration* daily, once we entered the War Zone. I asked Pills, our Naval historian and maritime encyclopedia, what a ration was.

"It's something that's supposed to be issued, when the right circumstances come along."

On the third day Tabor spotted a dot on the horizon and reported to the Skipper that it was the *1318*. After staring at it for a time through binoculars, Mr. Hiller said, "How can you be sure?" The Indian replied that he could tell by the way it was bobbing up and down. Sure enough about that time a second dot showed up, and soon there were four, altogether. "Well, when they get within range of your light, let them know where we are and invite them to join us. And, Tabor, be kind."

It amused me how cavalier Tabor was about sending and receiving messages. Of course, he was cavalier about everything; but you would've thought when it came to the ship's business, traffic handling between us and the rest of the world, he would have paid a little more attention to accuracy and detail. Because I could read the blinkerlight about as well as he could, and I knew the liberties he was taking. And I also knew where he stood with the signalmen on the other subchasers. The feelings were mutual, of course.

I just happened to be in the pilothouse and paying attention when the Tabor made the initial contact with Mickleby on the *1318*; and although I couldn't see what the Indian was sending, I had a direct view of what was coming at us. After acknowledging whatever it was that Tabor sent, Mickleby added: "Your offer is declined and you are to standby for a priority message from the Captain. I see that you still can't use the English language, Black Foot."

I had learned two things about Tabor: He was very good with a blinkerlight, and he had no fear for man or beast, including an officer of the U. S. Navy. How he had ever made it to Signalman First Class was a mystery to me, not because he wasn't a competent signalman but because he was incapable of doing anything according to Hoyle. His attitude alone should have kept him an Apprentice Seaman.

The signalman on the *1318* finally came back with a short message action addressed to us and rated Priority. The other subchasers were listed as information advisees. In brief, it said that a meeting of the skippers would convene on the stern of the 1318 at ten that morning.

I had a clipboard and wrote this down as it was sent to us, but Tabor summarized for the Skipper as follows, "They're holding a meeting at ten and you're expected to be there. They're not going to join us, we're going to join them."

"What makes you think that?" asked the Skipper.

"Well, if they was goin' to join us—"

"Where they anchor won't have a thing to do with us. We're close to facilities and therefore we'll stay here." After a pause, he added, "I wonder how I'm supposed to get over there?"

When I left the bridge, I was thinking that Mr. Hiller and Tabor were a lot alike, at least in one important way: They were both as stubborn as Missouri mules.

The four subchasers, led by the *1318*, made it to the entrance of the harbor about nine hundred hours; and, as expected, Mr. London chose an anchorage as far away from us as possible. It was close to ten when the wherry from the *1066* showed up for Mr. Hiller.

Practically the whole crew and the other two officers lined up to watch him leave, and it occurred to me that we were very fortunate to have a C. O. like him. I had never seen his likes before, and when I mentioned this later to Ace, the quartermaster said, "Yeah, and you'll never see his likes again. But he's playin' a very dangerous game, sparin' with London."

When Mr. Hiller was returned, he climbed aboard the ship with a big grin, saying that everything had gone about as he had expected. On the fantail that evening he entertained a number of us with just how it had gone.

It had started off, he said, right in the middle of the first glass of lemonade, which, by the way, was sweetened but tepid. Lt. London, a bit tight-lipped with him, had led off with, "Now, Bill, we've all been rather anxious to hear the details of—"

"Of my sub kill?"

"Not your 'sub kill'," London had said, testily. "Your temporary loss of sanity. What in hell were you doing, dropping charges and running about like a crazy person? I've got to send in a report on that."

"Yeah," agreed Lt.(jg) Virgil Wortham, skipper of the *1066*, "we couldn't see you very clearly; but I'd swear after that black smoke from your engines began to settle a bit your bow was out of the water a good two feet. I wanted to ask about that black smoke. Where'd it come from?"

Before Mr. Wortham could say anything else, he had jumped in with, "We made two depth charge runs. Then our bilges began to leak pretty badly and we had to back off and start pumping them." Then he had asked them if they hadn't picked up the sub on their radars.

"Bill, admit it," London pouted. "There was nothing to pick up. You just wanted to grandstand a bit. I'm afraid this isn't going to look very good on your record."

"What the hell, my record can stand it."

Then Lt. Wortham had wanted to know how we had managed to beat them to Suva, referring to what we had done as a little farce. "We were doin' twelve knots all the way here on a beeline and we couldn't even see you behind us."

All this time Mr. Patchen, of the 664, kept blurting, "Yeah! What I'd like to know is—!" But each time somebody would interrupt.

His story finally told, the Skipper lifted his hands in a gesture of resignation: "Well, then I told them we had a good wind all the way in. And that's the way I left it." After a pause, he added: "Oh, somewhere in there I mentioned that according to our radar they had all scattered in every direction, and we didn't know which one of them to follow."

*   *   *

On the fourth morning in Suva, following a breakfast of very weak coffee and cling peaches, Sharkey and Smith took up a position at the starboard lifeline next to the pilothouse. They were wearing nothing except shorts but already their shoulders were shiny with perspiration, and their motivation for hanging over the lifeline rather than backing up to the pilothouse where the shade was was the hope that a small breeze would spring up. Sharkey led off with:

"I'll bet that bitch has air conditioning in the crew's quarters. Look at that, they've got big canvas deck chairs back there under that awning! Have you noticed that we don't have a single chair topside on this ship? Can you beat that? Do you suppose they know there's a war on?"

Smith shifted his weight to his other bare foot but didn't say anything.

"How do you suppose they git away with leavin' all them lights on at night? And tell me this, why do they do it? Are they invitin' the Japs to try somethin'? You can see that thing for at least twelve miles, day or night. And what churns me is us bein' so close to it. If the Japs ever come over and strafe it, they're likely to strafe us by mistake."

"Maybe we chose this spot so we'd have a little protection from the Japs if and when they did show up," said Smith.

Eddie Jake, who rarely ever made it that far forward during the daytime, came up and leaned over the lifeline with them. He was smoking a cigarette and deep in thought. His quota of words for the week had been used up on the fantail the evening before, talking about Texas.

"How in hell do you stand wearin' so many clothes?" asked Sharkey. "I'd burn to death." No reply was expected, of course.

Eddie Jake inhaled and held it for a moment. "Actually, this little heat spell we're havin' reminds me some of home, only there you sweat a lot more and git all the poison out of your system. Here you just git hot."

"Where'n hell is 'home'?" asked Sharkey, sarcastically. He had not attended the session on the fantail.

"Alice, Texas," said Eddie Jake, proudly. "Where the skies aint cloudy all day."

"That sounds familiar, for some odd reason," said Sharkey. "Where have I heard it before, Smitty?"

"That's where Gilberto's from."

"My God, what are the odds of somethin' like that happening?"

"What's goin' on over there on the Aussie boat?" asked Eddie Jake.

The three of them stared at the frigate for a time. Suddenly, Eddie Jake commented off-handedly, "That one with the apron on just threw something over the fantail that wasn't scraps."

"It made a big splash," said Sharkey, like it was very solid. "What do you suppose it was?"

"I don't know but it looked like something wrapped in heavy paper. There comes somebody else with another one!"

They watched as a man, also wearing an apron, crossed the fantail of the frigate and tossed a heavy burden into the water.

Sharkey straightened up quickly, "Hey, they're throwin' lend-lease meat over the side!"

"What makes you think it's lend-lease meat?" asked Eddie Jake.

Sharkey whirled, looking up at the bridge and yelling over his shoulder, "I'll bet you ten bucks it's lend-lease meat from the States!"

He suddenly realized that Tabor was hanging over the bridge railing and looking down at him.

"Give me them field glasses!" shouted Sharkey.

"Why?"

"What the hell difference does it make? Hurry! We think the Aussies are throwing lend-lease food over the side."

"I could've told you that," said Tabor. "It don't take glasses to see that."

"We want to see what's stamped on the packages," said Sharkey, anxiously. "It could be meat."

"It says 'U. S. Beef'."

Eddie Jake was already running toward the stern yelling at no one in particular, "They're throwin' good beef over the side! In Texas that would be a hangin' offense!" And by the time Sharkey had given up on getting the field glasses and was back at the lifeline, Eddie Jake reappeared with Kwaitkowski.

"Get the Skipper, Tabor!" sang out Cookie. "Be quick about it."

At that moment the Skipper popped out of the pilothouse with a pair of field glasses. "What do we have that we could trade them for that beef, Cookie?"

"Mutton, Sir. Lots of it."

"No fooling? Why haven't you been servin' some of it?"

"I have been, under other names, Sir. The men won't eat it unless I disguise it, spice it up; so I was getting ready to have Tex throw it over the side."

The Skipper turned and looked up at Tabor. "Git on the light and tell them to hold up on that beef. Mention that we have some mutton." Then to Cookie he said, "I think I'll pay the Aussie a visit. Where do you suppose we could lay our hands on a wherry?"

"Where else?" laughed Cookie. "The only one in the *Splinter Fleet* is the one that took you to and from the *1318*. Maybe they'd lend it to us."

"I thought of them," said the Skipper, "but we're not exactly popular in those quarters right now. However, it won't do any harm to ask. Tabor, get on the light and see what our Australian friend says."

On the bridge Tabor had been whacking away at the blinkerlight. Now, he paused and called out, "I got their attention with that last word, Skipper!"

There was indeed activity on the bridge of the frigate, and rapidly this spread down aft to the stern. Along our own starboard lifeline at least half of our crew had assembled and were watching the scurrying about on the fantail of the frigate.

On our bridge the whacking had stopped. "Skipper, what do I tell the 1066?" asked Tabor. "They want it in the form of a message, with a date-time group, with the 1318 as a' action addressee."

"Just ask them if we can borrow their wherry."

After another round of whacking, Tabor leaned over the bridge railing and said, "Negative. The excuse was that they plan to make use of it soon."

"Tell them we've got a very sick man aboard and have to get him to the Base Sick Bay."

Thirty minutes later, during which there was an exchange between the 1066 and the 1318, Tabor reported that the skipper of the 1066 had agreed to send over his wherry but only if his own coxswain manned it.

"Tell them it's an *emergency*, that we need to borrow the boat for three hours."

Back came the answer: "Our coxswain will be right over. We were headed for the Base anyway."

"Not good," said the Skipper, suddenly red in the face. "We've got to figure something quick. The skippers agreed at that meeting to boycott the Aussie because of the lights and the music. I didn't vote for it, but all the others did. They evidently don't like Stateside music." After a pause, he said, "Tell them we have a very qualified coxswain aboard and we'll get the boat back to them in two hours."

When the reply to this came, Tabor summarized: "Take it or leave it. Their coxswain or no boat."

"Well, hell, tell them we'll take it!"

While Tabor whacked away, the Skipper fumed, "One way or the other we've got to get ourselves a boat!"

"Maybe we could swim ashore tonight and raid the Supply Base," suggested Sharkey. "I'll bet they've got lots of small boats and wouldn't miss one all that much."

"I'll take that under advisement," said the Skipper, looking at Sharkey suspiciously. "You're trying to be funny, aren't you? Well, let me tell you we're in this thing for keeps. And that wasn't all that funny."

When the smallboat put in an appearance, stopping just short of our starboard 'midships gunwale, the coxswain called out that his orders were to take the sick man in and drop him off at the hospital and then go on about his own business. He could take our Pills and one swab along.

"Now, you stop worrying about time schedules!" called out Mr. Hiller, irrelevantly. "I'll take full responsibility for the boat and you from now on." To Baldini he said out of the corner of his mouth, "Get a boathook on that thing. Round up some help. Don't let him drift off."

"That's what my skipper said you would say, sir!" called the coxswain. "But his instructions are—"

The coxswain, who had been in the Navy long enough to know that officers always behaved according to a strict code of honor, that Naval Regulations was their bible, was, nevertheless, a bit nervous. His skipper had said to him in no uncertain terms that he had better not let that boat get away from him. But, he wondered, how could it get away from him?

Baldini sized up the situation immediately, knew what his skipper wanted and knew what had to be done. He sent Leavy for the boathook while he explained his simple plan to Martinez and Roucloux, concluding with: "Don't hurt him. Just help him aboard the ship, and I'll take it from there."

Actually, it was Cookie who helped the coxswain aboard; but Baldini and his deckhands, working together with commando precision, had made the transition possible. Quite suddenly, in plain view of the seventy-five curious Aussies but well out of sight of the swabs on the other subchasers, Gilberto Martinez and Julius Anthony Roucloux were in control of the boat and the confused and frightened coxswain was on his way to the galley. He was, in fact, being supported by Cookie and Tex.

"Settle him down and give him something that'll cool him off," suggested the Skipper. "We won't be long." With that he climbed into the boat. Martinez had moved to the motor, and Roucloux had settled on the in the center of the boat. Baldini, with the bowline in his hand, wanted to know if the Skipper needed anymore help.

"Tell you what, Boats, let's take the Aussie skipper a peace offering. Have somebody bring up a few packages of mutton. Say a couple hundred pounds of it. I don't think we'll have any trouble getting it out of the boat." After Boats disappeared, he climbed out of the boat and headed for the pilothouse, saying over his shoulder, "I know something else I bet those fun-lovin' Aussies would like."

Within two minutes he was back with a heavy cardbord box, which he handed to Roucloux, Cookie showed him a wrinkled sheet of paper that he had found on the unhappy coxswain. It was the shopping list of the *1066*.

"Dad blame it, Cookie, we can't waste our time going all that way to that Navy Base in this heat! Let that accidentally drop over the side."

"They did lend us the boat," Cookie reminded him. "And we could use a few things from the grocery store ourselves."

"Oh, all right," said Mr. Hiller. "Go find Mr. Howorth and brief him on this. Tell him he'll take a work party of two men to the island as soon as I get back. Oh, and give him that list." To no one in particular he shouted: "Where's Baldini?"

As if the Boats had timed his arrival, he barreled through the crowd at the lifeline, clearing a way for Eddie Jake, who was carrying a heavy crate labeled, "Australian Lend-Lease; Mutton."

Tabor yelled from the bridge, "They're tryin' to git our attention on the blinker, Skipper!"

"Ignore them!" bellowed Mr. Hiller. "Communications blackout until I git back!" He turned and motioned to Gilberto. "Let's move out!"

At the starboard lifeline, Sharkey and Smith picked up where they had left off:

"What's that the Skipper was holdin' onto so seriously?" asked Sharkey.

"Barter," said Smith.

"Probably nude pictures of Fiji bathing beauties."

They watched as the Skipper and the enlisted man crossed the short stretch of water and nudged in alongside the frigate. After some scurrying about on the stern of the ship, a Jacob's ladder came down and they went aboard, leaving the pile of mutton in the small boat.

"There's one thing this heat will not damage."

"What?"

"That Australian mutton. It's already as foul and awful as it'll ever get. Look, they're leaving it right out there in this two-hundred-and-fifty-degree heat. And I know by now the Aussies know it's out there."

As they watched, Aussie sailors in spiffy summer uniforms hustled the mutton aboard the ship. And hardly had it disappeared before other Aussies were piling large, neatly-wrapped bundles into the boat!

"Now, do you suppose they had any of that beef left?" asked Sharkey. "They must've gotten rid of eight, nine hundred pounds."

"Look!" exclaimed Smith. "There's one that takes three men!"

Roucloux, naked to his waist and standing braced in the boat, accepted the package and with the help of Martinez, lowered it into the boat and, without breaking his rhythm, reached up for another.

"My God, that can't all be beef!" exclaimed Sharkey. "Wonder what it is, elephant?"

They watched as the Skipper skinned down into the boat and climb over the pile of packages to the bow. The two swabs then took their places, and the boat nosed back toward the *995*.

"We'd better move away from here," suggested Sharkey.

"I think I'll stick around," said Smith. "I'm curious about that biggest package."

As the boat came alongside, Mr. Hiller called out to those gathered along the lifeline. "Guess what we've got, men?" He pointed toward the mound in the boat, grinning broadly.

"God, I hate that kind of enthusiasm, this time of day," said Sharkey, who had decided to wait around, too.

"The skipper of that friggin' frigate was so thankful for the mutton and that package of Stateside music he sent over enough canvas to cover our fantail!" yelled the Skipper. "We've got ourselves a blahsted *bimini* for the fantail, me swabbies!"

Sharkey straightened up, speechless for once, staring at Smith, who repeated the word *bimini,* in a reverent tone of voice.

"Did you hear me?" shouted Mr. Hiller. "We're going to cover our stern with canvas!"

The news reached the fo'c's'le only seconds after it was being echoed about the after compartment, where the captive alien coxswain listened in stunned silence. I was in the radio shack when this earth-shattering news penetrated the latticework hatchcover beside the helm, and I immediately relayed it to the Exec and the Third Officer in the wardroom. The three of us then went topside on the double.

*   *   *

Once the canvas and the two hundred pounds of good lend lease American beef had been unloaded and stacked on the stern of the subchaser, Mr. Howorth was dispatched to the island with two want lists, taking Martinez, Roucloux, and the coxswain with him. Lt. Hiller then faced his happy crew and raised his right hand for silence:

"Men, we'll custom-make this sucker but put it up as quickly as possible! Baldini will be in charge, of course."

"Is it not perhaps the only *bimini* in the U. S. Navy?" asked Sharkey. When the Skipper turned and glared at him, he said, "Belay that question, Sir. I merely wished to imply the importance of our—."

"Is there enough canvas for the bridge, Skipper?" asked Ace.

"I believe there is, I believe there is," Mr. Hiller said with a sigh, nodding happily. "We'll waterproof it, and then we'll give it about six coats of paint!" Suddenly, his face became very thoughtful: "Oh, my god! All we've got is Canary Yellow."

"What'll Mr. London and the other skippers say, sir?" worried Pills. "I mean, won't they be a bit jealous?"

"They will just have to adjust to it," said the Skipper, tossing his head like a rakish female. "I know it'll be a thorn in their sides to look back at us bringing up the rear of the column lookin' like a million dollars, with an umbrella over our tail. But what can they do about it?"

"Maybe vandalism, late at night," suggested Sharkey.

Pills snorted, "Let 'em try. We'll be ready for them."

"Oh, I don't know," said Mr. Hiller, "put yourself in their shoes. They've gotten used to thinking of us as the ugly duckling. With a brilliant *bimini* on our fantail, we may be a bit hard to take."

"One thing for sure," snickered Wild Bill, "the *1066* won't ever lend us their wherry again."

"Which reminds me," said Mr. Hiller, "we've got to find one of those things. And since the Navy hasn't seen fit to issue us one, I guess we'll have to requisition one, somewhere."

None of us had ever known an officer like Lt.(jg) Hiller, and at this moment our admiration for him knew no bounds. I am certain that if he had called for volunteers to go and take by force the *1066's* wherry, there would have been nineteen takers.

That afternoon a thousand or so double-A's were sent in our direction, most of them from the *1066*. The captive coxswain had made it back to his ship around fourteen-hundred hours, taking with him the information that we now had an abundance of American beef and enough canvas for awnings over our bridge and stern. Tabor was far too busy installing canvas over the bridge to reply to the AA's; but, of course, he relayed to the Skipper the gist of what went on among the other subchasers.

Lt. London and the other skippers spent most of that blistering hot afternoon on their exposed bridges, discussing by blinkerlight, with the aid of their signalmen, Mr. Hiller and his crew of mavericks and misfits.

The signalman on the *1066*, for example, alerted Lt. London's signalman with an operational priority message around noon that said, in part, that the *Splendid Five* had commandeered *Splendid Six's* wherry, kidnapped the coxswain, and fraternized with the Aussie frigate. The other two subchasers had been listed as action addressees. Lt. London wanted to know just how the recalcitrant Lt. Hiller had fraternized.

The reply was quick and to the point: "He traded Australian lend lease mutton to the Australians for American lend lease beef, he bribed the skipper of the frigate with Stateside music for enough canvas to build awnings over his fantail and bridge, and he and his junior officers have been invited to the frigate for dinner this evening!"

Around fifteen-hundred hours, after a lengthy pause in the give-and-take on the blinker lights, Lt. London directed his signalman to send the following priority message, action addressed, to the *1066*, to be relayed to the other two subchasers:

"It is our belief that Lt.(jg) William F. Hiller has violated the Allied Agreement on Lend Lease. The Agreement expressly states that lend-leased commodities cannot be sold or used as barter." The *SC-995* was listed as an action addressee, but no roger was forthcoming from that vessel as of sundown.

By noon of the following day the canvas for the fantail had been cut and brass grommets had been strategically located around the entire piece. The *995* crew had worked steadily in the blazing hot sun the after-noon before and through most of the night and again that morning, with not one syllable of foul language being said the entire time. Sharkey had worked, shirtless and shoeless, alongside Baldini for a time with a pair of long-bladed scissors; and no one seemed to think it extraordinary that the one had not said a word about the uniform of the day or that the other had not used his scissors like a butcher's knife.

Wild Bill, Milleson, and Jines, hustling about like bosom buddies, had worked through the night on the awning supports, completing that job by the deadline. The rest of the crew (except Tabor, who, with Ace, Mr. Howorth, and Mr. Darling, was busy with the bridge awning), working in relays, had put the awning together, red-leaded it, and given the upper side six coats of hocky yellow, completing their part of the job just as Cookie and Eddie Jake began to send around platters of thick beef sandwiches.

The raising had been set for thirteen hundred hours.

Mr. Hiller, bare to the waist, had worked alongside the men on the stern. And it is altogether likely that he was aware that something magical was happening to his crew. For the very first time we were behaving in a civil manner toward each other. We were united against a common enemy, the blazing sun; and, perhaps even more importantly, we had taken a liking for our Old Man. And if we had been proud of him for engineering the heist of the Chrysler engines, we were bowled over by the gutsy way he had managed the acquisition of the beef and the canvas.

During the construction and raising of the *bimini*, nothing at all had been said about chowdowns and sack time. Cookie and Eddie Jake had circulated among us from time to time with thick beef sandwiches and whatever else they could find. This was helped along with very hot but weak coffee, which, surprisingly enough, went down like ice-cold lemonade in that blistering sub-tropical sunshine.

The dedication occurred around fifteen-hundred hours. The Skipper, happier than I had ever seen him, had one more surprise up his sleeve:

"Men, after the swimming party, which I think all of us need, we are invited to attend a little beer party on the Aussie frigate. Now, I'll warn you, it's going to be warm Aussie beer and they don't call it 'bitters' for nothing. Think you can handle that? About sixteen-hundred hours they will start ferrying us across. Be ready."

9

Kamikaze!

The convoy that came together in Suva Harbor was so big we could not see the end of it once we were at sea. We fell in on the port side with the other subchasers and half a dozen tincans, making up a second line of escort vessels for the big transports; and almost immediately the Skipper mustered us on the quarterdeck. This was surprising because the reading of the travel orders wasn't supposed to be until the next day.

"Two things," he said after we had settled down. "We'll be taking our orders from the U. S. Army, beginning today, which as far as I'm concerned can't be any worse than where we've been getting them. Maybe we'll eat better, who knows? At least we're traveling with an awful lot of food.

"The other thing is the assignment of battle stations. Mr. Darling will talk about that."

No one had ever seen our Third Officer smile or heard him make an off-hand remark to any member of the crew, so in a popularity contest with the other two officers he would have faired badly. As far as I was concerned he was a "typical Naval officer," remote and formal and strictly by-the-book. The closest I had ever seen him come to losing it was once with Tabor, when the two of them were on a bridge watch. And although the signalman ended up on report, I think Mr. Darling may have learned something from the encounter.

Now, he faced us with a sheet of paper.

"Beginning today we will be conducting a series of drills. All hands will participate. When General Quarters sounds, those of you not on watch will go quickly to your battle stations. If you're on watch when GQ sounds, stay there until you're relieved. Most of you know where your battle station is, but I have made some new assignments and will read them off at this time.

At this point I stopped listening to the ensign. My battle station, of course, was in the pilothouse at the Army transceivers. I may have been daydreaming about what it would be like going to General Quarters for real, or, more likely, I had just turned him off. Anyway, suddenly he was in my face, saying my name like it was a four-letter word.

"Hall! Are you paying attention?"

"Yes, Sir! Sorry, Sir!"

"Hall, you're assigned to starboard twenty, as gunner."

Somebody, Tracy perhaps, laughed. I cleared my throat and looked at Mr. Hiller. Then I looked at Mr. Darling

"Me, Sir? On a twenty?"

"The starboard twenty. Right there behind you."

Wild Bill was definitely laughing by this point, as were Sharkey and Smith and some others.

"Roucloux?" Mr. Darling now cleared his throat and repeated: "Roucloux, are you also deaf? You will be Hall's loader on the starboard twenty. Sharkey? Gunner on the port twenty. Smith will be your loader. Milleson, gunner on the after twenty. Martinez will be your loader."

Julius Anthony Roucloux, Junior, from San Antonio, Texas, had moved toward Mr. Darling and was shaking his head. The officer lowered his paper and waited. "Sir, I don't know one thing about that gun. Could I be assigned somewhere else?"

"No," snapped Mr. Darling. "Beginning today Tracy will be conducting Gun Drills. He will show you everything you need to know." After that had had time to soak in, he added, "We'll get additional training when we reach the Solomons." He then assigned Baldini and Carpenter to the forty, Leafdale and Kwaitkowski to the fifty-caliber machineguns on the stern.

After Mr. Darling dismissed us, I fell in with Sharkey and Smitty and we began to inspect the port twenty. Roucloux and Tracy joined us.

"Nobody will be expected to hit anything with one of these," teased Tracy, running his hand along the barrel of Sharkey's twenty. "But let's face it, putting Pinky on one is a joke. Leavy would have been a better choice."

"Putting me on one is no joke," said Sharkey, trying to get Tracy off me. "What do you mean, 'nobody will be expected to hit anything'?"

It worked. Tracy proceeded to explain in great detail just how difficult it was going to be to hit something with one of the twenties. The ship would begin to roll and pitch the instant the convoy began battle maneuvers, and just keeping one's feet planted firmly on the deck would become next to impossible. And since each gun had stops on it, would go just so far forward and aft, the chances of hitting a fast-moving target hurtling towards us was about a million-to-one against.

When I began to drift toward the pilothouse, after half an hour of this, Tracy called out: "Hey, Pinky Baby, I'm goin' to enjoy watchin' you fuck up!"

$$*\qquad\qquad*\qquad\qquad*$$

For the first three days our heading was north, northwest, with no zigzagging. The winds this entire time were steady and hard from the north, keeping us at a fifteen-to-twenty-degree port heel. During chowtime we were forced to hang onto our plates and silverware, and rely on Eddie Jake for seconds. And when we sacked out, just those that bunked on the starboard sides of the crew's quarters had to strap themselves in. Ordinarily, everyone would have needed straps.

The first leg of our journey had made us aware of a number of shortcomings and disadvantages; but for me going to sea in that small ship was such a novelty I paid little attention to them. Having to hang onto something always, being crowded together with twenty other men in such a small space, and waking up suddenly and realizing that my bedroom was rolling and tossing took some getting used to.

Unable to take much advantage of the *bimini*, with the ship heeling twenty degrees or more for hours at a time, we were forced to remain below when we weren't on watch; and for those of us in the Bridge Gang this was not so bad, but the deckhands and the Black Gang had only the fo'c's'le and, three times a day, short visits to the after quarters. Jines and I took turns at the radio position, below the pilothouse, looking for AFS shortwave stations and typing letters.

No one had received any mail in Suva Harbor, even though we had spent almost two weeks there. Most of the crew blamed Mr. Darling for this, since he was the official censor aboard and suspected of being capable of destroying whole letters. This was a bit extreme, I thought, but I had seen a few V-Letters he had cut up. Anyway, once we joined the long, slow convoy northward, almost all letter-writing ceased.

Our address was Comsopac, in care of the Fleet Post Office, San Francisco; but none of us had much confidence that the Navy was keeping up with us anymore. We had been turned over to the Army.

When the winds finally died down and the ship settled back to an even keel, Baldini began to make things miserable for us. He saw to it that there was no such thing as 'free time' for most of the crew between eight-hundred and sixteen-hundred hours. And knowing that aboard the other subchasers the men did nothing but stand their four-on and eight-off watches while at sea made it even worse.

Tabor, who was evidently no longer feuding with the signalmen on the other subchasers, volunteered the information that the *995* was the major source of entertainment for the other subchaser. Because of the way Baldini carried on. He said that a favorite pastime for the men on the other ships was to check out a pair of glasses from the bridge and watch Baldini run up and down the *995* deck screaming and waving his arms.

The consensus of seemed to be that Baldini was bucking for a Section Eight; but Pills had another theory, that our boatswain's mate was bucking for Fourth Officer. He never relaxed, never took a coffee break, and not once had any of seen him carry on a normal conversation with another member of the crew. To me he seemed ready to explode.

One morning about a week into the voyage some of us were sprawled out on the bow looking at the gray overcast that seemed about to drop down on the deck. We had not seen anything at all for a long time, except the dirty green Pacific and the gray overcast sky.

"Damn," sighed Sharkey, "I'm so sick of this nothingness I wish a Jap flyboy would come over and stir up somethin'."

Pills, the only one present not sprawling, grimaced, but kept looking with great interest upon his own hairy feet. "We'll git it soon enough, without wishing for it. I for one prefer this to being shot at." After a time, he added, "A wise man once said that this, too, would pass."

"Yeah, well, that's because the sonofabitch wasn't on a slow boat to China," growled Sharkey. "Who's to say this will pass? Maybe this is all that's left."

"All right, so maybe it won't pass," mused Pills, who had begun to scratch between his toes. "I think I've picked up what Ace's got."

"We haven't seen a sign of life since we started on this trip, and I for one would like know if anybody else in the world exists outside of this stinkin' convoy," insisted Sharkey. "I think we've all died and gone to hell."

At that moment every head turned toward the bridge. The distinct sound of a single shrill whistle had reached our ears.

Ace McCormick had joined us but was still standing.

"Now, who in hell's—?" he said, turning around and glaring at the pilothouse. Then, before he had time to take a step, somebody in the pilothouse yelled, "Bogeys! Tabor's spotted bogeys!"

We all leaped up and started for our battle stations, and I heard Tracy call out, "Tabor's probably mistaken a flock of gooney birds for Jap planes."

"Not him!" I shouted, racing toward my twenty.

Even before I had time to reach the quarterdeck and my gun, I saw three dots high in the sky, circling slowly and coming around from the north. They would be coming in on the starboard side, where my twenty was! I began yelling for Roucloux, but when I rounded the port side of the pilothouse I saw that he was already there, fitting an eighty-five-pound canister of ammunition on top of the gun.

Tracy was running from one of the three twenties to another, screaming, adding to the confusion. I had no idea what he was saying because General Quarters were going off all around us and a few big guns had joined with the anti-aircraft twenties and forties.

Everybody on the ship seemed to be swapping ends of the ship, wanting or needing to be wherever they weren't; and none of them was wearing a helmet or a lifejacket! Milleson came around from the engineroom hatch yelling something. I cupped my hand to my ear, heard Roucloux shout, "He ran up toward the bow!"

Then Milleson was shouting in my ear: "Which one of the guns is mine?"

"Not this one!" I screamed, pointing toward the port twenty.

He ran to it and strapped himself in. His gun was not loaded, of course; and his loader, as it turned out, was still on watch at the engine controls.

Then Tracy was in my face yelling something about gooney birds and what he was going to personally do to Tabor if that's what it turned out to be. I tried to get his attention and point toward the sky, but he kept right on, like a lunatic. This was our first encounter with the enemy, and I was thinking how curious it was that once I had strapped myself to the twenty I no longer felt crazy with fear. I caught Roucloux's eye, and he smiled; and I knew he was feeling the same way I was.

I became aware of the *burrrp-burrrping* of General Quarters on the big AKA on our starboard bow at the precise moment I saw a plane diving in for it. Tabor's voice broke through the chaos, "Bogeys, three of them! Starboard side, right on the water and coming in fast!" Then I realized he was speaking in his normal voice into the bridge PA system.

All eyes on the ship were on the three planes. They were so close to the water I remember thinking they would have gain some altitude to make it above the superstructures of the ships on our starboard! I would have to wait for the ship to roll before I could train the twenty on them, if they made it all the way to us! Of course, the 995 was rolling and bucking every which way, making it altogether possible that on a roll to starboard I might send some slugs into one of our own ships!

The bogeys, evidently having encountered more flak from the big AKA than they wanted, veered up and around to the northeast. One of them began to leave a trail of smoke, but soon all three of them were out of sight.

Suddenly, Roucloux was rapping me on the shoulder and trying to get my attention. He was pointing toward the west, and I heard him scream, "There! I see two more of them! They're headed straight for us!"

This time my twenty was facing away from the incoming planes, and Roucloux had to keep me posted on their progress. I was tight against the round shoulder braces and strapped in, making it impossible for me to turn more than a few degrees.

"Get ready! They're goin' to come right over us!"

I wanted to shout, "How do you get ready when they're coming in from the wrong direction? But instead I just pointed the barrel at twelve o'clock and waited, with my right hand loose on the trigger grip. The stops would allow me only about a thirty-degree sweep, a block of sky from two o'clock to approximately five o'clock on the horizontal, and on the vertical from just above a horizontal position to almost straight up.

Tracy came up, red in the face, and began shouting for me to stand up. I ignored him, waiting for Roucloux's go ahead to pull the trigger.

A lot of things were flashing through my brain about this time. I remembered having heard a gunner's mate on one of the other subchasers explain that the time the subchaser gunner had to fire at a low-flying plane, from the when it came within range and inside his thirty-degree arc until it was gone, was about twenty-to-thirty seconds, depending upon the speed of the plane. Maybe enough time for two or three short bursts, providing the gunner didn't blink. High-flying planes, he said, were of course a different matter. You might as well leave them for the big guns.

"Remember what I told you, July!" I yelled, certain the plane was right over us.

He put his mouth close to my ear and yelled, "I remember! Wait till I give you the word and then give it hell!"

By this time Tracy was all over me, yelling threats. I was not supposed to be sitting on the goddamned deck! And if I didn't stand up he was going to see to it I never got my hands on that gun again! I felt like saying, "Hey, that's exactly what I would like for you to do." But I knew he had already done his best to have me replaced.

"Here he comes! Get ready!" shouted Roucloux.

The noise was so great I could hardly make out what he was saying, and he must have realized this because suddenly he was down on the deck with me!

"Now! Now! Now!"

I clamped the trigger down and held it, aware that a great black shadow had flashed overhead and thinking about that twenty or thirty seconds I would have. Following the tracers rather than relying upon the big round gun sight, I could tell I was all around the rapidly retreating plane. There was no time to "lead" him, as Tracy had instructed; so I kept the barrel steady, very much aware that my barrel was about to melt!

Time seemed to stand still, and although I could see the blur of smoke and steel, and the tracers, and I knew I was still clamping that trigger.

The Jap Zero, one moment a sky full of blue-gray metal overhead, seemingly caught and fixed there for all time, suddenly lifted and began to circle, leaving a trail of smoke behind! The noise of the engine, when it arrived a moment after the hurtling plane itself had passed over, was deafening, drowning out all other sounds during that brief moment. I had ceased to hear my own gun, the barrel of which was beginning to turn red and smoke; and although I could see Tracy's big gaping mouth, no words seemed to be coming out. Then Roucloux was prizing my hand off the trigger mechanism, and slowly I became aware that all around me my shipmates were shouting and waving their hands and behaving like crazy people!

The plane rose high in the sky and heeled west, becoming a black ball of smoke. To most of the convoy this signaled the good news of the plane's death, but as we watched it became clear that the pilot had not given up. Instead of continuing away from the convoy and cutting back to the north in the direction his fellow aviators had taken, he was circling southward!

The skipper of the SC-664, Lt.(jg) Melvin Patchen, was so certain the air attack had ended, he brought his ship alongside to shout congratulations and something else about "the impossible having just happened."

Then Tabor was shouting through his megaphone, "Look out, here he comes back!"

Suddenly, the big guns across the convoy opened up again, along with a lot of small stuff; and soon the smoke of the wounded Zeke was difficult to distinguish from that of the convoy ack-ack. But through it all here he emerged, still leading a great cloud of smoke! From an altitude of about two thousand feet it began to heel slightly, heading back in our general direction! And when it became obvious that it would once again pass over us, I felt my insides do a flip-flop.

It was ridiculous and not a little vain, but at this time I was wondering if I had been responsible for turning an otherwise normal Japanese pilot into a *kamikaze?*

Lt. Hiller grabbed the megaphone from Tabor and shouted:

"All hands, return to your battle stations! Here comes a that blasted Jap back for more! Off the starboard bow, about one o'clock!"

Every eye became fixed on the huge black ball hurtling through the flak, beelining it in our direction! The pilot had practically circled the convoy with the others and perhaps could have limped off to safety, but here he came, like a very angry hornet!

Roucloux shouted, "Nobody in his right mind would bother with us when he's got LST's and PA's on all sides to pick from!"

The sky was again filling up with flak, and every gun in the convoy was pounding away at the lone plane, as it dropped from the sky.

We watched, our guns silent because of the distance. In what seemed like a very long time, the forward half of the plane, now a hurtling missile of death, materialized, angling downward through the flak! Down, down it came and just when I was convinced it was out of control and going into the drink, it began to level out, practically on the surface of the ocean!

It was lined up squarely on the *995!*

Until the convoy had gone to General Quarters, the five subchasers had been spaced about five hundred yards apart on the port side; and from the sky they must have looked identical—in size and shape— and very tiny from two thousand feet up. And while they were quite vulnerable to any size of bullet or missile, they undoubtedly made very difficult targets for a pilot hurtling through the air at better than two hundred miles an hour!

The instant General Quarters had sounded all of the ships of the convoy began maneuvering according to the battle plan. This, of course, had resulted in a very rough sea for the small ships; and now, as the lone bogey came in, the *SC-664* was bouncing along on our port side, away from the incoming Zero.

"He's right on the water!" yelled July Roucloux.

I had stopped breathing but I could hear myself saying over and over, "Oh, God!"

And Roucloux was saying over and over, "Here he comes!"

Not a single slug had issued from the plane, and now it was quite obvious that the lunatic flying the plane was going to use himself and his plane as a weapon! But it made no sense to me at all why he would want to do that.

A veritable wall of anti-aircraft fire had gone up on the starboard side of the convoy; but through it like a bullet, untouched, hurtled the black nose of the plane. It was so low by now it seemed about to crash into the water, and there was no way any of the flak would touch it.

Roucloux had replaced my overheated barrel with a fresh one still dripping with water and fitted a new canister of ammo. Milleson, on the after twenty, began cursing. His barrel had overheated; and his loader, while replacing it with another, had evidently lost it overboard during a heavy roll to starboard! Of course, it did not matter much because only during a roll to starboard would either one of us be able to get a slug into that thing.

On the bridge, the Skipper shouted into the voicetube. "Engines ahead full! Come right ten degrees!"

Suddenly, our powerful Chryslers belched, sending out great clouds of black smoke from both the port and starboard exhausts! I grabbed my shoulder pieces just as a great shudder went through the ship. A moment later I thought the after half of the ship was sinking! I saw July Roucloux's feet sliding sternward, and I yelled at him to grab something! And then I was certain we were about to be airborne, because our bow was out of the water!

Vanderveen's cursing, amplified to forty db over S9 by the flared hatch of the engineroom, reached us on the quarterdeck. I knew what he was trying to say, that the deck plates to which the engines were bolted would never hold together at this speed, and sure as hell the ship itself would come apart! The bilges would erupt and the ship would fill up with sea water!

There followed the sensation of moving rapidly through space, and I saw or imagined the missile of death passing behind us and disappearing for a split second into the black smoke issuing from our exhausts; and, all in that same split second, I *saw* it emerge—and knew even before the mighty explosion reached my ears, knew with a great sinking feeling in my stomach, *what terrible thing was going to happen!*

Obscured from my view by its own ball of black smoke, the plane had indeed missed us and slammed squarely into the starboard side of the *Subchaser 664*!

My mind simply stopped at that point. It would not accept what had happened. Still in my shoulder harness, I must have sat down on the deck and covered my head with my hands, as debris rained around me. I had no awareness of what others on the *995* were doing, while the bits and pieces of what had been our sister ship and *our comrades in arms* fell upon the deck!

The noise of the explosion I remembered later as sharp pains inside my head; and, when I was once again under some kind of control, I turned my eyes toward where the old *664* had been and saw in disbelief and horror a great cloud of smoke low on the water, surrounded by *debris*. Nothing else. It was like nothing I had ever experienced before; and it was too much for my brain to assimilate. Time, it seemed, had been compressed too far, and so the crash of metal against wood and flesh, the slow realization that some of what I was hearing, and perhaps imagining to some degree, were the agonized cries of my friends and acquaintances on the *664*—And what I was seeing, bits and pieces of the plane and the ship and human body parts, heads and legs and arms, that just moments before had been living human beings with hopes and aspirations.

The noise of the crash, in retrospect deafening, gut-wrenching, simultaneous with the incoming engine noises and the screams and cries of the sailors at the moment of their deaths—became etched indelibly in the minds and memories of every member of the crew of the *995*. Death for us would never hold the terrors it once had, for we had seen it up close and knew it for what it was: The inevitable calling in of one's number.

We should have been in the path of that plane; or, at least, the *Splendid Four* should not have been where she was.

That day and the next we did talk about the tragedy. Actually, we did not talk to each other about it ever. What was there to say? That I had been lucky with my bullets and was actually to blame for the deaths of our friends? That it was all a believe-it-or-not freakish accident that should never have happened? That in the blinking of an eye twenty-four good men had lost their lives because a lunatic Jap with suicidal tendencies was trying to take us out?

The if's went back all the way to New Caledonia: If we had not scavanged those MTB Chrysler engines, more than likely we would not have made the trip north (But even if we had managed to go north, we would not have had the engine-thrust to get out of the way, thus exposing the *664*...). If I had not shot that particular Jap in just that particular manner (from the back and at the last possible moment), he would not have circled back and therefore the 664 would been all right (But even if the Jap had circled back for whatever reason and the 664 had only remained on station...).

Reason and logic had gone out the window: coincidence and happenstance were the rule of the day. There was such a thing as *luck* after all, and, yes, *fate*.

                    *   *   *

Someone was talking to me, I realized, and had been for sometime. I looked up, trying to concentrate. It was Roucloux and he wasn't making any sense. I stood up and looked around. The sky had cleared up and, to my surprise, the water had some blue in it.

"What?" I asked, aware that our engines were making soft, gurgling sounds through the exhausts. We were treading water not far from the collection of debris. On the bridge the Skipper and Tabor were milling about, staring off in opposite directions. No one else was in sight, just

July Roucloux, and he was talking, talking. Then I saw Tracy sitting on the flag box and his mouth was not flapping.

I began to think about Laney, the kid who had mimicked Jimmie Stewart so well, and Michaels, the sparks who was always tapping Morse Code with his fingers.

So quickly and unexpectedly had the thing happened that no one aboard the 664 had had time to leap overboard. Indeed, at the moment when the Zero settled into what was to be its final heading, everyone topside had become transfixed, stopped whatever they were doing. It was as if they were waiting for the Zero to do whatever it was going to do. Perhaps they thought it was headed for the big APA, which was also in its path, certain that no pilot would sacrifice his life and a valuable aircraft for a lowly subchaser!

It was like watching helplessly as a neighbor's house bursts into flames, knowing that there was nothing you could do either to stop the thing from happening or save the victims from a sure death.

Then it was over and the world was suddenly very quiet, with only a great deal of white flak and a little patch of debris left to remind us of what had gone down. Up to this time we had joked about our vulnerability; but from that day forth we would joke about other things.

*   *   *

Soon there was not even a ripple in the ocean where the *Splendid Four* had been. And as the convoy re-grouped and fell back into its snail's pace toward the Solomon Islands, only a scattering of tongue-in-groove splinters remained behind for the gooney birds to investigate.

The next day Sharkey and Smith, after having been relieved from their watches, spread their towels on the starched white deck at the point of the bow and took up once again the sad state of affairs aboard the ship. I joined them, leaning over the lifeline and staring at the water. Sharkey was naked, except for ragged cut-offs and sandals, but Smith's

white, delicate skin could not take the one-hundred-ten-degree equato-
rial sun. He had on a pair of ancient undress white trousers, a tie-dyed
T-shirt, and was shielding his face with my *Radio Amateur's Handbook.*

Without preliminary, Sharkey led off the conversation with the
opinion that I was having a hard time forgetting what had happened.

"Um, yeah," agreed Smith, rising on an elbow and turning the upper
part of his body over for some relief. "Speakin' of which, would you ever
have guessed he was capable of shootin' down a plane?"

They were pretending I wasn't sprawled out a few feet away.

"What he did was aim his barrel at the heavens and pull the trigger,"
said Sharkey, with a shrug. "I could have done the same thing and so
could you. He probably had his eyes closed."

"You and Milleson had twenties, and Baldini had the forty," said
Smith, his voice neutral. "But they didn't shoot down a plane. And none
of the gunners on the other subchasers shot down anything either."

"It was pure de ole luck," insisted Sharkey. "It'll never happen
again in a million years."

"I think he ought to be given a medal for it," continued Smith in the
same voice. "The chances of somebody doin' that on one of these
matchsticks is about a billion to one against. Ask Pills."

"I'll tell you who'll get a medal if anybody does," laughed Sharkey
bitterly. "The Skipper. That's what always happens. The C. O. gets
credit for anything his men do."

"Why so?"

"Because he's the skipper of a vessel of war, that's why. Every good
and worthwhile thing that happens aboard it is his fault."

"How about if something bad happens?"

"Then it's somebody else's fault," grunted Sharkey. "Unless somebody carelessly runs the ship into something. Then it'd also be the
Skipper's fault, along with whoever did it."

"I'd recommend him for a medal, myself."

"Who, the Skipper?"

"Hell, no."

"I guess he's pretty fucked up about what happened."

"Who, the Skipper?"

"Hail, no!"

10

All Same Joe

According to McCormick, we were passing through some very hairy country. Jap-infested is what he called it. That first air attack on the convoy had occurred near the New Hebrides Islands, he said, showing me on the map, about halfway between Espiritu Santo and the Torres Islands; and we could expect more of the same all the way to the Solomons. We had to pass between New Britain and New Ireland, where the Japs outnumbered the coconuts. And then, if we were lucky, we would head through the Bismarck Sea.

He dragged his pointing finger across his throat, staring at me.

Outside the pilothouse the boatswain's mate was giving his four deckhands hell. Ace and I stopped talking to take in the dressing down.

It made absolutely no difference to Baldini that we might at any moment have to scramble for our battle stations, he was going to see to it that our topside was as white as snow and twice as clean. Every morning at the first sign of daylight he crashed down into the forward crews quarters and started banging and rattling things until he had us all up, regardless of whether we had stood the midwatch or not. And although he never pulled this stunt in the after quarters, the Department Heads were convinced that he was a lunatic and needed to be incarcerated in a padded cell. Their fear that any day now he would be elevated to the position of Fourth Officer was growing, and some of them, such as

Tracy and Sharkey, were beginning to suggest that something had better be done before it was too late.

What could be done about Baldini?

At least four of the old heads had gone to the wardroom, individually, complaining about something the boatswain's mate had done (Generally, it concerned noise and shouting and general disruption); but the Skipper and his two junior officers were of a mind, that the ship needed a strong boatswain's mate and Baldini was all we had. Could anyone blame him for wanting a clean topside?

Tracy's complaint was that the deck was already cleaner than Kwaitkowski's messtable in its best moment, that at least ten million gallons of sea water had washed and sanded it paper thin and the tropical sun had bleached it chalk white. Leafdale's worry was that Baldini was driving the crew insane, that one day they were either going to kill him or start in on each other.

There we were, heading north into the War Zone, and all we could talk about and bitch about was Baldini. We were spending less and less time worrying and fretting about such things as the shortage of food and water, our hot and humid and overcrowded living conditions, and the absence of such distractions as books, magazines, and playing cards. Indeed, most of our waking moments we were too occupied with this hateful man to give much thought to our miserable and hopeless existence.

It did not occur to any of us that without Baldini we would have more than likely died of boredom and apathy on our way to doing battle with the Imperial Japanese Navy.

We were beginning to spend a lot of time at General Quarters, what the officers called Condition Yellow; and although this forced us gunners and our loaders to endure long hours in the blistering heat in helmets and Mae Wests, it was made somewhat tolerable by the fact that Baldini was being forcibly detained in his bucket seat on the forty. Day after day we kept a wary eye on the sky for angry little black dots; and, with growing frequency, someone, generally Tabor, would spot planes off to the north or northwest; and about once a day, here two or three (sometimes half a dozen) would come, diving in and spiraling out. Invariably, American TBF's or perhaps P-38's would show up and take out one or two before the rest disappeared over the horizon.

One day the convoy was joined by a Fletcher Class tincan, one of the new ones straight from the West Coast. No prettier sight had I ever seen than this sleek, silver fighting machine, as it ploughed past us on the port side. Suddenly, Tabor was whacking away at the blinkerlight, and she was responding! The flashes came at us so fast I could barely keep up at times, but evidently the Blackfoot had no trouble at all reading it. He rogered eventually and turned to the Skipper:

"That was Splendid Leader. We'll anchor off Guadal for a couple of days, until orders come for us to move to Florida Island for gunnery practice." After pausing, he added off-handedly, "We'll need to relay that to the others."

The Skipper looked at me with a pained expression on his face. "Could you put that down on a message form? As complete and accurate as you can get it?"

What Tabor had not bothered to mention to the Skipper was that our *Splendid Leader* had chosen him, specifically, to relay this important message to the others. I suspected that the signalman had settled on Tabor because he had found someone who could read him without difficulty. Signalmen were temperamental characters.

When I had the message worked out on one of the yellow half-sheet message grams, I handed it to Tabor.

"Send it just like that, Tabor. No expletives."

*   *   *

Leafdale's attitude toward guns and noise was the same as it was toward the war and the Japanese, Wild Bill, Baldini, the Third Officer, and Cookie's food: He wanted no part of any of them. He did not even like for any of these subjects to be brought up in his presence. And the idea of going to an island with deckhands, grease monkeys, and common riffraff, like Sharkey and Milleson, and shooting off a variety of guns so upset him that he went to the Skipper and tried to get out of the one-day gunnery school we were supposed to attend on Florida Island. And when he had the Skipper's reply, he went about the ship assuring everybody that there would be no exceptions, that even Kwaitkowski and Eddie Jake, as well as Vanderveen, would have to take part in the shooting and carrying on

Sharkey, who was sitting on Pills' pillow in the after quarters, reached over and tapped the old pharmacist's mate on the shoulder (which was another of Pills' pet peeves). "Well, old buddy, I guess you'll just have to mingle with the peons and white trash over on that island. Don't feel bad, so will I."

"Take your hand off my shoulder," spat Pills. After he shook himself, as though ridding his shoulder of germs, he said, "It is no comfort to me at all that you will have to participate in that foolishness. You grew up with guns."

"I come from the north side, Pills, not the south. I hate guns as much as you do." Sharkey then took us on a pedestrian stroll of the various parts of his hometown neighborhood, ending with, "Pills, you've got me mixed up with old Studs Lonigan."

"I don't have you mixed up with anybody," snarled Leafdale. "Where the hell you from, anyway? What town?"

"Chicago!" cried Sharkey, plaintively. Then he made a yukking noise and whined, "I thought you knew!"

"That's right I should have known, the way you blow all the time."

"By the way," said McCormick, "I guess I will be the only one excluded from that little farce, huh, Pills?"

"You haven't heard a word I've been saying," protested Pills. "You, me, everybody on this ship, even the officers, will be in on it."

The run in with *Splendid Leader* had convinced us that we must be getting close to Guadalcanal and a temporary pause in our journey into the War Zone. And that very afternoon, the convoy began to split up. The big PA's and AKA's angled off to the right, and we continued straight ahead with the LST's and LCVI's. The following morning we found ourselves alone in the southern reaches of the Solomon Islands. Even the tincans and DE's, but not the *Hazelwood*, our *Splendid Leader*, had left us during the night.

I was on the radios in the pilothouse when Tabor spotted the first sign of land, Rennell Island, and shortly after that Ace made the announcement that we would make it to our anchorage by noon. Then land was on both sides of us, most of it low and covered with jungle. I asked Ace how much farther it was to Guadal, and he pointed ahead and to the left:

"That's Guadalcanal." Then, pointing ahead and to the right, he said, "Savo. We're entering "The Slot. The most famous piece of real estate (He nodded toward Guadal) in the Pacific."

For a very long time I had dreamed of one day seeing and stepping foot on that island. Which I had not even heard of until the Marines landed on it back in 1942. My first glimpse of it now was an extreme disappointment. It was flat and treeless, reminding me of a plucked chicken with the little pin feathers still there. What had been dense jungle was now nothing more than a lot of stumps ranging in height from two to six feet.

We anchored in plain sight of this, and about the time we were secured from our watches, air raid sirens went off on the island! We up-anchored quickly and watched a few Jap planes go over at a distance, too far away for our guns. Later that afternoon an LCVP showed up and took the crews of all four ships ashore. We were wearing cut-offs and nothing else, except the old salts, who, for the most part had not shaved since New Caledonia.

There was not one permanent structure on the island, that we could see, not even a quonset hut. And although the Seabees were in evidence, it was my guess that they were more interested in re-building the air field than building a base. They had put in an outdoor theater and a Recreation Tent for enlisted men, which looked like a tent but had a wooden deck and a screendoor. And the Army had put up two large tents, one a PX and the other a messhall.

We gawked about on limber legs, trying to get used to walking on an even keel again. Some walked almost out of sight down the beach, just to be doing something, while the rest either went over and sat in the metal folding chairs facing the movie screen or shopped at the PX. I checked out the "library" in the Recreation Tent. It was a single book-shelf with two dozen old battered hardback books.

For a week we stayed anchored just off Guadal, and the routine we fell into aboard the *995* was most tolerable one, despite Baldini. His loud complaining about the goldbricking that was going on and his frequent trips to the wardroom failed to keep most of us from going swimming when we liked, run back and forth to the Army PX on the island during the day, and see the outdoor movies in the evenings.

As it happened, by the time the radiogram about moving to Florida Island for gunnery training came, we had completely forgot that we had been waiting for it. So it came as a real blow to the morale aboard the ship. What was at Florida Island? everybody wanted to know. Did it have a movie theater and a Recreation Tent? We were assured by the girenes on Guadal that Florida was nothing but a jungle of coconut palms.

On the day of our departure from Guadal, Baldini came crashing down into the forward quarters before daylight and began banging on the metal bunk frames and punching us with a sawed-off swab handle that he had taken to carrying around with him. And, of course, all the time he was doing this he was yelling, "All right! Hit the deck! Topside on the double!"

Ordinarily, I would have beat him up by an hour; but the night before several of us had stayed up until well after midnight listening to Ace tell about the Battle of the Solomons, which included the Battle of Iron Bottom Bay and his part in it. His version of it was perhaps biased and focused a bit by problems he had been having with an officer aboard the tincan, but it was a good story and I did not regret staying up so late.

I went topside and lined up with the others along the port lifeline and watched Guadal disappear. Ace had told me that Florida was just a stone's throw away, that we would be there and anchored before morning chow. So when some of the others drifted aft for coffee, I stuck it out and watched one little island after another go by.

I had become used to thinking of the starboard twenty millimeter gun as my battle station, and the comradeship that had developed between me and July Roucloux was the best thing that had happened to me on the ship. But if I had been given a choice, I would have joined Harold Jines inside the pilothouse on the radios.

Ace turned out to be right about Florida Island being nearby. Just as Roucloux joined me at the lifeline, I realized that we were headed straight for a long white beach. The jungle behind it was the greenest I had seen. And although we could not see much of the island, it appeared to be round and almost flat, and the coconut palms came right down to the beach, in a straight line.

"Maybe after they see me shoot," I commented, "I'll be on the radios. I'll bet you qualify to be one of the gunners."

"Hah! Not me. But if we can't stick together, I'd like to be on the vertical of that 40mm. Maybe you'll end up in the other seat, on the horizontal."

Baldini saw to the anchoring from a distance, well out of the way of Leavy and Rincon, who had to do all the work. Unlike the larger ships, ours did not have an anchor wench.

An LCVP appeared from nowhere and came alongside, and the coxswain shouted to the bridge that he was there to take us to the island.

Baldini came running but was too late give Roucloux and me the order to board. Climbing aboard was tricky because the big clumsy barge kept rising and pitching, threatening to plough into the *995*. Eventually, we were all aboard that were going aboard. It suddenly became clear that some of the crew would remain on the ship, after all. The Skipper strolled down to 'midships, in response to Pills' waving and shouting, and told the coxswain to shove off. To Pills he said, casually, "Cookie needs to remain in the galley, and Ace can't be spared from the pilothouse."

"Well, how about Vanderveen?"

"He's needed in the engineroom."

The Exec and the Third Officer had joined us, dressed in khaki shorts and tie-dyed T-shirts; and Mr. Darling was carrying a small camera strapped to his left wrist. Two tourists trapped in a great wobbly sardine can on their way to a visit to one of the Solomon Islands.

We were farther out than I had thought, and on our way in we saw another barge picking up the crew of the *419*. Seabees, wearing nothing but shorts, were constructing platforms on the beach, three of them, about three hundred yards apart. Back in the edge of jungle we caught a glimpse of other Seabees working at some tables.

It was obvious that Pills was not the only unhappy volunteer for this project. Jines, standing near us in the barge, was particularly vocal about his feelings on the subject, and he did not bother to keep his voice down. Speaking primarily to Tracy, he said: "I'm the sparks aboard the ship, right? Why do I have to go through this? If I do well, can I expect to be pulled away from the radios. This is stupid."

"Maybe Pinky will qualify to go back to the radios, releasing you," snickered Tracy. "There is no way he will make a good showing on one of the guns. Have you ever watched him? I'll lay you odds he never shot a gun in his life until he came aboard the subchaser."

Jines' face was flushed with anger: "He's not supposed to be good with a gun, and neither am I. We're both needed on the radios."

"Well, at least maybe this will get people like Pinky off the guns. I can't wait to see him shoot at a towed target."

Jines, unaware that I was able to hear him, turned and looked at glared at Tracy, "Tell me, Bill, what do you have against Pinky? Has he ever done or said anything to you to make you so goddamn nasty mean to him?"

Tracy glanced at me and laughed: "Shit man, he deserves to be kidded. See, look at him, he's eatin' it up."

On my other side Sharkey was trying to work somethling on the two ensigns. To something Mr. Howorth had said, he protested, "No, Sir! I'm allergic to gunpowder. I break out bad. That's why I took up sonar work."

"Well, I guess we'll see just how bad your allergy is," said Mr. Howorth. "This sounds like a rather ambitious training and testing situation we're gettin' in on. I understand it includes all of the weapons we've got aboard the ship."

"Even pistols, Sir?"

"I don't know about pistols. Why?"

"No reason, except ever' since I was a kid I've had a phobia about pistols. My uncle was accidentally killed by one, and I was there and saw it happen. It was his son, my own cousin, that did it, and the thought of holding one in my hands makes me break out in hives."

"You'll be all right. Pills has some—uh—pills for hives." Mr. Howorth turned and winked at the other ensign, who did not appear to be enjoying the jostling in the crowded barge. "I was just kiddin', Shark," said Mr. Howorth. "As I'm sure you were, too. Anybody with a mentality like yours will have no problem with pistols and carbines and whatever."

"Sir, I really don't need to be involved in this thing."

The LCVP Army coxswain in charge of our boat was quite obviously a veteran of many such ferry trips and therefore perhaps a bit jaded, judging by the way he executed his run-and-drop routine. He full-throttled in, down-throttled all the way and, at the same time, threw on the brakes hard. Then while we were trying to disentangle ourselves, he released the noisy ramp in about four feet of water.

"All ashore that's goin' ashore!" he shouted.

The water was warm and we were all dressed for swimming, and so only a moderate amount of bitching took place. Mr. Howorth and Mr. Darling hung back, reluctant to get their white uniform shorts and tennis shoes wet; and after all of us enlisted had all cleared out, the joker at the wheel raised the ramp about a foot and eased on in to the beach.

There was a good mile of coral beach facing us, clean and white and absolutely virgin, except for the three platforms and the six gun emplacements. We waded ashore and fanned out, watching and gawking. The Seabees had no time for us but when confronted they admitted to knowing nothing about the day's schedule. They had built the platforms and set up the guns and hauled in the refreshments, and later they would feed everybody, but beyond that we would have to ask the instructors, when they showed up. If they showed up.

Was there a chance they might not?

Sometimes they showed up early, sometimes late, sometimes not at all.

Immediately, our spirits rose. Instead of a day of noise and stink and confusion, perhaps it was going to be a day of partying on the beach.

At one of the tables in the edge of the jungle a line had developed. Something was being served. I took off, followed by Roucloux, Sharkey, Smith, and about half of the *995* crew.

Later, bunched around a big palm tree some distance from the table, we drank our Nehi Orange Colas and tried to ignore Sharkey, who was complaining about the thoughtlessness of the Navy for serving us Nehi instead of beer. Then we became aware that something was causing a commotion down the beach. Half the crowd at the table had headed in that direction.

"Well, I guess they finally made it," said Pills, chagrined.

"From the noise I would say it's women," suggested Sharkey, who still had not moved. "Dozens of white women here on holiday, anxious to—"

Although nobody in our group was about to be taken in by Sharkey's spoofing, the stampede was on. I trailed behind, leaping as high as I could every few steps in an attempt to see over the heads of the crowd of sailors. And when I caught a glimpse of an outrigger canoe. I headed directly for the water and shortly was able to count five of the long boats, all loaded to the gunwales with bananas, coconuts, and naked natives.

About a dozen young black men with great bushy balls of hair had quit the boats and were dancing and shouting and pointing back toward their wares. The young women, who had similar hairdos but smaller bones in their noses and earlobes, were just as naked as the men. They had remained in the boats beneath large straw hats that were all brim.

The leader of the pack stood out from the rest in a number of ways. He was covered from his neck to his toes with tattoos, the large bones in his earlobes were resting on his shoulders, and he had a mouthful of very white teeth. Leaving nothing to chance, he danced well ahead of the others, crouching and maneuvering and putting out his hands toward the audience, as if he were inviting contact. And, of course, he was making more noise than anybody else.

All of these young men were built exactly alike and, without the ornaments and embellishments, had identical faces. They were all made from the same mold, apparently, and although everyone of them was smiling and obviously quite happy and peaceful, *they looked like cannibals!*

After the dance, which was evidently a ritual greeting, the leader began to speak to his captivated audience of about seventy-five swabs and eight or ten officers. More accurately, he shouted at us, in a very curious kind of English, that we were welcome to this place because we had chased the Joppinese away and we looked like velly good fellas and he had brought us some souvenirs of this place.

While he shouted in his halting, high-pitched Pidgen English, I studied the artwork on his face, neck, and lower parts.

Actually, the tattoos, when viewed up close, were welts that stood out from his skin about an eighth of an inch, and the initial impression was that he had wrapped his entire body with a thin, evil-looking snake. After meandering around his chest and shoulders, it rose to his neck, took two turns, and continued up to his face, coiling on each check and crossing at the bridge of the nose, and then rising to his forehead and coiling once again before disappearing into his great jungle of hair!

"Hey, you, G. I. Joe!" he yelled, looking directly at me. "You want much coconut and bracelet and necklace and mat to lay down on and take nap! What say? All same okay?"

He came racing up to me with his right hand out to shake. I let him take my hand, wondering where this was going. I did not have one thing this fellow could possibly want. He began to pump it, repeating, "What name?" It was becoming a demand. "Me all same Joe. What name?" Still hanging onto my right hand, he began taking an interest in my hair. Suddenly, he leaped and grabbed a handful of it and pulled my head down into his face! Then while I was making up my mind what to do, he began inspecting individual hairs!

"Wow!" he screamed. "Not for real? All same juice?"

I straightened up, taking him and my hair with me. "What do you mean, 'juice'?"

He whirled around and bent over to show me the back of his head. In the center was a large round area of brilliant orange.

"Juice, for the tickorice." He whirled back around, his eyes round with curiosity.

I said without hesitation, "No juice!"

We drifted down to his boat to look at what he had to trade, followed by the audience. He began lifting things up and showing them to us. Besides the tropical fruit and nuts, he demonstrated with great gusto a surprising number of "souvenirs" that we could take home to the "Stets." These included straw things, mats and hats and baskets; things from the sea, bracelets and necklaces and earrings.

The problem was we had nothing to trade, except the food the Seabees had brought for us. I glanced toward the tables and was surprised to see that they had placed down the center of each stacks of cold cuts, K-rations, sliced liverwurst and bologna, onions. On each end of the tables were pyramids of canned foods. Including cling peaches.

"Do you like peaches?" I threw out. I had grown to hate the sight of a can of that stuff.

For a moment his great smile disappeared and there was a pained expression on his face. He sounded out the word a few times, while I was getting one of the cans open. I handed him a slice on the blade of my pocketknife. He took it, smelled of it, stuck out his great red tongue and tasted it. Suddenly, a wonderful transformation took place on his face, and he began to leap up and down!

"Wow! Wow!" He stuck out his hands, palms up, and I slapped them, which delighted him and so we had to do it again and again. To put a stop to it, I began feeding him slices of peaches!

From this point on until the party was over, All Same Joe stuck with me like glue. We carried many cans of peaches down to his boat, indeed all that we could find on the three tables; and instead of eating the cold cuts the Seabees had brought, my shipmates and I filled up on bananas and coconuts and pineapples.

"Mebbe see you in Stets," he said when I mentioned that we would be around only that one day. "All Same Joe go Brooklyn after war. Brooklyn, you know?"

"Sure. What are you going to do there?"

He shrugged his massive shoulders and rattled his bones.

"Mebbe see you dere."

"Where did you learn to speak English so well?"

"Oh, wal, I go to mission school on island. Learn plenty good Anglis. Star pupple."

"Where did you learn about Brooklyn?"

"Oh, well, all same G. I. Joe. He come with ship, many time. Velly good mon. He sey las' time when he lef', he sey see me in Stets. I go see him, settle down."

I finally got around to asking him about the tattoo. Suddenly very serious, he explained that it had been his pleasure and privilege to have the great snake placed on his body. It was actually one continuous welt the size of a water snake, performed upon him by the professionals of his tribe. At the time it had been quite painful, but only a short section of it was done at any one time. And he was plenty much all same pleased with the beauty and majesty of it. No, the open sores here and there on it did not disturb him. They were part of the majesty of the thing. It was what made him such a famous man among his people.

"And you intend to live in Brooklyn?" asked Sharkey, who had happened along in time to catch part of what All Same Joe was saying. "They don't allow all same tattoos there, you know. You'll have to have that thing removed if you hope to live in Brooklyn."

All Same Joe's happy, proud face remained happy and proud while his mind worked out what Sharkey was telling him, a process that took a good minute. Then, suddenly, the import of the words finally having sunk in, he leaped to his feet and screamed, "All Same Joe beery much no same do! No can remove tattoo no how! Hurt like hell goin' on, hurt goddamn plenty worse comin' off! Mebbe so all same kill Joe!"

"And you'll have to put on clothes and a necktie and shoes, and take them goddamned bones out of your ears!"

At this point, I dived for Sharkey, who wrestled away and took off down the beach. All Same Joe finally calmed down after I had repeated a number of times that this evil sailor did not know anything at all about Brooklyn and the requirements for living therein.

*   *   *

That afternoon four Navy CPO's, two lieutenants, and a yeoman showed up in a Captain's gig and, rapid-fire, gave us instruction in the three types of weapons found on the subchaser. The yeoman was there to gather the records and make a report to the skippers of the individual ships.

All of us, we were told, had to fire each of the guns at a flying target before we could call it a day. Had we begun that morning there would have been no rush, but as it was the sun was on the horizon when the last bullet was fired. The remarkable thing was that the plane pulling the targets was not shot down.

At the boats ready to return to the *SC-995*, Sharkey pointed toward my great umbrella of a straw hat that All Same Joe had traded to me for a can of peaches. "You know, don't you, that Baldini will never let you wear that thing on the ship. Here, let me see it." He took the hat and put it on. "He'll throw it over the side if he gets the chance."

"How about those sandals you're wearing?" I asked. "Where do you plan to wear them?"

He handed the hat back, "We're talking apples and coconuts here. He won't say a word about these. Changin' the subject, I think you and Roucloux did right good on the guns today. Born gunners. Now, take Smith and me. We're meant for the pilothouse."

"What did you once tell me about Navy logic, Shark?" I asked. "I think the Navy way of looking at this will be that since you two are so lousy on the guns that's where you ought to be. Huh, July?"

"They will be assigned guns, no doubt about it."

"Hah!" shouted Sharkey. "One thing for damned sure, I won't be!"

Back on the ship (It was dark now and we were still milling around topside), the Skipper called us all to the quarterdeck with the news that he had the results of the target shooting on the island. By the dim light issuing from the pilothouse, he scanned a sheet of paper:

"These are the rankings on each gun, from the instructors. Therefore, I don't want to hear any bitching. Does anybody have anything to say before I make the gun assignments on this ship?"

I wanted to say that this day had convinced me that I belonged on the radios.

"All right. Permanent assignments are—Milleson and Baldini on the forty, Henderson on the port twenty, Hall on the starboard twenty, and Sharkey on the after twenty. Leafdale and Groth on the fifty-calibers. The loaders will remain the same." After a pause, the Skipper added, "Surprising how few changes had to be made."

*   *   *

That evening on the fantail Ace McCormick was in a talkative mood. While Roucloux and I settled down close by, he rolled a cigarette and, cupping his hands around it, lighted up. Everybody on the ship except the officers and Baldini, knew he did this kind of thing.

"I had a dolly once named Charlene, but when I was in the hospital down at MOB-Five Beach, I got a Dear John letter from her. So she's history. Did I ever tell you about the time I went to Japan, before the war, and learned about *geisha* girls?"

"Ace," I said, "tell the truth. Have you ever actually seen a *geisha* girl?"

"Yep, sure have, several of them. Used to make it to Japan about once a year back when I was in the Merchant Marines. You didn't know I was once a civilian sailor? Well, I sure as hell was. And that's probably what I'll go back to bein' when this shebang's over. But let me tell you about these *geisha* girls. First off, they're the prettiest things you ever saw. Pretty as porcelain dolls. They're so dad blamed pretty you don't dare touch one of them for fear she'll break."

He puffed on his cigarette for awhile, cupping the glow, and appeared to be giving this topic some heavy consideration.

"I heard they're just high-paid whores," said Roucloux. "Furnished free of charge to the cream of the Jap goldbraid."

"I heard they go wherever the Jap Army goes and sleep with the soldiers," I added.

"Wrong on both counts," said Ace. "In the United States we have whores, freelancers for the most part that go out and solicit sex for a price and give men things like clap and gonorrhea. But we don't have anything like the *geisha* at all. These girls are professional *escorts* and they don't give you one single thing but joy and happiness."

"Does that mean all they do is escort somebody around?" I asked.

"Oh, to be young and stupid again!" sighed Ace. "No, that's hardly even the beginnin' of it. These girls, carefully selected by the government for their beauty and intelligence and charm, are trained to be whatever a man needs during an evenin' or a given length of time. They're a man's fantasy, a rare and talented piece of artwork ready to do his biddin'. If he's needful of nothing more than conversation, she'll converse with him all night long. If he needs silence and a massage, that's what he'll git."

"Wow," I said quietly, genuinely impressed. "Will she go to bed with him if he needs that?"

"Sure she will! She'll give him a time of it he'll never forget as long as he lives. None of this hop on and hop off stuff. When she gets through with him he'll have a smile on his face for a week."

For a time the three of us gazed across the fantail toward the island. I liked to smell Ace's Chesterfield cigarettes, but neither July nor I had taken up the habit.

"To Americans having a whore in your family is a shame and a disgrace," said Ace. "But in Japan it's an honor and a privilege to have a sister or a daughter qualify to be a *geisha*." He threw his cigarette into the drink and got out a new one. "Did you boys see that pretty young thing today over on the island?" he asked, lighting the cigarette.

"What 'pretty young thing', Ace?" I asked. "I didn't see anything but some black natives with bones in their ears."

"I know the one you mean, Ace," snickered Roucloux. "She had tiny bones in her ears and went about flippin' her butt every which way."

"She had bones in her ears and boobs that would make ole Charlene sick with envy," said Ace. "Now, if you boys are put off by her color, let me remind you that that same chocolate color is what the girls back in the States try all summer for—and never achieve."

"Yeah, but Ace!" I sighed, faking disbelief. "She was—"

"Well, I'll be goddamned," moaned Ace, terribly saddened, "I'm talkin' to a couple of narrow minded, biased holier-than-thous! You didn't look at her because she's not quite like the girl next door. Now, tell me, have you ever *seen* a girl before with as many female attributes as this little thing had?" There was a mixture of dismay and disappointment in his voice.

"Ace, we just weren't brought up to—uh, look at girls the way you do," said Roucloux. "You see them as just something you can take to bed, a piece of woman flesh."

"And you don't?" scoffed Ace. "Now, let me tell you somethin', you bigoted and chauvinistic jerks. That girl we saw today has beauty, intelligence, and physique. What else is there?"

"How do you know she has intelligence?" I asked, shrinking into my shoulders and hiding a grin.

"Because I went over and held a conversation with her."

"Aw, come on, Ace, you can't talk native," said Roucloux. "And she sure as heck can't talk English."

"Now, what you boys need to do is hold your tongues till you know what you're talkin' about. That girl has been taught good English grammar in a missionary school near here, and even if she hadn't been I could've talked to her. In Pidgin English."

"Was that what All Same Joe was talkin'?" I asked, straight-faced. "I thought he was just—"

"Joe can talk both, if you noticed," said Ace. "When he wants to, he can talk better English than you or me."

"You actually went over and talked to her?" I asked, afraid Ace was about to drift off the subject.

"Yep, I did. She's sixteen, a virgin, and lookin' for a man. Her mother was with her and willin' to bargain with me for full rights."

"You're bull shittin'," said Roucloux, pretending to be getting ready to leave. "No mother would—"

"I'm tellin' you the truth. She wasn't a bit bashful, said she liked skinny types like me and had ambitions of goin' back to the States after the war."

"I'll bet she's slept with ever' man in her tribe," said Roucloux.

"She hasn't because she's the daughter of the king, and that means she can pick her man, an' once she picks a man she has to live with him from then on." Ace studied his long, bony right foot for awhile. "She's had her sixteenth birthday, though, and so she's got to choose real soon."

"What happens if she doesn't?" I asked.

"The king'll sell or trade her off to someone in another tribe."

"So, Ace, are you gonna marry her and save her from this evil?" laughed Roucloux. "If you take her back to the States, you'll probably want to remove the bones from her ears."

"Matter of fact I may do just that," said Ace with a nod.

At that moment we heard huffing and puffing from forward and knew it had to be Baldini heading our way. Ace got up, tossed his cigarette over the side, and headed for the after quarters. July and I scooted forward on the starboard side of the after gundeck just as Baldini barreled it down the port side.

11

Holystone

After the gunnery practice on Florida Island, we joined a convoy headed for parts unknown, the scuttlebutt being that this was just part of a much larger convoy headed north. In Sansapore, New Guinea, we anchored and waited. One night we were invited by the APA-32 to watch a movie, a real treat for us because we hadn't seen one since New Caledonia. It was a John Wayne war movie, about a Seabee Battalion that taught the Japanese a few tricks. We sat through it and left quietly, without a word. It would not have been polite for us to bitch about it in front of our hosts.

Finally, sure enough, a big convoy showed up and we joined it; and the next day, right on schedule, we mustered on the quarterdeck to hear where we were going. Mr. Hiller came out of the pilothouse with the Top Secret envelope. It was already open and after we quieted down, he said:

"The Palaus."

Needless to say, we had done a lot of speculating about where the next invasion was going to be. But no one, not even McCormick, had given this group of Japanese-occupied islands a thought. Landings had been already been made on Saipan, Tinian, and Guam over a month ago; so what was next? One guess had been Truk, the "Gibraltar of the Pacific," and Yap, another big Japanese stronghold.

"We don't know much about them, actually," said the Skipper. He glanced around at his two junior officers. "They're loaded with Japs and they've had plenty of time to get ready for us. I would guess they're the last hop before the Philippines, and if so maybe we'll be able to make that show, too."

"When is the present party supposed to take place?" asked Vanderveen, who had for once come up out of his hole.

"Well," said the Skipper, frowning, "since up until now neither we," he nodded around at his officers, "nor Ace knew where we were going, we haven't charted it; but off the top of my head, I'd say we've got about a week of ocean ahead of us. Why? Anybody got other plans for the near future?"

"How about some R and R before we git there, Skipper?" kidded Sharkey. "I'd like to play a game of softball and find out what warm Griesedieck tastes like ag'in."

"Is it true we're supposed to be gittin' a ration of one bottle of beer a day?" asked Smitty. "I heard we're supposed to be issued one beer and one pop ever' day we're at sea."

"Technically, that's right," put in Leafdale. "According to Naval Regulations, we're to get an allowance of one beer and one soft drink a day."

"That's not entirely ccurate," cut in Mr. Darling. "Small ships like this don't have the storage capacity for that much beer and pop. So when we get R and R it's up to the C. O. how much and what each man will be issued."

"Oh, Skippuh," said Mr. Howorth, "before evahbody scattahs, there's that little matter concerning Baldini, remembah?"

"Right you are. Men, let me have your attention again for just a minute. Mr. Howorth has something he wants to say."

Sharkey said, "Uh, oh."

The Exec raised his hand for silence: "As yall know, Baldini is the rankin' right-arm rating aboard the ship and theahfoah stands no watches. He's done a good job of keepin' the deck clean and evahthin' shipshape, but the Skippah has decided to give him a bridge watch. So while weah at sea, he'll—be standin' bridge watch."

Leafdale faced the Skipper. "The men won't stand for this, sir."

"Oh, I guess they will," said Mr. Hiller. "Baldini is already in charge of the deck. All he'll be doing is standing a bridge watch once ever twelve hours."

Pills was shaking his head and mumbling. Finally, he said, "This man is not qualified to run the ship, sir. If a psychiatrist ever gets a look at him, he'll be put in a straightjacket."

"You're out of line, Pills," said the Skipper. His face had changed from very white to very red. "I'll make the decisions on this ship, and I say that Baldini stands bridge watches."

Mr. Darling, who was visibly pleased by the opposition to Baldini's promotion to Fourth Officer, called out: "He will merely be sitting in for one of us—for four hours at a time while we're at sea. During General Quarters and whenever we're not underway he will be—what he has always been."

"A screwball," said Sharkey, quietly.

Calmly, Mr. Howorth began explaining that quite often at sea one of them (He cut his eyes around at Mr. Darling) was incapacitated, which worked a hardship on the other two officers. "Theahfoah, we need a fourth to insure a four-on and eight-off schedule."

Put that way, it sounded quite fair to me. Besides, I was thinking, how much more damage could Baldini do from the bridge than he was already doing running up and down the deck? And as for Sharkey's fear that he would run the ship into something, Ace McCormick would not let him do that.

The Skipper, looking a bit uncomfortable in his baseball cap and bright T-shirt, had one more thing to say on the subject:

"Now, I want to make one thing perfectly clear to all of you. I am still the Captain on this vessel, and it is I who will make the decisions.

Baldini will, until such time as I say differently, stand bridge watches, and he will have the same authority any other Officer of the Deck has while he's in charge there. When he gives an order, it will be carried out promptly. Is that perfectly clear?"

No one had a word to say to that. But on everyone's mind was the thought that our rock was, after all, an officer.

For at least two weeks Pills had been making regular trips to the wardroom with dire warnings about the crew's bitchiness and cruelty toward each other. He had indeed used specific psychological terms to describe the various maladies he had spotted, and on more than one occasion he had carried a medical text with him and read passages to the officers to prove his point.

"Most of them are so paranoid they're ready to kill one another!" he said on one occasion, just beginning to warm up. "They have lost respect for each other, as well as for most other things in this world; and they sure as hell don't respect authority of any kind. Every damned one of them is neurotic and psychotic and pathologically inclined, except maybe Tabor, and who the hell knows what goes on inside that block of stone he calls a head?"

"What do you mean by 'pathologically inclined'?" asked Mr. Darling.

"They're sick mentally and physically," Leafdale said, shrugging his shoulders. "They're pathological liars, and I think they're potentially—dangerous. And the principal reason they're this way is that goddamned Baldini."

The Skipper, on that occasion, had nodded sympathetically and said, "Yeah, you're right about them being under a lot of tension. I know what they're goin' through. These are pretty tryin' times for us all. But very soon now we'll park this thing near some sandy beach—"

"It'd better be soon, Skipper," the pharmacist's mate had warned.

*   *   *

Baldini's first O. O. D. watch was the eight-to-twelve the following morning, after we had been at sea a full day. To assure peace among the crew and ward off any accidents that might occur in the first part of the boatswain's mate's first watch, the Skipper and his two junior officers arranged with Cookie to have their breakfast trays delivered to the bridge precisely at eight o'clock.

But a good hour before this Baldini was agonizing over what he was going to wear. He had dumped his seabag on his bunk, searching for something to change into. His dungarees were, he had to admit, a bit sour, not to mention a mite slick from weeks of wearing. But all he could find was more of the same. Altogether, he had three complete suits of new dungarees, all very soiled and beginning to smell like rotting flesh.

Leavy waddled up and stood at his side, looking into the seabag.

"Does this mean I'll have to salute you?" he asked, his big Saint Bernard face registering real worry lines.

"Move back! You stink."

"Maybe now that you're an officer you won't have so much time to bother with Gilberto and me on the deck."

Baldini straightened up with a dungaree shirt and a pair of trousers, "Here, take these topside and put them in the laundry."

"Hell, I'm no laundry maid," complained Leavy, taking the clothes and turning toward the ladder. What do you mean 'laundry'? We aint got one."

"I mean tie a line around 'em and throw 'em over the side, Stupid."

"Oh," said Leavy, nodding. "Okay, I can do that. But what if they come untied or a fish gets them?"

Baldini cut his eyes around threateningly. "You'll go in after them and bring them back."

"Shee-ut," said Leavy, putting his hand on the ladder. "The way my luck's goin' lately—"

"Stay up there with them and pull them out in twenty minutes. Twenty minutes, got that?"

Leavy left worrying about how he was going to know when twenty minutes was up. The boatswain's mate immediately dug out his best regulation black shoes and began looking for his shoe-shining kit. Then he remembered that it had gone down on the *Portland*, which set him to thinking about the good old days. About twenty minutes later Gilberto Martinez drifted by, admitted reluctantly that he had some shoe polish and a brush, and proceeded to look for it in his pile of belongings beneath his bunk.

When Baldini showed up on the bridge a little past eight-hundred hours, he was wearing dungarees trousers that were white above and below but still a dark, ugly color where the rope had been cinched up just above the knees. The shirt was quite threadbare but very clean.

The three officers stopped eating and stared, but when Baldini avoided their eyes and went straight to where he was supposed to sit and run the ship, they went back to their powdered eggs and stale toast.

Tabor, not surprisingly, was sitting in the Captain's Chair gazing off at the horizon. Around his neck were the O. O. D.'s field glasses, and behind his right ear was a pencil. A package of Luckies was neatly suspended on his left shoulder by a single roll of his tie-died skivvy shirt. He did not look around when Baldini crossed the bridge and demanded that he vacate the chair.

When he received no response to his very first order, the Boats bawled into the Indian's face, "That's where I set!"

Tabor was concentrating on a point off the starboard bow and this outburst failed to get his attention.

"Did you hear me?" Baldini demanded; and, bending close, he whispered into Tabor's ear, "You goddamned sonofabitch, I said git out of that chair!"

Tabor's deadpan face swung around at this, and he said in a normal voice, "Go get your own cheer, Baldini. I got here first." With that he turned back toward the northern horizon.

Baldini's breathing was becoming labored, as he stood there hunched over, his lips not two inches from the signalman's ear. He straightened up a little, his small, beady eyes focused upon the defiant back of that Blackfoot's head; and for a moment he thought seriously of doubling his fist and knocking the disobedient piece of nothing over the bridge skirt to the deck below. But just in time he caught himself. He would deal with Tabor later, when there were no officers around.

Their breakfast finally finished, the officers stood up, surveyed the peaceful sea ahead, and, after insisting that Baldini have a good watch, went below to catch some shuteye. Not a single sign of rebellion or mayhem was there to be seen. The entire off-duty crew was undoubtedly sacked out until noon chow.

Baldini waited patiently until he was certain the officers had made it to the wardroom; then he wheeled, lost his balance, and lunged out of control across the bridge, catching himself just in time. Then, observing from his elevated position there on the bridge the various parts of the ship, he inventoried the scrounginess of the deck here and there and the general slothfulness of the two men who had just come out of the forward quarters and were beginning to goldbrick. A thrill of possession swept over him as he looked. For almost four full hours this was his very own ship! The whole shebang!

It occurred to him suddenly that everything had been *transformed!* When you're in charge, he thought, things look different. His gaze swept around and came to rest on Tabor again. Well, not all things, maybe. That knothead would get his comeuppance real soon!

He walked over to the starboard side of the bridge and removed the megaphone from its rack. Tabor glanced around but said nothing.

"Now hear this!" he said, pointing the megaphone toward the bow. "All hands on deck! Pass the word!" After a moment, he cleared his throat and said, considerably louder, "Now hear this! All hands hit the deck!" Nothing had happened except that the two deckhands had turned and were staring at him. He pointed the megaphone toward the stern and repeated the last order, adding, "This means left-arm rates, Department Heads, and all people on this ship below the rank of ensign! Git on deck on the double!"

He lowered the megaphone and surveyed the results. Leavy, half in and half out of the forward hatch, had frozen there, undoubtedly blocking traffic.

Baldini whirled and surveyed the area from the engineroom hatch to the fantail. Tracy and Jines had appeared just forward of the *bimini* on the port side, but like the two deckhands on the bow they were not moving. Nobody on the ship was responding!

Again he raised the megaphone toward the bow. "Now hear this! This is the O. O. D. speaking! All hands on deck! Leavy, git ever'body out of the fo'c's'le! And be quick about it! He turned and caught a glimpse of Roucloux, who was just disappearing beneath the awning. "Hey, Tex, pass the word! Roucloux, I'm talkin' to you! Hustle the Department Heads out of their quarters!"

Ten minutes later, after it had become abundantly clear to Baldini that no one was going to respond to his order, he slammed down the ladder to the quarterdeck and entered the pilothouse. Wild, isolated twigs of graying hair flared outward above his ears; and as he flung himself across the small compartment to the open hatch in the deck, his breathing was becoming a bit shrill.

McCormick was at the helm with a bare foot propped up on one rung of the wheel working on his spickitch, and I was sitting at the engine controls on the starboard side reading The *Radio Amateur's Handbook*, 1943 edition.

"What's up, Boats?" asked Ace, nonchalantly. "You musterin' the crew?"

Baldini had turned around and lowered himself to the top rung of the ladder that led to the radio shack and the wardroom. "Who's supposed to be in here?" he bawled, looking first at Ace and then at me. "I want all hands not on watch out on the deck!"

"I wouldn't bother the Old Man!" warned McCormick, not raising his voice. "He had the four-to-eight."

But Baldini was already banging on the wardroom door.

"You know," said Ace, "where common sense and logic has no chance at all with the Skipper right now, this kind of stupidity just might."

"Maybe," I said, lowering my book. "He should have waited a little longer."

Ace left the wheel and bent over the hatch.

"What're they saying?" I asked.

"Baldini's telling one of the officers that if he is to do his duty he has got to have respect, that the men aren't cooperating."

I joined Ace, just in time to hear Baldini say that the men would not obey any of his orders and the Skipper say, "What orders?"

"I'm tryin' to muster them on deck. They won't muster."

"Why do you need to muster them?"

"Because it's high time we had a real job done on that deck, Sir! It's dirty an' I intend to holystone it!"

"'Holystone'? Don't you think—? Right now?" After a pause, during which Ace and I waited, not breathing, the Skipper sighed, "Well, all right! I'll be right up!"

We scurried back to our positions just as Baldini's head appeared in the hatchway. His little pig eyes lined up on me, but before he could say anything the Skipper was prodding him from below and yelling, "Be quick about it!"

About ten minutes later, after all hands had been mustered on the 'midships gundeck and lectured to, the Skipper zipped back through the pilothouse and disappeared below, slamming the door of the wardroom on his way to his bunk.

"I've got to watch this," I said, putting my book down.

"My advice to you is to hide down there in the corner."

But I eased down the little passageway just in time to see Baldini mount the ladder to the bridge. Then we could hear him pacing to and fro up there.

Like a Napoleon surveying his troops before battle, Baldini paced back and forth on the bridge, his megaphone ready, glaring first at one of the crew and then another. Nobody was giving him the time of day, but it was obvious that he had won the first round. It was his moment in the sun.

He was most impatient to get on with things, but he had to give the officers time to settle down, lose interest in what he was doing. It had occurred to him that one bobble, one additional bobble that is, might cause the Skipper to stand his first watch with him or, worse still, dismiss him and stand it alone. But after a bit of sober contemplation that worry went away, replaced by the comforting thought that the Old Man badly needed some rest and would stay away from the bridge until it was his regular turn.

So Baldini paced, breathing easier, wondering how much time he should allow. He had to use his head.

What he had in mind was something that he had dreamed of doing for a long time, something that he had hinted at a few times to one or the other of the officers, but which until now he had not had the clout. The one time he had mentioned his plan to the Skipper he had received a vague, "Maybe, later."

Well, now was later.

"All right, men! Listen up!"

Baldini was now speaking calmly and confidently through his megaphone, using his deadliest tone of voice. And as his small, beady black eyes swept down upon the sorry sight below him, the megaphone moved like the barrel of a very big scatter gun, lining up first on one and then another of his special targets. All of them except McCormick, Vanderveen, and the Indian were down there. And, of course, the Skipper's pet. He aimed a volley at Leafdale's sour old upturned face:

"We're goin' to holystone this goddamned deck."

He waited patiently for the message to sink in. The loudmouths in the bunch like Leafdale, Tracy, Sharkey, and Milleson were, for once, silent. He pointed his weapon at Jines:

"Hey, you, Corndog, you ready to do a little holystonin'?"

"The goddamned deck is already bleached white, Boats!" yelled Jines. "A zillion tons of saltwater have seen to that!"

Baldini moved his megaphone a hair, "Leavy, you know where the stones are! Martinez, git the handles! Roucloux, git the buckets and soap! We're gonna have the cleanest topside in the goddamn Navy!"

Sharkey, just off a four-hour sonar watch, most of which he had spent asleep with his head on his arms, wanted to know just who in hell gave a damn what this little ship was going to have. Did anybody in the entire world care whether our deck was clean or not?

Like a mule driver driving a herd of recalcitrant jackasses, Baldini began to pop his imaginary whip, enjoying to the fullest the scene below him. He rushed about the bridge, now convinced that he was in full command, keeping an eagle eye on the Department Heads, who had begun to drift back toward the stern. He was anxious for his deckhands to return from the *lazaret* with the cleaning equipment, and it disturbed him that as long as he stayed on the bridge he could not see most of the stern because of that blasted *bimini*.

For a time the crew, especially the old heads, just milled about, bitching and threatening among themselves to do this and that, all the time watching Leavy and the other deckhands spreading the soapy water and positioning the buckets in strategic locations. But once Martinez had issued the long wooden broom handles, each of which had been sharpened at one end to fit the hole in the bricks, they began to come to life. Tracy lifted his handle and looked at it and then glanced at Sharkey. The sonarman took a short step backward and readied his handle, eyeing Tracy suspiciously.

Pills, always on the alert for overt as well as covert aggression, watched the two for a moment and then turned and looked up at Baldini, who happened to be standing just above him glaring down.

"You have made a grave mistake, Mr. O. O. D. These men are ready to kill each other with their bare fists and you have given them lethal weapons."

But Baldini paid no attention to Leafdale. He had looked forward to this day too long, and nothing any of the crew had to say was about to cause him to rescind his order. Nothing was going to make him forget about having the whitest deck of all the subchasers, yippy boats, and other kinds of wooden ships that the Navy might have.

A skirmish had broken out on the bow between Roucloux and Milleson. They had not been issued their bricks; therefore, having nothing better to do, the latter had playfully poked the former and made a disparaging remark about Texas. That, of course, had provoked retaliation. Hearing the commotion, Baldini raced to the front of the bridge and began shouting, "Stop that! Do you hear me?" They may have heard him but by this time there was a lot of noise topside, including that which they were creating themselves.

Only when the boatswain's mate began to threaten to tell the Skipper on them did the two lower their weapons and back away from each other.

Then someone on the fantail, out of sight of the bridge beneath the *bimini*, gave an ear-splitting rebel war cry; and instantly that was followed by loud whacking sounds that could be heard all over the ship. Baldini, of course, had to leave the bridge to put this new insurrection down; and the instant his bald head disappeared from above the canvas skirt, Milleson and Roucloux crouched, spears ready. Milleson opened the dialogue with, "On guard, you big ugly Texan!"

"I wouldn't talk, you scarecrow from Kans-Ass!"

On the other end of the ship, Baldini was screaming "Man the holy-stones!" into his cardboard megaphone. "Git to work or so help me I'll go git the Skipper!" This deadliest of threats, repeated a few times into the very ears of the combatants, finally brought the fighting on the fantail under control.

Having learned the hard way that the men had to be bunched so that he could keep an eye on them, he then began herding everyone forward, right into the heavy fighting on the bow.

Meanwhile, down in the wardroom no one was sleeping.

Just after the three officers had finally drifted off to sleep, the noise from above began. At first, only an occasional scream of pain managed to penetrate into their sanctuary; then loud thumping sounds and some splintering could be heard. This increased until the very boards above their heads seemed to be coming apart!

Baldini was on the run during all this, of course. Almost immediately after deciding that his holystoners had to bunched, he had learned that bunching was also not the answer. The trick was keeping the ones that hated each other separated. He raced about, staying clear of the flailing stones and deadly, sharp-pointed swab handles, breaking up the trouble spots, and, always, trying to keep his message before them, that he would tell the Skipper on them.

But every time he went to the stern and dealt with the situation there, a full-scale war would break out on the bow. Some of the men were beginning to bleed profusely about the feet and legs from the stones and sharpened spearlike weapons.

Coalitions and alliances had developed, among the Department Heads, the black gang, and the left-arm rates; and it was a frightening thing to watch one of these rush, phalynxlike, a helpless victim!

In time the battle lines were drawn, beachheads secured. On the stern the Department Heads ruled supreme, and on the bow the Forecastle Lowlies (a coalition of Grease Monkeys and remnants of the Bridge and Deck Gangs), baracaded themselves behind the forty millimeter gun. And while Tracy had become a youthful Achilles on the stern, Sharkey proved himself a crafty, aging Hector on the bow.

Of course, the Forecastle Lowlies (especially that part of it known as the Deck Apes) continued to fight amongst themselves, when there was no threat from the fantail. Trouble generally began with Leavy poking someone and snarling, "Hola! Baldini!" His weight had become that of a full grown Brahma bull, and his pokes were quite often rib-crushing. And while he had no clearly-defined enemies among the Black Gang or the noncoms, he could not resist the joy of using the pole on them during the lulls.

It was obvious to some of us, Ace and Pills particularly, that Baldini had not foreseen the danger of issuing the swab handles to the crew. He would later argue that he had known and was hoping everyone in the crew would end up dead or in the hospital. But Ace argued strongly that he merely wanted to clean the deck the best way he knew how. Others would suggest that he wanted to prove to the entire crew that he was Fourth Officer and to watch the high and mighty among them come down to the level of deckhands.

The fact of the matter was that even after it should have been obvious to a half-wit that sooner or later someone was going to kill someone, he did not go to the Skipper. Indeed, he was discovered hovering on the bridge when the three officers finally burst out upon the deck and brought the civil war to an end.

Later, on a midwatch, Mr. Howorth described to McCormick and a few others what it was like down in the wardroom. The harsh rattling and scraping sounds immediately above their heads were bad enough, but every minute or so a loud crash would bring the three of them to their feet. They were reluctant to interfere because this was, after all, a kind of test of Baldini as a watch officer. He and the Skipper, particularly, wanted to see the boatswain's mate succeed. Four-on and four-off was a real drag.

Then the Exec said that Pills should be given credit for having stopped the fighting.

The three of them were sitting on the edges of their bunks, trying to decide what to do when there came a frantic knocking at the wardroom door. The Skipper had leaped up and opened it wide.

Before him stood Pills, looking as wild as a banshee and bleeding from head to foot. His clothes were hanging from his body in strips and strings.

"Skipper!"

"What'n hell's goin' on up there?"

"Two things! They're killin' each other and for the first time in a very long time they're—gettin' some therapy!"

"How're they killing each other?"

"You'd better come up and take a look. Baldini has lost control!"

"Did he ever have it?" asked the Skipper.

In a flash Mr. Hiller was out of the ardroom and literally running up the ladder to the pilothouse, followed closely by the other two officers and Pills. McCormick took one look at him and decided not to say a thing. This was, as far as I know, only the second time anybody ever got through the pilothouse when Ace was on duty without being stopped by something Ace had to say. The Captain's eyes were bloodshot, his blond hair was disheveled, and he was in his skivvies!

On the quarterdeck he began to shout, "Baldini, front and center!"

Armed with their battle-tested lances, the holystones having gone over the side, the entire crew, except Tabor and McCormick, crowded about to hear what the Skipper had to say. They looked like half-naked, bleeding shepherds leaning upon their battered crooks. Not one of them had completely escaped the blood-letting.

"Where's Baldini?" bawled Mr. Hiller, red in the face.

The boatswain's mate slowly rose from beneath the canvas skirt that circled the bridge. He appeared to be in shock because for once he had nothing at all to say.

The Skipper's mouth was open but before he could get any words out, Baldini jumped in ahead of him, sounding almost hysterical:

"That was a' accident, sir. That loud noise, I mean. A brick got away, hopped into the forward hatch. I think it must've hit ever' rung of that ladder on its way down."

Mr. Hiller began to laugh harshly, bitterly. "Why, that explains everything, Baldini!"

Like Baldini, most of the crew had straightened up, to something resembling attention. And when the Skipper was satisfied that things were more less back to normal, he mounted the bridge and slumped into the Captain's Chair.

Ex-Chief Pharmacist's Mate Leafdale watched the captain climb the ladder to the bridge; then, scratching his head, he went aft to a quiet and sudsy spot on the fantail where he set up a First Aid Station. He was shortly joined by ex-Chief Commissary Steward Kwaitkowski, who had been flushed from his galley by the explosions on deck.

"You know, Cookie," said Pills, "I think something profound happened here today. I haven't had time to work it all out, but I think that holystoning fiasco just might have saved some lives."

"And I think you're into the rubbing alcohol again."

"No, I'm serious. For the first time since the Fijis I saw something in the faces of the crew besides chagrin and hatred and boredom. They may have been pretty rough with each other today, but it occurred to me that they were actually poking those spears at Baldini. And what's more, I think they know who their enemy is now, and if old Baldini don't clean up his act they'll one day nail his ass."

Kwaitkowski shook his head, "Baldini's not their real enemy."

"Who's to say?" asked Pills. "Maybe he's saved their sanity by making them hate him."

"I hate it when you become philosophical."

12

Peleliu

The curtain to Act One of the invasion of the Palaus was going down the night we he got there, which was just as well since our biggest gun was an old single-barrel forty-millimeter thing designed to shoot at slow, low-flying aircraft. It was the evening of September 14, 1944, and in the war literature of the time we were Task Force 58, and our job was to take Peleiliu, one of the principal islands of the Palaus.

The big guns of MacArthur's Fifth Fleet had been "softening" the landing beaches for four days and nights, and about midnight we began to see flickering on the horizon dead ahead.

Our orders were to assist in the landings on this Jap stronghold, which had not even been a name on our map two weeks ago. We had rehearsed this little drama at Savo Island, using five LCC's down near the beaches, a little detail that would have to be adjusted now that the 664 was no longer with us.

It was still not yet quite daylight on the eve of D-Day when Roucloux and I took front row seats on the bow of the subchaser to watch the fireworks display. What we could already see but not hear on the northern horizon were the fire flashes from 12-and 14-inch guns on the wagons and cruisers of the Fifth Fleet.

I had been relieved at three o'clock from my radio watch by Jines, who, like everyone else on the ship, was too excited to sleep. We were observing Condition Yellow; but since we had not seen a Japanese air-craft during the entire trip up from New Guinea, the feeling on this morning was something close to celebration. In my case *giddy* might be a more accurate term.

We had become convinced that the big guns up ahead and the car-rier-based fighters had rendered our little guns useless for this engage-ment. As a consequence, my battle station would be the U. S. Army transceivers in the pilothouse with Jines. Roucloux's would the twenty, as a stand by in case we sould come under attack.

The flashes of light on the horizon had been there since a little before midnight, but it wasn't until about the time Roucloux and I took our positions on the bow that they seemed to be getting closer. The sky was perfectly clear but we had to look hard to see any stars, and I had never seen the ocean so calm and glassy smooth. It was like we were floating in space, because it was impossible to tell where the water left off and the sky began.

"This is like watching a big storm come up, back home," I said, aware of a very peculiar feeling in my guts. "The really big ones you could see brewing for two days. At first, there would be some flashing way off in the west, but no sound at all, and it would seem as if you were in a vacuum."

*   *   *

The invasion force, made up of fleet transport ships, including APA's, AKA's, LST's, LCI's, LCVT's (and an endless number of other LC's), and the big Merchant Marine supply ships, fleet tankers, and repair ships, had been put together from all over the Pacific. Beginning on paper as an "Operation," it had slowly evolved into a viable fighting force of ships, vehicles, men and supplies attached to General MacArthur's Fifth Fleet. Actually, for the past month it had "busted its butt" to get into place in time to watch the carrier planes, the fighters and light bombers, put the finishing touches to the beach assignments.

Because the show had to go on, and it was scheduled to move front stage at daybreak, September 15, 1944.

We had been assigned an imaginary spot just out from Orange Beach, some five hundred yards from the extreme southern tip of the island. The other subchasers and a minesweeper (the *664's* replacement) were fanned out in a crescent formation inside the huge harbor, spaced approximately five hundred yards apart. And our orders were to remain on these stations throughout the landings and until we were ordered to leave them.

We had no idea how tricky it was going to be to stay on station during tide changes. And although we did not know it at the time, the Navy had no reliable schedules of the tides or, indeed, a single up-to-date chart or map of the Palau Islands.

It became obvious right away that we were going to have only two responsibilities: To serve as points of reference for the waves of landing crafts, which would rendezvous with us before setting out for the beaches; and as communications links with the Task Force Commander in the coordination of the landings. It was, for us, a simple operation, and as long as the LCVP coxswains did their jobs (circled us bow-to-stern with engines revved up for a quick take-off) and the radiomen did their jobs (received and relayed the TFC's execution orders instantly) and the signalmen did their jobs (hoisting the proper pennants instantly), there should be nothing to it.

Of course, we knew that the Japanese defenders would do their best to stop the landings, that well in advance of our arrival they had undoubtedly put into place mortars and field pieces trained on precise points out from the beaches, such as reefs which at low tide would become real barriers to the landing forces. We did not know that our TFC was working without up-to-date charts of the harbor, that coordinating the landings was greatly complicated by the absence of precise information about the tides.

I watched the first wave of U. S. Marines begin peeling over the gunwales of two big APA's while they were still underway. It was the first time I had actually seen up close how the troops disembarked into the Higgens boats, using Jacob's Ladders dangling from the lifelines. Twenty men at a time were able to work their way down the ten-foot-wide grids, turning lose only when their feet touched the foot-wide gunwales of the bouncing LCVP waiting for them.

It was a scene I would never forget, down to the tiniest detail. Men carrying full field packs, dressed in girene green camouflaged uniforms and black field boots, the short noses of their M-16's waving just above their heads. The sky already a bright silver on the eastern horizon, and for background music, the moment the pounding from the big guns stopped, TBF's and F6F's ripping and tearing up and down the beaches.

There was a lot of noise and commotion in the pilothouse around me, most of made by the chatter and sputter on the sixteen transcveivers; but my attention continued to be focused upon the loading of the bouncing, ugly Higgens boats out in the harbor. I noticed that once loaded a boat would move a short distance and begin to circle about with other boats until there were eight of them; then these would move off and tread water, waiting. To McCormick, I said, "Anytime now. They're just about ready to head this way."

Ace, at the helm (although we were not going anyplace), was softly humming his Dolly song, even while people were talking to him. He was trying to keep up with a number of things, the least of which was me with the binoculars. Smith and Sharkey, who had opened their closets up were settled in front of the sonar and the radar, were discussing the Coral Sea Battle, ignoring everything around them; the Skipper, who was evidently leaning on the bridge voicetube, was discussing with his fellow officers the strategy of island-hopping up on the bridge.

Tabor was standing by at the flag box. His first pennant, an orange one, was in place on the lanyard. It would become the signal that would kick off our part of Act Two.

On the beach, which seemed much closer than it was, an occasional Japanese infantryman, naked down to the trousers and wearing no shoes, could be seen for brief moments scurrying from one foxhole to another. We were well out of range of their .25-caliber rifles, but who could to say they didn't have something a bit larger on this occasion?

The voicetube emitted a shrill whistle and McCormick leaned in to it and said, "Pilothouse, aye."

"Got your glasses handy? I want you to tell me what that sign is over on that outcropping on our port. We can't quite make it out."

Ace reached for my field glasses, but I said quickly, withholding them: "'Kilroy was here'." He relayed this to the bridge.

"Now, that is a curious thing," said Ace. "No American could have done that, and no Jap would do it. So what do you think?"

"Here they come!" I shouted, waving toward the line of LCVP's headed our way.

Through the voicetube came the Skipper's excited voice, high-pitched and urgent: "This is it!"

Each ship in the *Splinter Fleet*, and the minesweeper, became the focus of eight landing barges, which came fast and began to circle, biding time until the signal to go would be hoisted by the signalmen. The camouflaged and helmeted occupants in the boats stood shoulder to shoulder, their heads showing just above the gunwales. At first they just looked at us and we them, as round and round they went. Then somebody on one of the LCVP's shouted, "Anybody there from Texas?" Roucloux yelled, "San Antone!" And in no time Eddie Jake let it be known he was from Alice. This led to a number of other exchanges, one between me and a young Marine from Commerce, Oklahoma.

"Hey, aboard the yacht! How about Oklahoma?"

I was standing in the pilothouse door with my clipboard, because we were expecting the five-minute alert from the Task Force Commander at any minute, which I would relay to Tabor. But I could not resist a look at the Higgens boats to see who was from Oklahoma.

I began waving the clipboard and yelling, "Seminole County!"

"Why don't you give him your mailing address?" asked Tabor, who was not about to admit to a stranger that he was from Blackfoot country in Oklahoma.

The kid in the boat yelling that he was from Tulsa, appeared to be about fourteen. Each time his boat reached a point on the starboard side, he would shout something and I would reply. He swore, crossing himself, that he was eighteen, and that he had been in the Marines a year and had fought on Guadalcanal. He was, of course, loaded down with gear; and the only parts of him I could see were his face and his hands.

"You look too young to be a sailor!" he yelled. "What're you doin' on that boat?"

We both laughed at this because these were almost exactly the words I had shouted at him..

"I'll be nineteen in three days!" I called back. "Want a chocolate bar?" I held up a Tropical Hersey, still in the wrapper.

He waved excitedly and raised his hands, and I was certain he was mouthing, "Affirmative!" But, of course, the noise from the eight LCVP's and Milleson, who was right beside me screaming at somebody from Wichita, was far too great. I went out to the center of the quarterdeck for more room, wound up like a baseball pitcher, and threw the rock-hard piece of chocolate high into the air.

Up, up it went and when it came down a dozen pairs of hands were reaching for it. When it fell squarely into that kid's hands, I could hear old Pills saying that according to the Probability Theory doing what I had just done was about a million to one against. I began leaping up and down and waving my clipboard even before the bar reached its destination, and the instant the kid had it he began doing the same thing.

Milleson was yelling, "What part? I'm from the north side!"

"Where the bums all live, huh?"

"No, where the best looking girls in town live!"

"You ever run into a blonde named Maizie there on the north side?"

"Sure did! Went out with her a few times in fact!"

"Did you know she had the claps?"

"Not Maizie, not the one I knew! Musta been some other gal!"

"Her name was Maizie and she came from the north side!"

"Well, you must've got the clap from some other girl!"

At this point I heard Jines shout, and I turned to relay but Tabor had already sent the orange pennant zipping up to the yardarm.

It seemed like no time at all until we were braced for the go ahead signal, for the First Wave. In this short period of time I had, indeed, exchanged home addresses with the kid from Commerce, Oklahoma, and promised that I would look him up after the war.

Then I came to attention, because from inside the pilothouse had come the pop and crackle of a mike clearing up; and I surely knew what that meant. I looked around for the young girene from Oklahoma, waved wildly at him, and dashed inside, just in time to hear the Task Force Commander shout:

"Attack! I repeat, Attack!"

Once again Tabor did not wait for me to relay to him. The instant Jines sang out, he began hoisting his red pennant up to the yardarm with lightning speed, and simultaneously the angry loud brrrrup-brrrup of the LCVP engines being accelerated engulfed us from all sides.

Away they went, peeling away from us and and all eight of them lining up, side-by-side, loaded with eighteen-and nineteen-year-old U. S. Marines. The best we had to offer.

The beach was a good three hundred yards away, and up to this time not a single boom had I heard from a mortar or field piece. The way was clear for the Marines to go in, and we on the subchaser had the best seats in the house.

I caught Jines' eye and he nodded, relieving me to go out and join Roucloux. We fell in with Milleson and Eddie Jake on the after gundeck and watched the distance shorten between the first wave and the brilliantly white sand of Orange Beach.

"No sweat," observed Milleson. "Looks like we're goin' to take this island in no time flat."

As he spoke, eight more landing barges began to circle us. We waved at the silent Marines, who, like us, were watching the first wave go in. Then, turning back to watch the First Wave, we saw the bow of the boat on the left end of the column, the very boat that was carrying the kid from Oklahoma, rise high in the air, and, in that same instant, watched it explode into a million pieces! From just above the beach a ball of smoke had appeared, and then we heard the unmistakable sound of a cannon!

Stunned, disbelieving, we watched as the bits and pieces of the barge and a few recognizable parts of human bodies flew into the air; and before these had returned to the water, we saw another and another of the boats rising in the water and exploding!

The entire first wave to hit Orange Beach was stranded on a reef!

It was a turkey shoot. The Japs had indeed prepared a reception for our landings, and no doubt they had counted on our misjudgment and our consequent failure to synchronize with the tide. We could not have timed it worse. The tide had gone out and the reef, now was just below the surface of the water, was a jagged line of white caps!

In a state of shock, I continued to watch the explosions, feeling my insides turn to mush. I had a sudden urge to leap into one of the barges circling the subchaser and go in with them in the next wave. I heard Milleson mumbling incoherently and Roucloux touching me, trying to get my attention.

Then I was in the pilothouse and Jines was talking to me.

McCormick was staring at me and wanted to know what had happened. "You're white as a sheet," he said.

While he continued on about how I looked, I sat down beside the transceivers and strapped on a pair of headphones. I was unaware that I was tearing badly, because all I could feel was shock and disbelief. Jines took one look at me and told Ace to let me be. That is what I saw him say; but the roar in my head was blotting out all other sounds.

Of course, I could not watch the landings that followed. The second wave made it in, established a beachhead, and eliminated the field mortars; and from there the landings on Orange Beach proceeded according to schedule.

Roucloux came into the pilothouse and said, "When are you goin' to learn you don't make friends out in this god-forsaken War Zone?"

From the chatter on the transceivers, the taking of Peleliu had slowed almost to a halt. For a time the Marines had made steady progress into the island, but by the end of the first day it had begun to lose its momentum considerably with each passing hour.

Like so many of the islands in the Pacific, especially the ones the Japanese had converted into fortresses, Peleliu was honeycombed with caves. Scuttlebutt began to circulate that the enemy had gone underground in great numbers, and that the Marines had brought in a new weapon, designed for just this kind of operation: the flame-thrower.

*   *   *

It made no sense to any of us why we were still down close to the beach. All of the landing forces had gone in, and for the better part of a week vehicles of all kinds, including tanks and half-tracks, had moved past us. Scuttlebutt, of course, abounded. Peleliu had turned out to be a sonofabitch for the Marines, primarily because of the caves. After every square inch of top soil had been wiped clean of Jap soldiers, thousands of caves, most of them still inhabited, remained to be dealt with. For this purpose the Marines were moving from cave to cave with flame-throwers.

There had been absolutely no news of the invasion, good or bad, either on Armed Forces Radio or the International Press. Tokyo Rose had not mentioned the Palaus. Her attention was directed at MacArthur and the Philippines.

But one thing was clear: The island was still not secured.

One morning from the TFC came a radio message, action-addressed to all units, asking for trained radio operators for a beach assignment with the Marines. Specifically, it was calling for volunteers to assist in the cave explorations as "Com Units."

"Skipper, I would like to volunteer for that," I said, showing him the message. "I want to find out what it's like over there."

Jines, down in the radio shack, almost broke his neck getting up the ladder, and even before the Skipper had said a word, he opened up on me:

"What do you know about this? Do you know what a 'Com Unit' is? You go over there and some Jap will shoot you full of holes."

"We're not doing a thing here," I said, glancing at the Skipper, "and I want to find out what it's like on the island. Skipper, I want to go."

"And I don't want to be stuck here with all these radios," blurted Jines.

I pointed out to him that the landings had ended and along with them a need for U. S. Army transceivers.

The Skipper grinned at me and said to Jines, "Yeah, you sure are busy these days, Sparks. Is that the only protest you've got?"

Jines suggested that we might get our orders to join a convoy; and if that should happen while I'm gone, I would be left behind.

"Skipper, I want to go," I repeated.

"All right. See if you can find out what you'll need and how long you'll be over there."

Within the hour an LCVP showed up at our starboard gunwale and I hopped aboard. Roucloux, Sharkey, and Smith were there to see me off. They had about the same attitude Jines had; but when I waved goodbye, Sharkey called out, "Bring me back some good old girene chow. My favorite flavor of K-ration is vanilla."

At the beach a Marine lieutenant gave me a heavy backpack that turned out to be a walkie-talkie and told me to follow him. We were going to the unit's temporary operations tent, he said, where I would join two Marines on their way to a cave. My job would be very simple: I was to report by radio whatever they told me to report.

"Don't get in their way. And, Navy, keep your head down."

At the operations tent a Marine corporal went over the walkie-talkie with me, gave me the two frequencies the unit was using, and assured me I would have no difficulty.

Two big hard-looking boys named West and Eagleberger showed up, and held their hands out to me. When they turned and headed toward the nearest thicket of scrub trees, the only ones left in the area, I followed, staying back about thirty feet. Each of them was carrying a semi-automatic rifle with the bayonet attached.

The first caves we came to had already been cleared. This was evident from the tiny yellow ribbon markers displayed near the openings and by X's on a chart that the two men were carrying. The first two unmarked caves, after a thorough and lengthy check, turned out to be empty. At this point, West and Eagleberger decided to call it a day. We had covered about three miles of rough terrain that still showed signs of heavy fighting, and by the time we made it back it would be chow time.

Back at the camp, over cold beans and Spam, I learned that this unit was a platoon that had seen a lot of action the first two days. As some kind of reward (They joked about it being the Marine equivalent of Navy R & R) they had been given the task of checking out caves. They had no flame-throwers but when they found a cave that required more than rifles and hand grenades, one was brought in from another unit.

The next day turned out to be a great deal more of the same, except that we were closer in to the fighting and therefore considerably more of an adrenaline flow for me. Stray bullets zinged overhead occasionally, prompting me to stick closer to West and Eagleberger and keep a lower profile. And when the day was done, I was glad to get back to camp.

By evening chow on this second day I was beginning to feel a part of the team. There was still very little talking around or over the cold cuts, but in the actions of the men I felt a closeness that I had not felt before.

And stretched out under the stars listening to the sporadic rifle fire in the distance, I told myself I had done a good thing by volunteering for this assignment.

The next day turned out to be a whole new ballgame.

We were deep inside a cave that I had already decided was empty, and was turning to get out of there when I heard from beyond West and Eagleberger what sounded like someone trying to cough. It did not sound like a man. Curious, I moved up behind the girenes, who were blocking something from my view. Eagleberger was crouched, with his bayonet ready. Then I caught a glimpse of the terrified face of a young girl, her mouth full of blood, and on top of her a white, humped body! West's rifle appeared to be balanced, wavering in the center of the back; but, of course, it was the bayonet—

"That's the way to go," said Eagleberger, straightening up.

"How better?"

I made it to the cave entrance before I exploded; and when I thought my insides were coming out, one of the girenes appeared beside me with a canteen and told me to wash my mouth out. I took it, staring at him. He appeared to be quiet pleased with himself.

"Report this cave secured. Two unfriendlies, one a female national. Both deceased. Here's the soldier's identification."

We were perhaps five miles from the Marine camp, but I made it by myself. I had not reported the cave and the dead bodies.

"What's the matter?" asked the lieutenant. "Why are you here?"

I had rehearsed what I was going to say, and in a gush it all came out.

"All right, Red, control yourself. You're going back to your ship right away. What you saw out there today was two dead Japs. Tell anything else to your captain, and you will be sorry. I promise you that."

*   *   *

The fighting on Peleliu continued, mostly in the caves; but day followed day and no orders came for us. Without permission the Skipper had ordered Baldini to drop the anchor, since there had not been a sign of enemy aircraft. The minesweeper pulled out one morning, along with most of the big ships in the harbor, triggering something close to panic aboard the *995*. We were in serious need of food supplies and fresh water; but even while the harbor was full of supply ships, the Skipper's requests had gone unanswered.

Early one morning, to get out of the sun and away from the bitching on the fantail, Sharkey and Smith went up to the bridge.

"You know what the problem is, don't you?" asked Sharkey.

"Well, I would say that it has to do with chow."

There was a scramble for the Captain's Chair, and Sharkey won out, as usual. He got settled and put his feet over the front railing. "This is a' Army show. We've been transferred from the Navy to the Army, and you-know-who don't give a damn if we starve to death."

"Most likely you're right," nodded Smith. "Show me a dogface and I'll show you a dog beneath it." Nothing followed this for a time. Finally, Smith added, "The General has forgotten us, no doubt it."

"Naw," scoffed Sharkey. "He didn't forget us. You have to be aware that something exists before you can forget it."

"You're right, of course."

"The point is we're caught between MacArthur and Halsey."

"How so, if neither one of them knows we exist?"

"We were assigned to Halsey's South Pacific Fleet, right?"

"I guess we were but who the hell knows for sure?"

"Then Doug decided to island-hop across the goddamned Pacific, and so we were suddenly attached to his invasion forces."

"So what's your point, if I dare ask?"

"Does the Army lose any sleep over the Navy?"

"And *vice versa* , huh?"

"Well, that's why we're not gittin' anything to eat. We're attached to the Army, which doesn't care whether we starve to death or not. And the Navy doesn't know we exist any longer. We git the bottom of the barrel ever'where we go."

"I think we ought to up anchor and go find some food," said Smith, without conviction. "If what you say is true, then no body'd miss us. We could paint this dude the color of the Pacific Ocean, which is an ugly dull green and declare ourselves a frigate of some neutral nation and—" Suddenly, from the voicetube next to Sharkey came an ear-piercing whistle.

"God, how I hate it when Ace gets hold of that thing," complained Sharkey. "Hell, all he'd have to do is speak to us in his normal voice and forget about the tube."

"He gits a kick out of breakin' eardrums," nodded Smith.

Sharkey lifted the tubular brass whistle from the voicetube and put his face into the cradle and blew with all he had. "I hope the S. O. B. had his ear cocked for that."

From below came Ace's laugh, "You may huff and you may puff, Shark Butt, but right now there's priority traffic from the Task Force Commander! Is the Skipper up there?"

"Well, by God," said Sharkey. "In answer to your question, are you completely blind? Look out through your front windows."

The Skipper, having been alerted by the whistle, received the message from Jines in the pilothouse. It was indeed from the TFC, and it was addressed to all four of the subchasers. He lifted the half-sheet and looked at it.

"Is it our travel orders?" asked Mr. Howorth.

Mr. Hiller handed it to him and turned to McCormick: "Pass the word to the engineroom that we're getting underway." To Mr. Howorth he said through clinched teeth, "This has got to be the shit detail to end all shit details."

Mr. Howorth looked up from the message. "My God, Skippah, we'ah to pick up these dead bodies that've been in the heat for a week?"

"More like ten days," Mr. Hiller said with a nod. "Pick them up and bury them at sea."

"How are we goin' to do that, I'd like to know?"

"I guess we'll figure that out when we find the first one."

Toward McCormick's retreating back, the Skipper said. "Inform Mr. Darling he's wanted on the bridge."

We had heard a story about the final pitched battles on Peleliu, the last one above ground, that is. The Japanese ground troops, knowing very well that the First Marines did not take prisoners, had fought to the last man, many of them backing out into the shallow waters of the Pacific before they went down. Their bodies were eventually picked up with the outgoing tides and carried out to sea. There was no official estimate of the number of bodies that had to be found and given burials.

Now that the bodies had had time to bloat and rise to the surface, it had become our responsibility and the responsibility of the other subchasers, to find them and, somehow, bury them at sea.

We up-anchored and got underway, still with no charts or maps of the area. The message had said, simply, that we were to patrol the area around Peleliu for Japanese military personnel. The words "proper burial at sea" were repeated.

Tabor, without benefit of field glasses, found our first body almost immediately. Or, rather, it made itself known to him remarkably soon after we left our anchorage. Mr. Darling and the Indian were on the bridge, and the *995* was clipping along at twelve knots toward the southeastern end of the island. The Indian suddenly straightened up and glanced at the tell-tale on the yardarm.

"What are you doing?" asked Mr. Darling, frowning. "Don't you know it's unsanitary to put your finger into your mouth?"

Tabor was eyeing the horizon two points off the port bow and did not respond.

Mr. Darling then said, with a slight lifting of his nose, "I think I just got a whiff of something dead. It's coming from straight ahead, I'm pretty certain." He pointed toward the bow, to reinforce what he had said. "Either point your glasses in that direction or hand them to me!"

He waited, sniffing, but Tabor was looking at a spot slightly left of dead ahead.

From the pilothouse voicetube came a whistle.

"Bridge," said Mr. Darling, bending and being careful not to touch the voicetube with his mouth. The neutral look of a moment before had disappeared from his face, and now his pale blue eyes were mere disapproving slits.

"Anything yet?" called Ace.

"Sir!" screamed Mr. Darling into the tube. "Address me as 'Sir'!"

"I was askin' for the Skipper. He wants to know, Sir."

"There's somethin' dead just off the port bow," said the Indian, leaning to the tube. "Come left ten."

Mr. Darling's high, anxious voice replaced Tabor's in the voicetube: "Captain, it's coming from dead ahead. Stay on the present heading."

"Skipper!" Tabor barked, not botherin' to bend to the tube this time. "Do we go to that Jap or circle it?" McCormick had no trouble hearing him, and immediately he passed the word through another voicetube to the wardroom. He also corrected the heading.

By now the smell was filling the pilothouse and beginning to penetrate into the radio shack. It was a sweet, sickening odor that put the smell of a dead horse to shame. No one, with the possible exception of Tabor, had ever encountered such an abomination before.

"Since neither you nor I have seen whatever it is that's stinking like that, how do you know it's a Jap?" demanded Mr. Darling. "Give me those glasses."

Ignoring Mr. Darling, Tabor leaned into the voicetube and said quietly, "Two more degrees left. We're almost on it."

"We'll do no such thing!" cried Mr. Darling, exasperated. "McCormick, did you take it upon yourself to alter the heading?" To Tabor, he spat, "Give me the glasses!"

At this point the Skipper arrived on the bridge. "Have you located him yet?"

"I can't see him yet," said Tabor, "but he's dead ahead."

"Cap'n, he's guessing," said Mr. Darling. "We need to come back to our original heading."

"Let's give it a couple of minutes," said the Skipper.

Some five minutes later the body finally showed up on the horizon, a great mound of stench so deadly most of the crew quickly disappeared below decks. Those still topside, as they watched the body approach, tied handkerchiefs about their faces and tried to breathe as little as possible. Finally, there were only McCormick, Tabor, the Skipper, and me left topside. Mr. Darling had reasoned that since the Skipper was on the bridge he would take five in the wardroom.

Some fifty yards from the corpse, the order was given to stop engines. It was face down in the water and still clad in pale green fatigues that looked as if they were balloons. The smell had completely filled every nook and cranny of the ship, and most of the crew had reappeared and were hanging over the lifelines.

"Well," Mr. Hiller said to the Indian, "somebody's got to lower that thing. We've got orders to bury it at sea."

Tabor nodded. "Maybe a forty millimeter ammo canister." He went to the starboard side of the bridge and called down to Roucloux, who was trying to puke over the side, "Git me an empty ammo can and a rope!"

July's long tragic face came up slowly. "Empty?"

Mr. Darling suddenly appeared beside Roucloux, gasping and trying to vomit. Tabor's grave misuse of the term *rope*, which, has no meaning in the Navy, brought his head up slightly, but he decided to let it go uncorrected.

The Skipper nodded approvingly to Tabor. "Good idea. You think you can handle it alone?"

The signalman nodded, showing no signs at all of the agony everyone else was going through. He crossed the bridge to the ladder, kicking off his sandals as he went, and descended to the quarterdeck. He was wearing nothing but a pair of faded dungaree cut-offs and one turquoise earring. From his waist dangled a long-bladed knife in a sheath, something that he had not picked up at Ship's Stores. Over his shoulder he said to me, "Here comes a big ship sailor."

I glanced up at the bridge in time to see the Skipper, as sick as he was, smiling. For Baldini had made it out of the forecastle and was now wavering beside the open hatch. On both sides of him, lined up at the lifelines, were Leavy and Martinez, feeding the fish.

The Skipper called weakly to him, "Post a lookout on the bridge with a carbine, Boats, just in case there are sharks about."

At close range Baldini's looked like that of a dead orangutan, but he managed to push himself away from the hatch cover and head for the wardroom, where the carbines and pistols were kept.

At about this point I joined the Skipper on the bridge and was on hand to see Tabor lower an ammo case over the side.

Mr. Hiller nodded to me, looking a little surprised. "Glad to see you're handling this smell okay."

"I thought dead cow was bad," I said with a grin. "But this has got anything I ever smelled beat a country mile."

We watched as Tabor pushed away from the ship, his sheath knife clamped between his teeth.

With a tie-dyed skivvy shirt wrapped around his face, Mr. Howorth managed to make it up the ladder and stagger over to the Captain's Chair. With a little hacking cough between each word, he said, "Ah've come to the conclusion thaet people from Oklahoma aint quite like the rest of us, Skippah. They smell as well as we do but they never learned to distinguish between what's a good smell an' what's a bad one!" Looking at me sadly, he said, "I sweah, have you even puked once?"

"Not yet, Sir."

"I mean in your entire life."

We followed Tabor's progress as he swam out to the body. He had removed his shorts and was wearing nothing but the half-inch line, one end of which was tied about his waist and the other to the ammo can.

"What's the knife for?" asked the Captain? "You suppose he has doubts about whether that thing is dead or not?"

Mr. Howorth tried to laugh and talk at the same time, finally got out that Tabor probably didn't trust Milleson with the carbine. "Everybody remembers Milleson's record with a rifle, suh." When the Skipper's head came sharply around, he added, "I guess I didn't tell you about the Gooney Bird Shoot-out on the fantail one day. Milleson had a hard time hittin' the wake."

"Begging your pardon, sir, but Tabor has something else in mind," I said. "He plans to get that fellow's teeth."

The two officers turned and stared at me but didn't say anything.

           *   *   *

The burial procedure Tabor had worked out with that first corpse soon became a kind of gothic ritual—his towing an empty forty millimeter ammunition can out to the corpse, tying a line that was attached to the can about the neck of the corpse, filling the can with sea water, and letting go. In the days to come, instead of the operation getting easier or even more tolerable, it grew considerably worse, since rotting flesh does not improve with time in hot, tropical weather.

For that reason, it was sometime before word got around to the crew in general just what the Tabor was doing. Most of them knew he always swam out with a Bowie knife between his teeth and some kind of sack tied to his waist, but only the Skipper, Mr. Howorth, and I knew that he was collecting souvenirs, that indeed he was taking a pillow case out to the bodies and bringing back whatever he found.

"All right," Sharkey said to me one day between corpses, "but what about the goddamned knife? What does he need it for?"

"One thing for sure is he doesn't cut much of anything with it," I evaded. "He *pries*, I would imagine."

"What does he pry, for chrissake?"

"How about false teeth? Gold false teeth."

But even after I admitted this to Sharkey, no one wanted to believe that Tabor was actually opening the corpses' mouths and removing teeth, while the flesh was falling from the body.

Then one day Tabor exhibited his newly-created solid gold necklace during morning chow. It was the only meal anyone ever ate anymore, and so it was of great importance to those at the table that no word be spoken concerning the burying of the corpses or indeed anything at all about our present circumstances. His presence at the mess table had not been expected, because as far back as anybody could remember he had never bothered to eat there before. And although he did not say a word about the hideous symbol of abomination around his neck, he didn't need to. Everyone quietly rose from the table and went topside to the lifelines.

We continued the search for another week, until what we were finding had very little flesh left to bury; and then, just after our travel orders came, we found one in very good condition.

Actually, we didn't find this one at all. It had no smell about it, and if Tabor had not been on the bridge we would no doubt have run right over and kept going. But like several of the others it was floating in a great island of debris and looked very bloated; but, and this was curious, it was on its back, and the face and arms were covered with what looked like rain-proof gear.

Martinez volunteered to swim out to this one, insisted on it; and since Tabor had all of the souvenirs he wanted (and more than he would be able to take home), he gave the nod. Milleson, as luck would have it, was the one assigned to the carbine on the bridge, in case there were sharks about.

I was on the bridge, taking a break from the radio shack, and watched Gilberto strip down, tie a line around his waist and to a forty mm. canister, and clamp Tabor's sheath knife between his teeth.

Later, we would all admit that we had simply let our guard down, that we should have known what we were looking at was not a corpse that had been killed on Peleliu two weeks before. That what looked like bloating carcass was bulge of arms crossed on the chest and the live grenade. We had been very careful in the beginning, but with the arrival of our orders telling us to get out of this terrible, stinking area and head for R & R, we had become careless.

That a man, even a Japanese, would float on his back for a week in shark-infested waters just for a chance to take out one more American did not make sense to us at the time. But then that happened in September. Our education into the *Cult of the Divine Wind* would not actually begin until the following month, when Japan revealed her truly scary secret weapon, the guided missile known as the *kamikaze*.

Gilberto Martinez survived the experience with the incredible story that Mary, the Mother of Jesus, had suddenly appeared telling him that it was a booby-trap. He would give neither Milleson nor any of us who had shouted warnings any credit at all. And then he showed Pills his middle finger and said, "Your number theory stinks, Peels."

13

Man Overboard

The rain hadn't let up for two days, and even beneath the awning on the fantail it was impossible to relax and smoke a cigarette without getting soaked. Which (the soaking) wouldn't have been so bad if the rain hadn't been so cold, but to Sharkey it felt like the first biting rain of winter back in Chicago. And it never let up.

It had been a miserable day, as usual, beginning at three-thirty when Leavy had awakened him by feeling of his face. The excuse had been that it was so dark in the compartment he couldn't tell whether Sharkey was in his bunk or not. Where in hell did that big lunkhead think he'd be at three-thirty in the goddamned morning? He'd unstrapped himself and stepped out onto somebody's wet clothes, which kicked to the other end of the compartment only to find out they were his.

Finally dressed and completely miserable, he'd gone topside and used the bathroom overboard, preferring that to the smelly telephone booth of a head in the forward quarters. McCormick came loping along the lifelines humming his Dolly song and said something about poisoning the fish. And from four until breakfast he'd sat in the swivel chair in the radio shack with his head on his arms and tried to ignore the humming and whistling of the quartermaster above him in the pilothouse.

Every five minutes Ace would call out something to him or ask his opinion about something.

Chow wasn't chow at all but a lousy bowl of cling peaches and as many graham crackers as he could eat. Cookie was even rationing the coffee. If he ever made it back to the States, there were two things he would never touch again, peaches and crackers. If he ever got married and his wife put any of that stuff before him, he would knock her flat of her back and then divorce her.

The crew hadn't had anything else to eat for so long their teeth were falling out. Even little Johnny Carpenter, that once upon a time could've posed for a toothpaste ad, was spitting up blood and teeth, because, according to Pills, he wasn't eating anything to massage his gums.

Following chow he'd hung around the after quarters for awhile shooting the bull with Tracy. But when he (Sharkey) suggested they get the dice out and shoot some craps on their beer futures and the asshole had refused, he'd climbed the ladder and lighted a cigarette. And there he had stood ever since, not up to facing the smell in the forward crew's quarters, and getting wet from his knees down from the slanting rain.

And, of course, the worst part of the weather was that everybody had been forced below, where they lay strapped in their bunks and argued and griped at each other day in and day out. There was absolutely nothing to do, since the disappearance of the last deck of cards on the ship. Tracy's dice might've been a diversion, but almost everybody aboard the ship had already lost the next six months of their pay. The only books on the ship were translated Greek and Roman classics, not even fit for toilet paper.

He figured the four subchasers had just about reached the halfway point between the Palaus and Hollandia, or Hell and Purgatory, whichever you preferred. Neither place had any recreational facilities. But he had to admit that Hollandia had more to offer than that hell hole, Peleliu. But give the Seabees another month or so and there would be a country club for the officers, a recreation hut for the enlisted, an outdoor movie theater for everybody, a Ship's Store, two airstrips, and avenue of quonset huts.

It really didn't matter very much where exactly they R-and-R'd, because all of these God forsaken islands had about the same to offer. It would be real nice to walk on dry land once again. The way the subchaser rolled and dived all the time it took you two full days to walk straight once you got off. You'd be walking along, subconsciously reaching for a lifeline, and catch yourself leaning to starboard or port on perfectly flat ground! And your little bubble upstairs was always goofed up and causing you to feel light-headed. Then about the time you could walk straight again on land the ship would take off for Timbuktu and you'd spend two days crawling from bow to stern until you got your sea legs again.

Baldini did not mind the cold rain at all, evidently. Every five or ten minutes here he'd come barreling it down the side of the ship, mumbling to himself and trying to figure out some crappy thing the men could be doing besides sleeping or just lying on their backsides. For a time after the farce he had perpetrated as the Fourth Officer, he had kept to himself, delegating all his shit details to Leavy and Beck and Martinez. But even before Peleliu he was back into his old habits and getting worse with every passing day.

His last kick had been the drills. Every morning and afternoon here he'd come yelling out which drill it was going to be. If it happened to be raining, it'd probably be something like the Boat Drill or the Abandon Ship Drill. On perfectly pretty mornings when everybody would want to be outside, it'd probably be the Gun Drill, a little two-hour exercise of taking the Navy Colt .45, the carbine, and the 50-caliber machine-gun apart and putting them back together blindfolded. Altogether, there were about a dozen stupid drills, which on a big ship might have made some sense but a subchaser made none at all. With the Skipper's permission, old Baldini would spring these upon the men at any given moment, day or night, generally right when most of the crew was trying to get some sleep.

*   *   *

Tracy stuck his head through the after hatchway, blinking right in Sharkey's face.

"Got a cigarette to spare?" he asked, yawning. "What's with this fuckin' weather? I didn't know it ever got this chilly this close to the Equator."

Sharkey handed him a cigarette, and Tracy lighted it off his butt. "Maybe we're off course and up around the Aleutians," he said. "The weather we can't do anything about, but I know something we can do something about."

Tracy stared at him through his cigarette smoke.

Baldini's rasping voice swept back to them from the bow, "All right, pass the word! On the double! Git the lead out!"

"It's another drill of some kind," moaned the gunner's mate. "That lousy sonofabitch."

"Remember all that shinola you peddled about the crew gettin' rid of that gorilla?" asked Sharkey.

"Baldini?"

"Yeah, Baldini. Who the hell else? You was just blowin' wind up our assholes with all that shit about drawing straws. I say it's time somebody did something besides talk."

Tracy didn't say anything for awhile, but finally he nodded and said he had been intending to talk to Ace McCormick.

"Hell, McCormick has no gripes against Baldini. He's got some kind of diplomatic immunity from that gorilla."

"Maybe so but he's got to be in on it, along with everybody else. One no vote and it's no good. And it's got to be planned out well ahead of time. And who do you know that can do that better than Ace?"

McCormick had never been known to lose his composure, what Sharkey called his 'don't-give-a-shit' attitude; but then of all the enlisted men on the *Subchaser-995* he probably had the least reason to. He was unaffected by the ravings and rantings of Baldini, he believed sincerely in Pills' Number Theory, and he was doing essentially what he liked to do most in the world. Which was take care of the pilothouse, his little sanctuary, and keep track of everything that was going on.

He was like an old gossipy man, Sharkey felt, poking his nose into everybody's business. But you had to admit he was a damned good quartermaster.

Unlike everyone else on the ship, Ace had no home address, no attachments on land at all; so the love and possessiveness that most people bestow upon some landlocked residence he bestowed upon the pilothouse of his present residence. And although he had a cozy bunk in the after compartment next to the coffee pot, he preferred to sleep in his little chartroom with his head on his hands.

To him coming down to a one-hundred-and-ten-foot boat from a mighty destroyer had not, in the long run, been such a tragedy. His beloved *Bryan* had been shot from under him in the Solomons, and the transition to the small wooden ship had been made easier by the knowledge that his tincan's number had come up and that there was nothing he or anybody else could do about it.

He had actually come to feel a kind of proprietorship over the entire subchaser and its crew without fully realizing it, and so what went on on deck with Baldini did concern him very much. Kids like Carpenter and Olson needed looking after, he felt.

And that is why, as things had gotten worse and worse with the crew, he had come to dislike Baldini and worry. How much more could they take before they all went Asiatic?

While standing his long helm watches, with one bare foot hooked through the spokes of the ship's wheel and singing or humming his Dolly song, he did a lot of thinking about the welfare of the ship, how vulnerable it was in such a great big ocean during wartime, how small and ill-equipped it was to house twenty-one men and three officers for an extended period of time. There was little he could do about the war, other than to stand his watches fully awake and keep the ship on the right heading. But as he watched the little crew, some of whom he liked very much, he began to identify with their most pressing problem, which he had come to believe was not the Japs at all but the evil megalomaniac Baldini.

From his central and slightly elevated position in the pilothouse, Ace kept track of Baldini's every move, heard his soliloquies as he paced to and fro on the deck, and came to realize that he was a true creature of habit. Indeed, he had come to know Baldini so well he could predict with great accuracy exactly what he was going to do (and therefore say) each hour of the day. It was a little scary at times just how well he could anticipate the old boatswain's mate next move and mouth his every word.

Ace knew that Baldini's little ritual at the 'midship's gun deck after evening chow lasted through three cigarettes, rain or shine, and that the boatswain's mate would invariably lean against the lifeline and stare at the water. It did not matter what the weather was like or how badly the ship was heeling or bucking, Baldini would spend as much as an hour smoking cigarettes there, all the time muttering to himself.

In foul weather he would wear a poncho and keep his cigarette from getting wet by holding one side of it out like a lean-to shelter. Ace, standing just inside the door of the pilothouse, would sometimes catch a glimpse of the bright red glow when Baldini took a draw from his cigarette. And because it was a major violation of the blackout rules (during any kind of weather) to smoke on deck, the boatswain's mate would cup his cigarette away from the pilothouse, bracing himself against the lifeline as he did so.

*   *   *

Late one black, stormy night some three days south of Peleliu the crew of the *995*, wearing hooded rain gear, crowded into the pilothouse, ostensibly to discuss "morale problems" in the crew. Actually, most of the old hands on ship knew what the morale problem was and was not surprised when the get-together turned out to be a drawing of straws to see who would do what.

The man at the helm began to talk in a normal voice, which immediately put an end to all noise in the compartment. He defined the problem, referring to Baldini as "the subject," and pointed out that the crew could no longer trust to luck or accident or a "Navy solution." A decision, he said, had to be made this night. Then he asked someone standing beside him, whose face could not be seen, to describe the "subject's" nightly cigarette break at the starboard 'midships. This second speaker was brief and to the point, and when he had concluded, the man on the helm said, "Frankly, I'm surprised the sonofabitch hasn't already slipped on that wet deck and gone into the drink on his own."

A new speaker said, "I'm more surprised that one of the crew hasn't drifted by there one stormy evening and given the subject a shove."

The helmsman then explained the procedure that would be used, saying that it had been worked out sometime ago.

Someone said, "I don't think we better do this unless everybody is in on it."

There was general agreement to this. Another someone suggested, "As long as we keep this anonymous, I'll go along with it. We've got make sure whoever does it is anonymous. No one should be able to point the finger later on."

"Okay, it's settled. Now, listen good while I explain how we'll decide who does what has to be done. This weather will probably hold all the way to Hollandia, but I think it ought to happen tomorrow after evening chow. If everybody agrees, then there should be no one topside except the subject. He eats with the Starboard Section then goes straight to his favorite spot for a long smoke break. No matter what the weather is, he'll be there for a good thirty minutes to an hour. The snap on the lifeline has got to be fixed by someone in the Port Section during chow. Two anonymous volunteers have already agreed to see to that. If it's raining or there's a lot of wind, the subject will light his cigarette beneath his poncho. The odds are that's the way it'll be. If so, that's when somebody's got to happen by and accidentally bump him overboard. We will draw to see who gets to do this. Are there any questions?"

"How about he doesn't put his head under his poncho?" asked a raspy voice, obviously a disguise.

"He'll turn facing the drink in that case, with his hands cupped over his cigarette. That would make it even easier."

"Maybe whoever gets the short straw will need a back-up," came a muffled voice from the shadows near the engine controls.

"Hell, no!" blasted the helmsman. "One person does it. And it's not going to be a straw and nobody is going to know who it is. The one that gets the number thirteen out this helmet does it. The rest of us won't even know who it is. That way nobody can—"

"If the lucky man fucks up, we'll never git another chance," came a nervous voice from the chartroom. "I suggest that we put two *thirteens* in that cap."

"Nope, just one," insisted the man at the helm. "And I want to emphasize how important it is that the one that gets the lucky number keeps it to himself. Swallow it at once. Nobody is to know who gets what. Is that agreed?"

There were no *nays* to this.

"And for that reason nobody else goes near starboard 'midships for about an hour after evening chow tomorrow."

It had become hot in the room, and steam was beginning to rise from beneath the ponchos. Someone called for adjournment, and someone else called for the drawing,

The helmsman lifted something for all to see (It was too dark to be certain what it was): "We'll draw from this as we leave."

"How we gonna see in the dark?" complained someone.

"That's your problem."

          *   *   *

The following day the clouds dropped even lower and turned the rain loose in great sheets, and the *995* pitched and bucked like a Texas maverick. Visibility had dropped to nothing by mid-morning, making it impossible for us to make out the *419* ahead of us; and since the radar was on the blink and had been since before Peleliu, Sharkey and Smith were taking turns the sonar, four-on and four-off.

The alternative, which was raised by Sharkey and hastily squelched by the Skipper, was to post Tabor on the bow with a handie-talkie. So the day passed, with most those not actually on some kind of watch strapped in their bunks. I spent the day in the radio shack copying high-speed press releases and listening to Armed Forces Radio for stories I might be able to use in the newsletter. About noon Cookie passed the word that anybody interested in and/or capable of a bologna-and-liver-wurst sandwich was welcome to visit the galley and get it. Evening chow would take place at the usual time.

On the midwatch that night Eddie Jake delivered a tray of chow to the pilothouse, where I was manning the radios and listening to Sharkey talk about *northside* Chicago. The tray was loaded with big ugly Dagwoods made out of stale bread and the usual cold cuts, and the coffee tasted like roasted cottonseeds. Ace and Milleson, who had strayed up from the engineroom, were fantasizing about jumping ship in Hollandia. When Tex slammed through the door with his gifts, Milleson called out:

"We could take this big galoot along to use as a bribe with the head-hunters back in the hills."

Eddie Jake was not known for his *repartee* or his sense of humor, ignored the remark completely. "Anybody seen Baldini?"

"Who the hell wants to see him?" demanded Sharkey.

"Well, generally, he's runnin' up and down the deck gettin' in ever'-body's hair. Maybe he turned in early tonight."

"Did you check his bunk?" teased Roucloux, on engine controls. "I thought I smelled him just before I left the quarters to go on watch."

Baldini did not put in an appearance at morning chow, which provoked Leafdale to say to the Kwaitkowski, "It couldn't be because he's seasick. He's the only man I ever knew that insisted on eating when he was so sick he couldn't hold it down."

"He usually puts in a couple of appearances down here before chow," said Cookie. "I wonder what he's doin'."

"Probably brown-nosing the officers."

When Leavy, Roucloux, and I crowded into the after quarters at the head of the Port Section chowline, Kwaitkowski asked us point blank where Baldini was hiding out. "It's not like him to miss a chow call."

"I'm not his keeper," grumbled Leavy.

"Come to think of it," added July, "he was out and gone before I got up, an' I didn't see or hear him topside. Must be down with the officers."

"Or maybe he's visitin' Davy Jones," grinned Leavy, brightening up. "Wouldn't that be a kick?"

The day turned out to be a duplicate of the past three, except for the quite noticeable absence of the boatswain's mate. Cookie, who had as a high school student seriously considered acting as a career choice, kept bringing Baldini's name up as the day progressed, doing an excellent job of appearing to be concerned. At morning chow he strutted and fretted, worrying coquettishly because one of his biggest chowhounds had boycotted breakfast; by noon chow, he was an angry King Lear ready to disown a thankless offspring.

The truth was, of course, that Kwaitkowski, like McCormick, had not been greatly affected one way or the other by Baldini; but while Ace wanted him put out of his misery for the sake of the crew and the safety of the ship, Cookie wanted him put out of his misery because he was a most unhappy man crying out for help.

After evening chow of this first full day without Baldini, Kwaitkowski headed for the bridge with a covered tray of food for Tabor, balancing his way along the narrow passageway on the starboard side. He was wearing only a pale green skivvy shirt and a pair of CPO khaki shorts, despite the chill in the rain, which was slanting in at a thirty-degree angle from the southwest. The ship was, as usual, rocking and rolling and bobbing like a cork, but he kept a loose grip on the lifeline with his right hand and did a masterful job of keeping the tray horizontal with his left. At the 'midships his hand suddenly found no lifeline, and had the ship been in a starboard heel, he would surely have gone headfirst into the drink.

"My Gawd!" he burst out. "I must be losing my mind!"

But, as luck would have it, the ship was heeling to port and so Kwaitkowski found himself sailing past the engineroom hatch toward the other lifeline! Being very agile (Some of the crew used the word *prissy*), he and the tray survived and shortly thereafter, in the pitch darkness, mounted the narrow metal ladder to the bridge and worked his way around to where he knew the Captain's Chair had to be.

"Chow down," he said in his soft, cajoling voice. "Hope you like it, Chalmer."

"Don't call me that." The voice came from the other side of the bridge.

Cookie was so startled he almost dropped the tray. "One of these days I'm going to stop doing this for you. Then you'll either come to my table or you'll starve."

"Cookie!" came a soft Southern voice from the direction of the Captain's Chair.

Kwaitkowski almost dropped the tray for the second time; and, despite all he could do, he did lose the cover, which went flapping across the bridge deck!

"Mr. Howorth? Is that you?"

"I've already eaten," chuckled the officer. After a pause, he asked, "How did this get started, you deliverin' food to an enlisted man?"

"Not just any enlisted man, sir. Just Tabor. When he first came aboard back on the East Coast, I started missing all kinds of things out of the galley. Then one day I noticed that he never ate with the men; so I went to him and he would not deny that he was raiding the pantry late at night. So I told him to stop it."

"And when he didn't, you started a delivery service." After a pause, Mr. Howorth asked, mysteriously, "Has somebody else been avoidin' your table lately?"

Kwaitkowski almost choked at this. "Sir, it's funny you mention that. I think something's happened to Baldini. He's not been aft all day, and the deckhands are saying that he's not in the fo'c's'le."

Mr. Howorth removed the whistle from the voicetube and blew into it. When he heard McCormick's "Aye," he said, "Pass the word to the Skipper that Baldini's missing! And tell him I'm on the bridge."

"Sir, I just about fell overboard on the starboard side a few minutes ago," said Kwaitkowski. "The lifeline at 'midships was unhooked. Could Baldini have fallen over the side during the night?"

The Exec, sounding almost like a Northerner, said, "Baldini is not one to go fallin' over the side, but we have been heelin' pretty bad to the starboard the last few days."

"And the deck's awful slick there."

"Uh, huh. Well, let's see what the Skipper has to say."

Within five minutes the entire crew was romping about topside, apparently oblivious to the rain and the sheets of salt water coming over the starboard side of the ship. Most of them seemed to be trying to get inside the pilothouse. Those that couldn't get inside, where the Skipper and Mr. Howorth were discussing the disappearance with various members of the crew, were humping about on deck like children, and from the tone of their voices, more than the words they were saying, they seemed to be feeling rather good about this surprising turn of events.

"I can't imagine how it became unhooked," the Skipper kept saying. "Or how Baldini failed to realize it was unhooked."

"I'm surprised about that," nodded Mr. Howorth. "You think we ought to go back and look for him?"

"I'll request permission from Lt. London, but there's no way he'll okay the search. None of us has enough fuel to turn around and head back the way we came, for any length of time. And, since we have no idea how long ago this happened, London won't go for it." The Skipper frowned, his face pale, "And we can't endanger the rest of the crew by using up what little fuel we've got by goin' it alone. But, of course, it it's not up to me."

Because of blackout regulations, Mr. Hiller reminded everyone, the blinker light could not be used until daylight; and, of course, radio transmissions day or night were out. We would, therefore, have to wait until daylight to notify the *SC-1318* of Baldini's disappearance.

Tabor, who usually spent the night on the bridge whether it was raining or not, in port or underway, this night sacked out like a normal human being in the forecastle. He was awakened before daylight by Carpenter, who was finishing up the graveyard shift on the engine controls.

The Skipper was on the bridge with his clipboard when Tabor tripped up the ladder.

"I want it sent exactly like I've got it here." He handed the clipboard to Tabor. "With nothing in between or on both ends." Then he added, "As soon as possible."

Tabor nodded: "As soon as the two farm boys between us and the *1318* can relay it. I'll have to send it to that turd on the *419*, and he'll have to pass it on to the *1066*, and—"

The Skipper cleared his throat, impatiently, "Don't antagonize them anymore than you have to. We need to get this to Mr. London right away, and it's very important what is sent. This will be used in the hearing."

"Could we ease over to one side or the other? That way I could send it direct to the *1318*."

"Just do it, Tabor, the way you're supposed to do it."

Tabor showed no signs that the Skipper had said anything. Without looking at the clipboard, he began sending A's in the direction of the *419*, which at the time clearly visible some three hundred yards ahead. It was slowly coming daylight and, for the first time since the trip started, the sky was beginning to break through the clouds. Occasionally, it was even possible to catch a glimpse of the *1066* and the 1318 when one or the other of them was on the crest of a great wave. The ugly fantail of the nearest ship was deserted, of course, and there was no sign of life on the bridge.

Tabor continued sending A's until, finally, a swab wearing an apron appeared on the stern of the subchaser ahead, caught sight of the blinking light, and ran for the bridge.

Tabor glanced around at the Skipper, handed him the clipboard, and waited. Minutes passed.

"I want that sent the way I put it down on that paper," said the Skipper.

From the 419 came three flashes, a long, a short, and a long.

Tabor lost no time sending: "We lost Baldini over the side. Relay to London and be quick about it." After the *419* man rogered, he added, "Who pushed him, you?" Tabor sent: "Don't fuck it up."

Mr. Hiller asked, "What did he say?"

"He got it and he's relayin' it."

At fourteen hundred hours that day a reply finally made its way back to the *995* from Lt. London:

"Maintain present heading. Interrogate the entire crew and have full report ready upon arrival at destination."

There was a postscript to this one, too: "Why does it always have to be you, Bill?"

14

Showdown

The instant word was passed that land had been sighted, I went topside to get a look. It seemed like twenty years since we had visited dark, smoky, mysterious Hollandia Harbor and heard the awful ruckus of the birds and beasts of the jungle that surrounded it.

July Roucloux was right behind me, and what we saw when we reached the deck was nothing but just a lot more water and maybe a thin line of something in the distance.

On the doubtful horizon ahead a jagged dark shadow had begun to take shape. We stared at it a long time, aware that it could be a range of mountains; but it was more likely just some more dark clouds, like the ones overhead and behind us.

"That's not land," said July, skeptically. "Who reported it?"

"Tabor's on the bridge," I said, with a knowing look. "Care to make a bet?"

Roucloux laughed and took another look. "It's probably land."

"Sure it's land!" I said. "I can smell it."

"What does it smell like?"

"Like the Fijis, like Melanesians and whatever it is they're always cooking or at least burning, something yellowish-brown."

"It sure is good to get back to some land that's got trees and nobody's shooting at us," said July. "I like the sea a lot, but this rowboat gits mighty tiresome at times."

We went up on the bow and sat down, with our legs over the side of the ship. I stretched out full length on my stomach and put my head over the gunwale and stared at the green water. It was actually a dirty green, which told me that we were not all that close to land.

"I can't remember," I said. "Is the water green like this in the harbor at Hollandia? I've always heard that the only place where there's blue water is close in to land."

"Hollandia Harbor is green, just like this, probably because it's so deep in there." Suddenly, Roucloux sat up and looked at me: "Tell me something. How much longer are you goin' to take old Tracy's pranking and teasing? He's onto you all the time and you don't do a thing about it. What would it really take for him to get you mad enough to fight him?"

"Like I've said every time you bring this up, I don't intend to fight him at all. No matter what he says or does. He's just a big-mouth and a practical joker. Fighting never solves anything."

"It might git him off your case." After a time, Roucloux added, "Well, he sure is braggin' a lot lately about what a coward you are and what he intends to do to you. Are you scared of him? I wouldn't blame you if you are. He is really something with his fists, and I for one want no part of him. He put Jines in the hospital, back when we was in New Caledonia, remember? And one time he came close to killing Martinez up in the fo'c's'le. Would have, I think, if some of us hadn't pulled him off. And I've lost track of the ones he's beat up on the other subchasers."

"I haven't fought that loudmouth because I just don't think fighting's the answer. This is a very small ship, and what I want is for all of us to get along. Now, with Baldini gone, we can have a pretty good thing. Beating him or being beaten by him would not solve a thing."

"He's tellin' everybody behind your back you're a coward."

I nodded, "He will say anything to make somebody angry. It doesn't mean anything. Everybody knows I'm not a coward." I looked him in the eye. "Do you think I'm a coward?"

"No, but he sure as hell better not call me one."

For a time neither of us spoke. I leaned over the gunwale and studied the water, while July lay on his back and looked at the clouds overhead. The surface of the sea had become glassy smooth, and the clouds had lifted and thinned out considerably. Little patches of blue sky could be seen to the right of the jagged dark line on the horizon.

"That's New Guinea," I said, turning over and sitting up.

"All I smell right now is Leavy."

Sure enough, the sun was blocked out and I looked up into the face of Big John Leavy, who had moved his great weight up from the fantail and was standing in front of the pilothouse looking in our direction. When I lifted my hand slightly, he shuffled on toward us, getting as far as the fo'c's'le hatch, where he sprawled out.

"Hollandia's dead ahead," he said, wheezing. "Hey, Pinky, I just heard Tracy talkin' 'bout you to Jines."

"What's he saying?" asked July.

"Jines is takin' up for Pinky. Never thought I'd live to hear him dispute ole Tracy's word about anything, after what happened."

"Well, Fat, spell it out," demanded Roucloux. "What was Tracy saying?"

"Oh, same ole thing. He started off sayin' Pinky's got a yellow streak down his back. Jines told him to can that kind of talk, that Pinky has already proved he's not afraid of anything. Then ole Tracy said, 'When we git to Hollandia, I'm goin' to prove he's a big momma's boy'. 'How're you gonna do that?' ast Sparks. 'I've figured out a way to git him to fight me', said Tracy. 'A sure fire way'. Sparks ast him again how he was gonna do that. He said, 'How you gonna do that, Pinky?' But ole Tracy wouldn't tell him."

"Did Jines call me 'Pinky'?" I asked.

Leavy's big, sagging face took on a troubled look for a moment, a sign that he was trying to get the wheels turning in there. Finally, He shook his head, "Come to think of it, I don't think he called you anything."

"What do you suppose he meant?" asked July. "Mark my word, he's up to something. If I was you, I'd watch out for him."

*   *   *

Our arrival in Hollandia seemed a little like going home. We had never been anyplace twice before. And while I knew it wouldn't be a real R and R place like Noumea, New Caledonia, or even Suva, it would be a very welcome change from the Palau Islands.

This great sprawling, seemingly always fog-shrouded harbor out of a Tarzan movie was still within range of Japanese fighters and bombers, and surrounding the harbor on three sides were untold numbers of starving Japanese soldiers who had not been able to escape when the Allies re-took the place in the summer of 1943.

For twenty miles along the wide flat gray beach that surrounded the harbor there appeared signs of energy and activity. Spirals of smoke drifted upward in a number of places, marking the spots where clean-up and jungle-clearing was taking place, where some kind of human activity was going on. (Any kind of human activity in this part of the world was a welcome sight to see.)

In the harbor itself small boats, LCVP's and Captains' gigs mostly, raced about, delivering people and supplies; and ship traffic was so heavy we had to single file it very carefully on the way to the still-unfinished submarine base.

Everywhere I looked something was happening, and behind it all in the jungle I knew there were starving Japanese soldiers who were more afraid of the New Guinea natives than us. These headhunters, we had been told, preferred white meat to any other kind but would settle for yellow. Rumor had it that the Japanese stragglers quite often chose suicide or the American stockade over fighting it out with the Melanesians.

We crossed the harbor at eight knots, so close behind to the *419* we could carry on a conversation with the swabs on the fantail without much trouble. The surface of the water was like a mirror of the sky, so blue it looked unreal; and I looked about for July Roucloux to tell him he was wrong about the color. He was pretending to paint the K-gun rack back on the stern, but when I waved from the bridge he saw me and stood up, ignoring the critical eye of Bill Tracy.

On the bridge with me were Tabor and the Skipper. The other officers had gone below, probably to avoid watching the little farce we had to go through every time we tied up at a dock. But my hungry eyes couldn't get enough of this wonderful change of scenery. For a very long time we had seen nothing but water, sky, and gooney birds.

Tabor was carrying on a conversation by blinker light with the signalman on the *1318*, through and around the masts of the other two subchasers. Through the side of his mouth he kept the Skipper filled in on whatever scuttlebutt he was picking up, plus some serious stuff, like where we were going to tie up, when the enlisted men's recreation hut would be open, the new rules of the base about shore leave, and what would be showing at the outdoor movies that evening.

I was reading the blinker light along with him, and before he had a chance to tell the Skipper what the movie would be that night, I shouted back at July, "There's a wild West movie tonight!"

Tabor's black eyes met mine for a split second, "Don't they have flicks back in Konawa?" To the Skipper, he said, "As I was sayin', they've got their screen up and tonight we'll see Charley Starrett in *Home on the Range*."

When we reached the submarine docks, we had to stand off, with engines idling, until the others tied up. Jim Pauley, the boatswain's mate, tossed the monkey's fist himself, almost knocking the man on the dock flat. Shortly after that I heard him yell, "Roll out the gangplank!"

The *995*, of course, was the last to tie up; and, as usual, there had to be one or more frustrating delays before this could take place. According to a rule Lt. London had thought up, no subchaser came in until he gave the word; and he was never in a hurry to share the dock with anyone. Once his ship was in and tied up, his gangplank in place, and half of his men already on their way down the beach, he would then have his signalman give the go ahead to the *1066*. Stiff-backed and looking a great deal like a battlewagon skipper, he insisted on remaining on his bridge until the other ships were secured, a little thing that infuriated Mr. Hiller and his two officers.

After cursing for a time and threatening to one day forego Jackie London's little ritual and outrun the other subchasers in and tie up first, Mr. Hiller would wait patiently until the ship was finally secured then lead Mr. Howorth and Mr. Darling below to the wardroom, where they would sulk or stall, or whatever, for an hour or so in protest. This just in case Lt. London should decide to hold a skippers' powwow on his ship. Which happened almost every time the ships tied up at a dock; and when it did happen, Mr. Hiller had his revenge by forcing Lt. London to send a messenger to him and then stalling for an hour or so over a bottle of brandy (or whatever they had in the wardroom to drink).

Half a dozen dock workers, seamen from the submarine base, were on hand to assist in the mooring of the first two ships. One of them raced down the dock, caught the monkey's fist like a baseball, and quickly rolled up the small line attached to it until he reached the heavy mooring line. Then as the ship came in, he shortened it up until the boatswain's mate on the ship signaled for him to cinch it down and tie it off. When it came our turn to move in next to the *1066*, Leavy threw the monkey's fist short and it landed in the drink!

A swab on the fantail of the *Splendid Six* called out, "Would you like to borrow a bosun's mate?" Another suggested, "How about you mail that thing to us?" Finally, Leo Meyerson, their boatswain's mate, tossed us a monkey's fist.

The submarine base was still very much as we remembered it, in a state of confusion. This despite the fact that a great deal of Seabee construction had taken place since our earlier visit. In addition to a new enlisted men's recreation hut, equipped with three pool tables, a phonograph, several comfortable chairs, and a few battered books stacked inside and on top of an orange crate, there were now an outdoor movie theater like the one on Guadalcanal, and a large quonset hut messhall back in the trees.

It was a well known fact among swabs during this time that the U. S. Army ate well back in the States, the U. S. Navy ate well wherever it was, and the U. S. Marines, when they were not bivouacked in the bush, ate considerably better than almost anybody else. I had never heard how submariners ate, but my attitude was that anything had to be better than what Kwaitkowski served up.

                    *   *   *

Bill Tracy, as it turned out, was counting on the Skipper doing what he had always done when Lt. London pulled one of his stunts, hiding out in the wardroom, plugging his voicetube, and refusing to answer any and all summons from the pilothouse.

Roucloux, having soaked his head in freshwater and combed his great mass of wavy light-brown hair severely back above his ears, emerged from the fo'c's'le and walked back toward the quarterdeck, where I was doing a chore I had put off much too long, checking the acid in our sixteen batteries beneath the quarterdeck.

"Need any help?" he asked.

Talking loud for the benefit of the swabs on the dock, Tracy called out from the bridge, "Hey, Tex-ass, aint this the very spot where you and Pinky fell in love?" He joined in with the bystanders for a good laugh.

"Ignore him," I said, kneeling and tugging at a deck plate. "See if you can get hold of that other end."

"Ever'body knows you two're bunkin' together."

"Listen," said Roucloux, looking up, "I'm warnin' you. Leave me alone. Nobody's botherin' you."

I got down on my knees and began testing the first brace of batteries, reminding July that as along as he paid attention to Tracy he would keep up the banter.

The gunner's mate called out, "You always bother me, Julie Honey! You and that pink mama's boy you're in love with! You two think you're hot shit on this ship, but let me tell you I'm goin' to stomp the crap out of both of you, right here on this dock! Your sweetheart's yellow through and through, Tex-*ass*, and I'm beginning to think you are too!"

"You're wrong, on both counts!" called out Roucloux, red-faced.

For a long time the crew of the *995* had waited impatiently for Tracy to pick on the wrong man. Most of us felt that Roucloux just might be the one to put an end to Tracy's trouble-making. I, for one, knew that he was capable of picking Tracy up and tossing him overboard. The way he handled the heavy 20mm. canisters had convinced me that if he ever became angry enough he just might kill this pugnacious gunner's mate.

The tall, thin kid who had come aboard in New Caledonia was now broad and thick in the shoulders, three inches taller, and fifty pounds heavier. And there wasn't an ounce of fat on him.

Tracy was shorter by a good six inches but built solid from his ears to his feet, like a tree trunk. His head, lacking a neck, rested squarely on round shoulders, with nothing in between; and when he turned any part of his body, his head swung around, too, like a tank turret.

Swabs from the other subchasers and a few strays from the base had begun to drift down the dock toward us, curious about what was going on. Tracy's reputation as a fighter was well known on the other subchasers, and on our previous visit he had endeared himself to the submariners by whipping their base champion.

All the time this was going on, I was puzzling over why it was that men love a really good fistfight the way women love to dance and go to parties. Most men, if the truth were known, would rather watch two of their friends beat each other's brains out than make love to a beautiful woman. Of course, most brawls aboard the ships in the *Splinter Fleet* could hardly be called fistfights, especially when they occurred at sea. There just was not enough room for a knock-down, drag-out fistfight. So what usually happened was like a barroom brawl, with gouging and biting and kicking. And more often than not they did not last more than a minute, at most.

William Tracy, of the *995*, loved to fight and was uncommonly good at it, as every man who had watched him in action was quick to admit. And by the time we reached New Guinea he had either fought or backed down almost every enlisted man on the four ships. I had seen him take on and beat unmercifully men much larger and tougher-looking than he was.

Bill continued to badger Roucloux ruthlessly. Suddenly, just as I stood up to get the kink out of my back, July ripped off his shirt and said what everybody on the dock had been waiting for him to say:

"I've had it with you, Tracy! Let's go out on the dock!"

Roucloux, with his shirt on and not upset about anything, looked like a big, easy-going kid. He had large, kindly eyes and a face that told everything that was in his heart. For his height, about six feet, four inches, he had rather short arms; but his shoulders and chest were massive. Lined up in front of Tracy with his shirt off and his big, slightly bulging eyes signaling hatred and death, he looked formidable. Even some of the men on the other subchasers, who had seen Tracy whip Jim Pauley, a former Navy middleweight fighter, began to switch their bets.

July had caught me off guard with this sudden outburst and was halfway across the *1066*, which was tied up inboard of us, before I realized what was about to happen. I left my test equipment and two jugs of battery acid on the quarterdeck and took off after him.

Everybody was making bets on the fight, but I had no intention of doing that. Like most if not all of the men on the *995*, I really did not think July had a chance; but I was not about to bet that way. I heard Ace McCormick putting my sentiments into words as I leaped across the other subchaser. "I would die and go to the hell before I would put money on that big-mouth, but I think too much of my money to waste it bettin' on July." Then he added, for anybody that might be paying any attention to him, "Is the carbine still on the bridge?"

Sailors had begun to crowd in from all directions, but not one officer was in sight. Our three, of course, were locked inside the wardroom; and the others were probably listening to Lt. London.

When I reached the gangplank, I heard Tracy badgering Roucloux.

"Where's your honey, Julie Baby? Aint he comin' to help you?"

Then I caught a glimpse of him jabbing at Roucloux's chest. "I want your sweetheart to see me rip that soft gut of yours apart!" He had begun to dance about, faking jabs while moving slowly backward, down the dock.

It was obvious to me why he wanted to take the fight down the dock. He did not want Mr. Hiller and the other officers on the *995* to hear the noise. And it was going to get very noisy soon.

Some of the spectators from the base interpreted Tracy's retreat as a sign of weakness. One of them called to Ace McCormick, asking why so many swabs were betting on the "short one." His reply was, "Because he's the undefeated champ of the *Splinter Fleet.*"

The crowd was backed up all the way to the gangplank of the *1318*; and on the bridges of that ship and the *1066* there was standing room only by this time, and swabs from the other ships had crowded aboard and were lined up two-deep along the port lifelines.

There was no getting through the crowd quickly, and for a time I could only guess what was going on. The bets were almost split, apparently, with the submariners backing Roucloux and the Splinter Fleet sailors backing Tracy. I overheard one of the submariners ask a subchaser sailor, "Who's your money on?"

"Hey, I'm for the kid."

"Yeah, me too. And it ought to take about ten seconds."

While I was shouldering my way up the dock beside the *1066*, the cry from the spectators went up, "Come on, you two! "What're you waitin' for?" To me this meant that Tracy was playing with July, making a show of it. Suddenly, I could see a bit of what was going on.

As if waiting for this challenge, Tracy dropped into a crouch and began to weave from side to side. Roucloux remained as he was, looking awkward and uncertain about what to do. It was obvious that he was not a fighter, and to me it was painful to watch. In all the time I had known him he had never taken a poke at anyone.

One of the submariners near me cried out happily, "Look how sure that big kid is of himself. He's not even botherin' to protect himself!"

Tracy, a low, fast-moving target, was loving every minute of this. He straightened up from time to time and strutted from one side of the dock to the other, then went back to his weaving and bobbing. Roucloux followed him around clumsily, his hands clenched and ready. After throwing half a dozen powerful swings that missed the gunner's mate a mile, he began to crouch a bit and put out his left tentatively. To Tracy these preliminaries were just fun and games, a kind of ritual that had to take place before the serious business. He ducked easily to safety each time one of the sledgehammers came his way.

I was able to see above the heads in front of me, but I still could not wedge my way through the wall of bodies.

Testing the waters, Tracy ducked in and, with his left, a One-Two, *spat-spat* against the ribs, and with his right, a Three, wham! hard into the gut. I had seen him begin a number of fights this way.

This, I told myself, was likely to be short and ugly. But, of course, it all depended on just how long Tracy wanted it to last. He was capable of ending it in a flat minute.

Suddenly, Tracy was no longer teasing. Dancing in, with his left hammering away at July's ribs, he landed solid rights again and again, receiving nothing in return. July took it like a man, however, and tried desperately to reach the grinning face. He tried haymakers and short jabs and flurries of wild punching, but nothing he threw touched Tracy. At one point, while flat on his back, he tried desperately to kick the cavorting, laughing, teasing gunner's mate.

The submariners could not believe what was happening. They began to shout angrily at Roucloux, calling him names; and some of them began to question whether it was a rigged fight. But shortly it became quite clear that Tracy was trying to beat the big kid to death.

The fight continued, long after the outcome was certain. July would not give up, and Tracy was having too much fun. It occurred to me that the gunner's mate just might not have a knockout punch in him. He was as very quick and powerful, but it would take a mule to lay my friend July Roucloux out.

The end came, however, shortly after that. Tracy dived in, did his One, Two, Three; and down July went, all of the wind knocked out of him. Everybody as far away as the *995* gangplank had heard the sound of one or more of his ribs snapping! His face had been torn open in a number of places, and he had begun to clutch his left side.

At this point I broke through into the circle and leaned down to July, followed at once by Jim Pauley. The old Chief Boatswain's Mate suddenly stood up and faced Tracy and told him to back off.

I began to look around for Leafdale. "Somebody get Pills! I think his ribs are broken!"

"Leave him right there, Pinky," said a voice in my right ear. "I think we'd better get a stretcher."

Leafdale, sour-faced and cursing under his breath, knelt down and began to pull at Roucloux's hands, to get them away from his ribs. Over his shoulder he said to no one in particular, "Go get my satchel. Not you, Pinky. Stay here and help me keep everybody back." Then, as he examined July's midsection, he said through clenched lips, "I was watching Tracy when he deliberately hit this kid below the belt. I could tell by the look on his face he meant to rupture him. And you know, he just might've done that."

"How's he doin'?" asked Pauley, bending down again.

"Not good," said Pills. "Keep everybody back, will you?"

Pauley straightened up. "All right, everybody! Clear the dock! Go on back to your ships!" He was dressed in faded dungarees, with a salty old CPO cap pulled down over his eyes; and instantly the swabs on the dock did as he ordered.

Leafdale stood up and faced Pauley. "If you want to do something, Chief, send someone for a pharmacist's mate and a stretcher. We'll take this kid to the Base Sick Bay."

When the stretcher showed up, accompanied by a pills from one of the other subchasers, I followed along to the Base Dispensary. I hadn't even looked at Tracy. The sight of him sickened me, and I wasn't certain what I might do.

For the next two hours, until a doctor showed up, I stuck around with Roucloux. After glancing at the X-rays Pills had ordered, he said:

"Good job, Chief. He'll be all right if he takes it easy for awhile. Fist fight?"

Leafdale nodded, bristling. "Some folks might call it that. I would call it a slaughter."

When I was able to get Leafdale's ear, I said, "Listen, Pills, I'll see you back at the ship."

Pills nodded, eyeing me like a hawk. "Listen, Hall, you go back and do what you're planning to do and Tracy will probably kill you. You're too mad to fight him right now. Wait till you've calmed down." When I wheeled to leave, he added, "Then hit him with a club from behind."

Capless and out of breath, I crossed the gangplank of the *1066* running. Pedersen, the Sparks aboard that ship, wanted to know what was up. I brushed past him and leaped over the gunwales and landed on the deck of the *995*. Only Eddie Jake Groth was in sight, and when the big messcook looked up from the bucket of potatoes he was peeling, he yelped:

"Hey, Pinky! What's the hurry?"

"Where's Tracy?"

"In his bunk, I reckon," he said, nodding toward the after hatch. "Nobody would eat chow with him, but it didn't seem to bother him much. You know, Pinky——"

But I did not wait around to hear what he had to say. I dived through the hatch opening and fell most of the way to the deck below.

Eddie Jake, as slow as he was most of the time, leaped up, spilling his potatoes, and started shouting, "All hands on deck! This is goddamned D-Day minus nothin'! Tracy has made Pinky mad!" Then, apparently, he ran about all over the ship yelling, "Tracy finally got Pinky mad at him!"

The after crews quarters of a subchaser was no place for two men to thrash out their differences. Even with the table leaves down and the bunks all up there was just enough space for one-way traffic.

As I was banging down that narrow metal ladder, I heard Kwaitkowski's shrill voice yelling something about the galley being off-limits to rough-housing. Then I landed on both feet and ducked around the island into the quarters, just in time to see Tracy rising on one elbow in his bunk!

I was so angry I was actually blubbering, and tears were streaming from my eyes!

"You made a mistake, ole buddy!" I cried, grabbing a handful of his hair in my left hand and hitting him squarely in the nose with my right fist. Down he came from his second-tier bunk to the cushioned seat that ran the length of the bulkhead. His fists were striking thin air as I jerked him about, and if he hit me at all I did not feel it. I continued to beat him about the head and neck with everything I had.

He was all muscle and bone, and for maybe a minute or two he held out in his struggle to get up. Then he began to bawl like an enraged bull, and with his arms and legs he began thrashing crazily about beneath me. I must have hit him fifty times before it was over.

Later, Eddie Jake described some of what he saw from the ladder: "It was like Hall had a rag doll by the head an' was beatin' hell out of it for doin' a bad thing. He kept hittin' old Tracy in the head till there wasn't much left but a bloody stub!"

Milleson and Jines were the first to join Eddie Jake at the bottom of the ladder. The three of them, with Cookie doing more talking than anything else, got me away from Tracy and out of the compartment; but all three of them paid a price for their trouble. Eddie Jake wrapped his arms around my feet and the other two pinned my upper body, and somehow they managed to poke me up through the hatchway. Other members of the crew, including the Skipper, finally settled me down on the fantail.

Vanderveen then led a rescue squad back down into the after quarters for the battered gunner's mate. They took him to the dock and sent for a pharmacist's mate and a stretcher. By fifteen hundred hours Pills was back at the Base Sick Bay visiting with Roucloux when Tracy was brought out from surgery and lined up beside his gunner's mate striker.

"These boys off the same ship?" asked the doctor from an open doorway.

"Yes, Sir. Same ship," said Pills. "That one," he nodded toward Roucloux, "ran afoul of that one." He glanced at Tracy, who was bandaged from head to foot and still unconscious.

"I'm a bit confused," said the doctor. "If that one ran afoul of that one, then who in hell did that one 'run afoul' of?" The doctor was waving his hand first at Roucloux and then at Tracy.

"Somebody on the ship that used to be called Pinky. From now on, I venture to say, he will be called something else."

15

Abandon Ship!

Sharkey insisted on taking the first watch because he hated the mid-watch and knew I liked it. There were times when this big Windy City fellow seemed almost like family, like somebody you could trust even if you didn't much like them. Of course, almost without exception, I felt this way about the whole 995 crew.

He poked his head down through the radio shack hatch and yelled at me to sign out, that he would be back to take over as soon as he got a mug of java from the galley.

McCormick was on the helm in the pilothouse, and without trying I had been listening to him and Leafdale carry on about the "liberty" Ace had had in Hollandia. According to Pills, he had caught the clap our first night there, even though there wasn't an eligible woman anywhere within five hundred miles. Pills allowed as how Ace was always catching something, regardless of the scarcity of opportunities. The worst thing the quartermaster had ever caught, as everybody well knew, was spick-itch, which he bitched about all the time but nevertheless enjoyed.

Also according to Pills, *spickitch* was a South Pacific fungus infection something like athlete's foot and leprosy. Unlike the former, it wouldn't go away, and unlike the latter, it wasn't life-threatening. But like both it involved rotting flesh. Ace never gave it time to fall off. He was always digging at it, with an expression on his face like a pampered pussy cat.

I hadn't heard a single *dit-dah* during my four-hour watch; so I logged in sixteen "No Sigs" at fifteen-minute intervals, and signed my name at the bottom of the page. The Army transceivers in the pilot-house had been noisy, but not one single word had come through any of the speakers. Ace had kept an ear on them while I worked on the ship's newsletter below in the radio shack.

Press had come in at thirty words a minute, in Morse Code sent over a teletype; and since I had had no interruptions and the ship wasn't giving it hell bobbing up and down and rolling about the way it generally did, I copied that stuff straight, right off onto the newsletter, with no mistakes.

When Sharkey came back from the galley and leaned over the open hatchway, I pulled myself away from the typewriter and reached up for the two big Navy mugs of steaming black coffee. Then he skinned down into the radio shack and fell into my chair.

"I wish the Skipper would let us in on where we're goin'," he complained, taking the coffee from me and sipping noisily. He turned around and looked at the No Sigs in my log. "Why we've got to wait for twenty-four hours is more than I can figure out."

"Ace says we're headed for Manus Island, in the Admiralties."

"Yeah, I know. Ace says that and so does Tabor. But they're both guessing. That's where they hope we're goin'."

"What difference does it make? It's R & R and one atoll looks pretty much like another."

Ace had found out from someplace that Manus was a good R & R island. According to him there was an Officers Club and an Enlisted Men's Club and tennis courts and two outdoor theaters, one just for officers. Armed Forces Radio had put in a relay station there. But the place did not have any women at all, except maybe a few Navy nurses. The big thing was baseball and warm beer, provided you had saved up your daily allotments.

Sharkey had taken it upon himself to keep track of the days since he had had a beer so that when and if the ship ever anchored at an R & R island, he would not be short-changed.

Up to this time we had never stopped at an island for R and R. Therefore, not one of our beer or soda pop rations had been used up. And since the allotments of beer were much like our Navy pay, promised but seldom if ever delivered, most of the crew had been playing poker with I O U's, using Sharkey's calculations like "beer futures." The market had climbed steadily since New Caledonia, and at this juncture, one Griesedieck beer was worth ten American dollars.

A bottle of Pepsi Cola, which in Suva Harbor had been worth about what the Navy paid for it, had, by the time we headed out of Hollandia for the second time, risen on the market to about a dollar. Sharkey and Smith and other old salts would not accept it in their poker games as a thing of value; but since all of us were accumulating it just as fast as we were beer, most of the beer drinkers were willing to trade their (paper) rations of it at a rate of ten for one.

Roucloux, who had decided he liked beer (even though he could not remember ever having tasted one), wanted to exchange with me bottle for bottle, one Pepsi for one beer. And since we were good friends and I had no interest in the foul-smelling stuff, I went along with that agreement for a time—until he admitted to me one day that he had lost all of his beer futures, including the ones I had traded to him for Pepsis, to the sharks on the ship, meaning Sharkey and Smith and Tracy.

"I guess I lost quite a bit of your beer, too, old buddy," he said.

"Sorry, old buddy, but we don't do business that way. I've decided when we get our allotments, if we ever do, I'm going to sell my beer to the highest bidder, for cash money."

"You want me dead?" he protested. "I've got your vouchers!"

*　　　　　*　　　　　*

I went up the ladder from the radio shack and paused for a moment at the radar cubicle to see what New Guinea looked like after three hours out. The E. T. D. had been fifteen hundred hours, and we had been plodding along at ten knots in a perfectly calm sea. Smitty was dozing inside his cubicle, with his head resting against the port bulkhead; so I leaned over him and studied the green screen. There was nothing at all on the screen, which surprised me until I realized he had accidentally turned the thing off. I straightened up and looked at Ace.

"Oh," said the quartermaster, faking a tragic look in my direction and raising his long, skinny foot to dig between toes that had not seen a sock or a shoe for months, "I've got a dolly with a hole in her stockin'."

"Ace, why don't you get some ointment from Pills?"

"An' her knees keep a knockin'."

He was just saying the words. There was nothing in his voice or his delivery that suggested he was singing.

"An' her toes keep arockin'."

"Who's relievin' you?"

"Leavy the Lard Ass."

"I'll go get him. Want to brave one of Cookie's sandwiches?"

"Shore thing. I missed his last attempt at chow."

I went forward and found Leavy right where I knew he would be, sound asleep in his bunk. I slapped him on the shoulder. It was wet with perspiration. "Hit the deck!" I yelled, imitating Baldini.

He opened one eye, groaned, and closed it. "Quit kiddin' around, Red."

"Get up, Leavy. Ace has been on watch four hours!"

"Okay," he said, without moving. "I must've dozed off ag'in. It happens to ever'body once in awhile. Go away."

"I'm not leaving." I poked him in a sore.

"Okay! Geez!"

"I'm not leaving until you get out of that bunk. Ace was right, you are worthless. If I have to, I'll drag you out on your butt."

"What's your problem, Red? I said I'd git up!"

I stood there waiting, but he didn't move.

Leavy had gained several noticeable pounds in the short time since Baldini had disappeared, and with each passing day he was becoming harder and harder to unglue from his bunk.

He had begun to snore; so I grasp him by the wrists and jerked part of him out over the deck. It was like pulling on a full-grown hog. "I'm turning loose, Leavy!" I said. "Think about it!" When he just grunted, I let go.

When we showed up some five minutes later in the pilothouse, McCormick was laughing. "Hot damn, I do believe this is a record, Big John is only twenty minutes late this time!" Then he glanced at me. "Was that what I heard and felt?" He nodded toward Leavy. "Whatever you did to get him up actually threw us off course about two degrees."

"You should've been in the bow when it happened," I said with a grin.

*　　　*　　　*

At noon the second day out of Hollandia Harbor word was passed for all hands to muster on the quarterdeck. This, we knew, was the official reading of our travel orders. I followed the Skipper out on deck and settled next to my twenty. He mounted the ladder to the bridge and waited, and in his hand was an official-looking manila envelope.

After getting as much drama out of this mock heroic event as possible, he held up the envelope with the TOP SECRET stamped across the front side, which more than likely had been opened back in Hollandia, and signaled his desire for silence by clearing his throat noisily. Ace kept humming his Dolly song.

"Nobody interested in where we're goin'?" he asked, looking disappointed.

"Manus!" burst out Sharkey and Smith in unison.

The Skipper folded the sheet of paper, taking his time, and replaced it in the envelope. Obviously a bit hurt, he said, "This means R and R, men. Maybe a couple of weeks of it. How would you like that?"

"Yeah, and then the Philippines," said Sharkey.

"Back to the old grind," put in Pills.

We were headed into a storm. Heavy black clouds were rolling in from the north, the direction we were headed; and any minute we were going to forced inside. But looking at the Skipper's face I was quite certain the a much bigger storm was even closer to home. The Skipper was working up to something, and I thought I knew what it was.

To my surprise, however, the C. O. began to speak calmly, almost affectionately, about the ship and the crew and our part in the war. However, there was nothing in it at all about the "big picture," which was what we were all braced to hear. Just as the rain came, he closed with, "We're going to come out of this thing, men. One of these days this war'll be over, and we'll go back to the States and pick up where we left off." Then he added, "After we kick the shit out of the Japs."

"Skipper," broke in Leafdale, "pardon me for saying it, but our chances of comin' through this just aren't all that good. We've already lost one subchaser with all hands aboard, and we've come awful close to losing a couple of others."

A great howl of protest arose from the crew, but the Skipper held up his hand for silence. We had almost escaped his *gung ho* speech.

"Now, Pills, I want you to keep that kind of talk to yourself. We've got a very good chance of coming out of this. Besides, what good does it do to dwell on the bad that could happen. I want you to think positively."

On and on he went, with the big picture speech, while the tropical storm raged around and upon us. And Leafdale's stock dropped considerably on this occasion.

*   *   *

The third day out dawned finally, in the middle of a downpour. The heavy dark-blue clouds were right on the water, and visibility at mid-morning was about four feet. By morning chow the bridge had been informed that the radar had decided to go on the blink. Smitty, who practically lived in that little radar cubicle, cut his chow short and set in immediately to take the thing apart and look for the problem. Which he said he probably wouldn't be able to fix if he found it. There were no spare parts aboard the ship.

The Skipper had stood the midwatch, going to the wardroom around five, after a long chat with Mr. Darling on the bridge. They were in high spirits, despite the weather, and looking forward to getting a glimpse of land within two days. At that time the radar was still operating properly. But by the time Eddie Jake delivered two trays of food to the bridge around eight, and passed the word for the Starboard Section to chow down, Mr. Darling was thinking seriously of waking the Skipper and breaking the bad news. Visibility, already bad, was getting worse.

"See if you can git the *Splendid Three* on the light," Mr. Darling told Tabor. "Tell them our radar's out." Then he looked at his wristwatch. "It's time for my relief. Would you check on that, after you send the message?"

The Indian had already started sending A's, which he continued to do, ignoring the officer. Mr. Darling glared at the back of his head, fidgeting. For a time he stood at the front bridge railing and stared through field glasses. Then, with great sighs, he began pacing the bridge.

"What's wrong with them?" he cried out at one point. "I think they've increased speed."

The fantail of the *419* was now barely visible, and the rain was coming down in sheets and swirls, at times completely blotting out the other subchaser. Visibility had been so consistently bad they hadn't seen the *1066* and the *1318* since shortly after leaving Hollandia.

The Exec's head appeared at the top of the bridge ladder.

"How's it goin', My'on?"

Mr. Darling's face was pale and drawn, and when he spoke his voice betrayed his anxiety, "Our radar is malfunctioning and visibility is about three hundred feet, maximum."

Mr. Howorth tripped up to the bridge and went directly to the front railing, taking the glasses from the other officer as he passed.

"My God, Tabor, are you sure the *419* is still dead ahead of us?"

"It's there," said the Indian. "But their bridge can't see us."

Mr. Howorth turned around and said to his fellow officer, "You're relieved, Sir. Would you be so kind as to wake the Skippah?" Then, stepping to the voicetube, he cupped his mouth into the opening and blew.

"Pilothouse, aye."

"Engines ahead one third. And stand by to back 'em off quick."

"Aye, sir."

Mr. Howorth turned about and saw Mr. Darling. "If yuh don't have anything better to do, My'on, I'd appreciate it if you'd go down and inform the Skippah we've got a slight problem on our hands."

"Right now? He just got off at four."

"Right now, suh. If you don't min'?"

When the Skipper reached the bridge, Mr. Howorth explained why he had increased the speed to one-third.

Mr. Hiller nodded, rubbing his eyes. "Have Tabor send a message to *Splendid One* requesting permission to reduce the distance between us and the *419*."

"That's just it, we haven't been able to raise anybody."

Tabor, still on the blinker light, glanced over his shoulder and said, "I see it now."

Then the two officers saw the other ship. It was weaving and bobbing crazily, apparently dead in the water. Mr. Howorth barked into the voicetube, "Back 'er off, Ace! Tell engine controls to stand by to put 'er in reverse."

"Roger. Engines stop."

"Who's on engine controls, Ace?" asked Mr. Howorth.

"Leavy."

"Who else is within shoutin' distance?"

"Hall's on the radio."

"Have him take over at engine controls."

Finally, the blinker light on the other ship opened up, and Tabor said, "'Bout time." He sent the message so fast the signalman on the *419* had to ask for two repeats.

"Calm down," said Mr. Howorth.

"It's not me. He just can't receive worth a damn."

The Skipper grunted, a sign he was not pleased. To Mr. Howorth he said, "Well, all we can do is hang in as close to the *419* as possible and hope we make it to Manus Harbor before heavy fog rolls in. Our biggest problem, if we lose sight of *Splendid Three*, is going to be charts. We don't have a single one of the Manus region. Even with sonar, we would be up a creek."

When the reply came from Lt. London, it was not what anyone had been expecting. "Maintain a distance of five hundred feet minimum from *Splendid Three*."

"Send this!" shouted Mr. Hiller. "Relay to Mr. London we'll lose visual contact at that distance! And tell him our radar's out!"

Back from the convoy leader came, "You have sonar and a navigator. Use them!"

At noon chow that day, Leafdale, looking like a very pale Ancient Mariner, burst into the after crew's quarters and encountered Mr. Howorth, who was on his way out. "Could you tell me why, Sir, since we're the one ship without charts of the region, we were picked to bring up the rear?"

"None of us have charts, Pills. But I feel a bit paranoid, myself. We are, of course, rather insignificant and undeservin' in the eyes of those that make the decisions." After giving that time to sink in, he added, "All these islands out heah in the Pacific belonged to the Japs prior to the late misunderstandin', an' I reckon they'uh the only ones with up-to-date maps an' charts."

"The *1318* has charts," Pills insisted, argumentatively.

"Well," sighed Mr. Howorth, "my understandin' is that Mr. London is the convoy commandah."

"I was on the bridge when the signalman—"

"Then yuh know more'n I do," grinned Mr. Howorth, ending the conversation. He disappeared into the galley, leaving Pills with his mouth open.

For the next two days nobody got much sleep or rest on the *995*. Everything was battened down, of course, including the men not on watch. Heavy sheets of rain, borne along on winds that reached gale force at times, swept constantly across our little deck, taking with them everything that was not lashed down or holding on for dear life. Eight- and ten-foot waves lifted us to giddying heights and dropped us with a suddenness that left us gasping for breath and hanging onto stanchions and whatever else was handy.

The *419* had disappeared the afternoon of the third day, was spotted only once briefly on the fourth day, and then disappeared for good on that same day. Ace McCormick would not give up the helm, which I thought was a good thing. When I asked him if he had any hope of finding Manus in all that soup, he grinned sadly:

"Well, my boy, I'll tell you. Manus is a mighty big pile of black rocks and a little bitty piece of flat land. With me on the wheel, we'll find some of them rocks. That's not the problem."

"The problem is getting through the black rocks to the flat land."

"Right on, my boy!"

The galley closed down entirely beginning with the fifth day, and Cookie and Eddie Jake began delivering sandwiches once during each watch to the various compartments and to the bridge. They took turns working their way from the galley with their large buckets of sandwiches and coffee; and they were greeted with cheers and slaps on the back when they would fall through the door of the pilothouse, looking like drowned rats.

Mr. Hiller, maintaining his usual calm, piped down to the pilothouse that our E. T. A. had been amended to about dark that day. Then he added that everybody had better pray that we reached the harbor entrance before the fog moved in for the night.

McCormick, beginning to look like a corpse, had remained at the helm for thirty-six hours. And so powerful were the wind and the waves, when he was finally pulled away from the wheel, two men were required to replace him.

Within thirty minutes after the quartermaster was strapped into his bunk, Tabor yelled through the voicetube from the bridge, "Land ho! Land dead ahead!" He had remained lashed to the Captain's Chair for longer than anyone knew; and, so, when he began shouting that land was dead ahead, the consensus among the bridge watch was that he was either crazy or his eyes were playing tricks on him. Nobody else could see a thing but billowing clouds and heavy sheets of rain.

All three officers had taken up positions on the bridge with field glasses, while at least half of the crew had crowded inside the pilothouse. Tabor's announcement brought shocked silence. I shouted at Jines, who was on the helm with Tex, "I think it's easing off a bit!"

At that moment from the bridge came a shout, the words lost in the wind; then Jines relayed from the voicetube, "A mile-long strip of rugged coastline has taken shape! Tabor was right! Rocks fifty to a hundred feet and more in height are rising from the water on all sides of the ship!" Then, without a pause, he shouted, "Stop engines!"

During lightning flashes we could see killer boulders that one after another kept popping up out of the mist and fog.

Then, during a momentary lull in the storm, we heard the Skipper shout, "Tabor, go to the point of the bow! Take a megaphone and keep us off the rocks!"

"There's the *419*," said the Indian, pointing into the cloud bank. "She's just this side of the harbor entrance!"

"Are you sure?" somebody shouted hysterically.

Tabor, on his way to the bow, spoke through the megaphone, "I just got a glimpse her! And what looked like the entrance to the harbor!"

Mr. Howorth raced for the blinker light and began sending A's in the direction the signalman had pointed.

Tabor's presence on the bow, coupled with his assurance that the *419* was nearby, helped relax the crew of the *995* a bit at their positions along the lifelines and on the bridge. Time was running out for us, however, for it was already well past sundown; and in a very short time it would be impossible to see a thing without radar. The sonar was going crazy, of course, and could not be relied upon as long as we were among the boulders at the entrance to the harbor.

"Steady as she goes!" shouted Mr. Hiller into the voicetube. "It looks like we've made it! Keep your fingers crossed, but by the miserable gods of the sea, I think we have! Tonight we'll get some decent chow and some decent sleep!"

Between towering black rocks we moved cautiously, our speed back up to six knots; and ahead in the gathering shades of evening was the unsteady butt of the *419*. Ahead, we knew, was the mouth of Manus Harbor; and beyond that sanctuary and a return to something like normalcy. The water inside the narrow entrance to the harbor was considerably calmer than what we had been traversing, and it was easy to imagine that we were quite close to some substantial dock.

In the pilothouse one of the Army transceivers began to spit and sputter, causing me to quit the engine controls. It was the *Splendid One*, calling Manus Base, requesting permission to enter the harbor. Manus came back loud and clear:

"*Spendid One*, you are cleared to enter the harbor. Stand by for a priority message. Do you roger?"

The *1318* rogered.

The date-and-time group, precedence, and place of origin followed. The message, from the Base C. O., was that one of the subchasers would have to remain outside the harbor and patrol until eight hundred hours the following morning. The others would be allowed to enter. The C. O. of the *1318* was to make the choice and advise Base.

The *Splendid Eight* rogered.

For a good minute there wasn't a sound in the pilothouse of the *995*. Mr. Hiller seemed to be tongue-tied. He sputtered, turned red in the face and began shaking his head vigorously. "There is no damned way we'll git saddled with that!"

I was holding the mike, waiting for instructions. He snatched it from me, looked at it, and shouted, "How do I turn this sonofabitch on?"

"*Splendid One* is going to call us any second, Sir."

"I don't want to talk to them! I want to talk to Manus Base Radio!"

Jines, down in the radio shack, shouted, "It won't do any good, Skipper! That radio operator is just following orders."

But Mr. Hiller began flipping switches on the Army transceivers, and seeing a light come one, he shouted, "Manus, this is *Splendid Five!* Tell your C. O. it's impossible for us to remain outside the harbor tonight! We have no charts of the region and our radar's on the blink!"

After a moment there came the hiss and a crackle of a transmitter opening up, then a crisp, authoritative voice said, "*Splendid Five*, there will be no further plain language on this frequency! Manus Base Radio off and clear."

"That didn't sound like an enlisted man!" shouted Mr. Hiller.

At that moment, the Splendid One came on with a very short, succinct message: "The *Splendid Five* will patrol outside the harbor until zero-eight-hundred tomorrow."

In the dim light of the pilothouse the Skipper's face was registering shock. But he calmly handed me the mike, "Tell the *Splendid One* we will not remain outside the harbor tonight! We're going in!"

I rogered the message, using plain language, and added, "We are unable to comply with the order to remain outside the harbor. This ship has no chart of the region." Then I put the mike down and stood back.

"Ready on the engines controls," said the Skipper.

Ahead in the gathering dusk we could still make out the fantail of the *419*; and as Martinez came awake at the engine controls, we saw two big ocean-going tugs nose toward each other from opposite sides of the harbor entrance. The timing was perfect. Within seconds of the *419's* entrance into the harbor, the tugs joined and secured the nets! Then, as the Skipper fumed and shook his fist at them, they beat a hasty retreat back the way they had come.

Manus, it seemed had just become submarine-and subchaser-proof for the night!

"Well, that did it!" Mr. Hiller shouted. Then he ran frantically out of the pilothouse and up to the bridge and shouted through a megaphone, "All right! Somebody's going to pay for this night's work!"

In the pilothouse, a new arrival, Leafdale, said caustically, "Yeah, and I know who it's going to be."

It was at about this point that the realization of our predicament began to strike home. We were outside the harbor, easy prey for any Japanese sub that might happen along. We had no radar, our sonar was useless, and a pitch black night was upon us!

The message had said, "Patrol outside the harbor." It was unclear just how we were supposed to do that. Any movement on our part was likely to end in disaster. With radar we might have been able to avoid running into something, and with up-to-date charts perhaps we could have stayed in deep water; but with neither we were blind and lost. The sonar gear was double-pinging and quadruple-pinging its message of death from all directions.

Someone suggested that we anchor right where we were. Maybe there was no Jap sub in the area, and if there were maybe it would not see us!

"Let's get back out to sea!" yelled the Skipper. "At least let's do something! If we had enough fuel oil, we'd sure as heck go back to Hollandia!"

Mr. Howorth observed quietly to the bridge watch, "We can't stay still an' we can't move about. Looks like that Base Commander has done put us in a fix."

"Sharkey! Stay on the sonar!" barked the Skipper, returning from the bridge. "We better ping for subs tonight!"

Sharkey's head and shoulders came out of the sonar cubicle: "Okay, but I gotta tell you all I'm gettin' is solid pings—from all directions."

We cautiously reversed the ship's heading and began to work our perilous way back out through the quarter of a mile of entrance. It was so narrow it gave the appearance and feel of a canal, and the lookouts knew we had to keep to the center or we would run aground. Darkness was settling in fast, along with a heavy mist that seemed to be coming in from the sea.

"We're not going to make it!" moaned the Skipper. "Git Tabor up on the bow again!"

But just as the words came out of his mouth the ship's keel touched something solid momentarily, causing a shudder to run from bow to stern. It was nothing and yet it sent a wave of fear through everyone of us that dwarfed anything we had experienced during the last three stormy days.

"All engines stop!" shouted Mr. Hiller.

But as the controls clicked and the engines died, again we felt a shudder run through the ship. We were scraping the bottom! And this time, just as we came to a dead stop in the water, we felt rather than heard something snap beneath us! The ship seemed to be balanced and resting solidly on the bottom! Then we heard the slow grinding sound of rock against the ship's keel!

McCormick was back, wanting to know what that sound was. He was certain something had broken off. Jines' terrified voice came up from the radio shack, "We've lost our sonar head! And there's a big water-spout down here!"

This information I shouted into the voicetube, for the Skipper, who was back on the bridge.

Through the tube from the bridge came, "Get Vanderveen on the double! Tell him to get the bilge pump set up in the radio shack!"

As if he had expected just such an emergency, the motormack showed up almost instantly with a big, clumsy pump that had to be manually operated. He began cursing and shoving his way through the pilothouse. The huge pump went through the small hatch, but only barely.

"Gang way!" he kept shouting.

At the hatch opening of the radio shack I grabbed one end of the pump and maneuvered it down the ladder to the deck of the radio shack. Vanderveen's big butt squeezed through the narrow hatchway behind the pump. Across the room, a four-inch column of water was spouting almost to the ceiling! There was already a foot of water in the shack and the level was rising rapidly on the bulkheads and the wardroom door!

"This pump will never handle that much water!" screamed Vanderveen, trying to reach the Skipper, who had come down to the pilothouse. "We're not going to make it!"

"What do you mean?" Mr. Hiller bawled at the hatchway.

"I mean, Skipper, we're sinking! We're goin' down!"

"Vanderveen, just start the pump and shut up!"

"We're not goin' to make it," Vanderveen repeated to me. "You better get on that radio quick!" To Jines, who was at the top of the ladder, he warned, "It's gonna git crowded in here in about a minute!"

At that moment the Skipper leaned through the hatch and yelled, "Hall, get on that Navy radio and call Manus and tell those half-wits we're goin' down! Evidently, they turned off their harbor frequencies, but on that thing you should be able to get them!"

"You mean use C. W., Sir?" I asked, doubtfully, already flipping switches on the big TDE transmitter. "This thing just might short out any minute, with all this water down here!" I had stepped up into the only chair in the shack, a swivel rocker, and Jines was clinging to the ladder right above my head. Vanderveen, grunting like a large hog, continued to thrash about in the rapidly rising water.

"I'm just in the way, here on this ladder," said Jines. "Let me know if I can help."

Mr. Hiller shouted over his shoulder, "Stick with that damned thing, Hall! Start sending S. O. S. and don't stop till I say so!"

"It won't do any good!" complained Vanderveen, struggling to get the bilge pump up to maximum. He had moved the pump to the other end of the narrow compartment, in Carpenter's little office nook, and so had to relay messages through me to the Skipper, except when the Skipper was hanging through the hatchway opening.

"Tell the Captain I think we better abandon ship," said Van.

I relayed the message and received a quick reply from the Skipper.

"Tell him to git the lead out and stop being so negative!"

The water was well above Vanderveen's knees by now, and I had moved on top of the radio desk, still trying to dip the final of the old transmitter.

"We're going to lose our main power source any minute," announced the motormack. "Tell him that and if he intends to do anything, he'd better do it quick."

Working frantically at the Neanderthal transmitter, I managed to dip the final tube and zero-beat the Navy's calling frequency, to which the Hallicrafters receiver had been tuned. This despite the water, Vanderveen, and the chaos. Using the brass key, which had seen very little use since World War One, I began to tap out *dididit dahdahdah dididit,* the international distress signal, S. O. S.

"I haven't sent code in so long this sounds like a ham novice playing around with a manual key," I said to whatever head was hanging through the hatch.

"What're you sending?" called the Skipper. His head and shoulders were hanging through the hatch opening. "Send our position every once in awhile. To hell with radio silence!"

"It won't do us any good," said Vanderveen. "We'll be sunk in thirty minutes."

"You want me to send the word *Manus*, Sir?" I asked.

"Send the sonofabitch! We're in a bad situation and *Manus* is to blame for it!"

"We're goin' down with this sucker!" laughed Vanderveen, his voice high-pitched, almost hysterical. "You realize that, don't you, Hall?"

I shrugged, "Probably. But we're sitting on a rock already."

"Hang on there, Hall, as long as you can!" called the Skipper from the pilothouse. "It may not do any good, but it's worth a try!" After a long pause, he added, "That goddamned brass over there on the beach couldn't care less whether we sink or not."

"We're taking on about four inches of water every ten minutes!" said Vanderveen, raising his voice just loud enough for the Skipper to hear him.

"Have you got it working right?"

"It never was meant to handle Old Faithful!" laughed the motormack bitterly.

"Nevertheless, get it up to maximum!"

Van began to curse and complain, but it wasn't directed at the Skipper, whom he admired a great deal, and not at me, whom he still thought of as a kid recently out of boot camp, but at the slings and arrows he had suffered aboard the ship since the first day he stepped across the gangplank. He gave Baldini top billing despite his absence, and spent some time on lousy chow and the cramped quarters aboard the ship and Milleson and Tracy and Pills, who were canker sores that he was being forced to live with. I half-listened, shaking my head, getting my little distress message down pat.

Then the lights went out, and Vanderveen, anxious to leave, sloshed through the water to the voicetube to the engineroom, which was just inside the wardroom door. I heard him tell Milleson to throw the emergency power and then get the hell out of the engineroom.

"How deep is it?" called the Skipper. "Think we ought to abandon ship?"

"You astin' me?" came Vanderveen's voice from the darkness. "I made that suggestion thirty minutes ago. Hell, yes, and be fast about it!"

"What do you think, Hall?"

"I think we ought to get the crew off, just in case, Skipper."

"You're right," he said. "That's exactly what I was thinking." He disappeared and a moment later he was heard giving Tracy and Milleson orders to lower the life rafts and prepare to abandon ship. When he came back, he said, "I told them to stand off a distance and get ready to pick us up. Everybody's leaving but us three."

"Wait a minute!" said Van, sounding excited. "Something's goin' on."

"What?" demanded the Skipper.

"The water flow's slowin' down."

"The hell you say!"

I could tell by the sound the water was making it had settled a lot. It was definitely no longer coming through like a geyser!

"I think we're settlin' on top of somethin'," said Van.

Then, while we stood in the waist-deep water with the Captain leaning down through the hatchway, we heard the unmistakable sound of the ship adjusting itself!

"Well, can you believe that!" exclaimed Vanderveen. "Whatever we're sittin' on must fit us pretty well! The water's just about stopped!"

"Some god of the sea—" began the Skipper, happily.

"Skipper," I pleaded, "if you don't mind, I would just as soon you did-n't get the attention of any gods of the sea again! That could have been what started all our problems in the first place!"

"Nah!" laughed Mr. Hiller. Then with a lusty laugh he went to notify the crew to return aboard.

"Of course," said Vanderveen, "we could slide off this rock at any minute and that'd put us right back where we was before."

"You mean you think we're on a *small* rock?" I asked. "Couldn't it be the bottom of this channel?"

"Not likely. Can't you feel the ship kinda pivotin'?"

Indeed, the ship was wallowing just a bit, as though it were perched on top of a rather pointed rock, a rock just big enough to fit into the sonar hole! The thought caused me to laugh.

"You better be serious, kid! We're not out of this yet!"

While the motormack removed as much water from the shack as he could, I turned off all the radio equipment and climbed out to the pilot-house. I heard the Skipper telling Cookie to get his ass below and cook the crew some food. "By God," he said, "we'll eat and sleep tonight as well as anybody inside that damned harbor, sitting here on solid ground. Aint no Jap sub comin' in here to git us in water this shallow!"

"If he only knew what a little pebble we're sittin' on!" Van wise-cracked.

*   *   *

Unbeknownst to me and the others on the *995*, an amateur radio operator in Seattle, Washington, had picked up my S. O. S. message on his civilian receiver well before midnight, Manus time; but since it was wartime and hams couldn't fire up their transmitters, he was unable to respond directly to the call for help. Instead, he made a phone call to Navy Radio in Seattle, informing a startled WAVE telephone operator of the *995's* predicament. Seattle hastily relayed the information to San

Francisco, whence it was booted out to Honolulu. Comsopac, just before daylight Manus time, fired an angry plain language missile westward, addressed to the C. O. of the Manus Naval Facility. This message was not picked up by Manus. Luckily, a Navy radio operator on a tincan anchored at Guam rogered for it and, an hour or so later, managed to pass it on to a cruiser steaming off Hollandia, New Guinea. Finally, just as the harbor nets were about to be withdrawn in Manus Harbor (The tugs were already on their way down the long approach to the gates), my S. O. S. reached Manus Base Radio!

Suddenly, our little pilothouse was filled with a mighty blast from the main transmitter at Manus Base:

"*Splendid Five*, are you there?"

It was never clear to anyone aboard the *995* what kind of dressing down the Base Commander received for forcing a ship without charts and radar to remain outside the harbor during a pitch-black night, or whether he was even reprimanded at all. But on that bright, lovely morning that followed our memorable night of hell, there occurred the following exchange between mighty Manus Base and our lowly subchaser:

"Calling *Splendid Five*. This is Manus. Over."

The chipper voice was issuing from one of the Army transceivers in the pilothouse, where Sharkey, Tracy, McCormick, the Skipper, and I were standing around sipping weak coffee.

The Skipper had just remarked that the only thing he knew to do was gun the shit out of the Chryslers and try to hop off that rock and make it well inside the harbor before we sank. Whoever was on the helm could maneuver in close to land so that we wouldn't have far to swim. We would miss the first landing on the Philippines, but sure as hell we would get some R and R.

"Who said that?" demanded the Skipper, looking at the rack of transceivers. "Did he say 'Manus'?"

I nodded, picked up the mike, and said into it, "This is the *Splendid Five*. Go ahead, Manus."

"Hey, we just got the dangedest message about you guys! Are you still afloat out there?"

"Are we still 'afloat'?" shouted Mr. Hiller, getting redder by the second. "Tell that two-bit that through no fault of his we are!"

"It's evidently someone at Manus Radio who hasn't been brought up to date on last night," I suggested, trying to decided how to translate the Skipper's message.

Just as I lifted the mike to speak, the Skipper lunged for it and wrestled it from me.

"Yes, you stupid jerk! We're still afloat and we're still 'outside the nets'! We're sitting on a rock, and when we git off, we're going to ram that damn building you're in!"

For a long moment there was only a frying sound in the speaker; then a conciliatory voice said, "This is Manus. We had no idea you were sinking! I've got to tell you the night shift here pulls some good ones. What's your situation right now?"

"Sir, could I reply to that?" I asked, reaching for the mike. "He's just a radioman."

But Mr. Hiller wasn't quite finished with the mike. He nodded to me, grinned viciously, and shouted into the mike, "Our situation is critical here!" With that he tossed the mike to me and left.

Within minutes Manus Radio had apologized profusely. The two big tugs at the mouth of the harbor were reportedly on their way to give us a tow, and the world's largest sea-going drydock just happened to be available to take us as soon as we could reach it!

I went up on the bridge, where the Skipper was looking moodily off in the direction of the harbor entrance.

"Sir, the nets are opening now, and we're supposed to stand by to be towed to the drydock about halfway up the harbor."

Mr. Hiller wheeled about with a disgusted snort, "If they think we'll fart along with those slow ass tugs while we're taking on a foot of god-damned saltwater every five minutes, they're crazy. We'll show them a thing or two!" With that he leaned over the voicetube and shouted, "Engines ahead full! Mack, let's go to that drydock!"

16

Tokyo Rose

It was five stories high and the subchaser looked like a rowboat inside it. We had seen it the instant we came barreling around the bend in the harbor, and there was no doubt in anybody's mind about it being the world's largest sea-going drydock.

Without backing the engines off a knot, the Skipper took the water-logged *SC-995* right up to the drydock, within range of a monkey's fist, before putting her in reverse and killing her. And from that point on she was out of his and Vanderveen's hands.

With the engines dead and two feet of water in the wardroom and radio shack, all hands lined up along the lifeline to watch the giant mouth swallow the ship and ourselves. Once the enormous sliding door closed us in, the water level began to drop rapidly; and within an hour the ship was high and dry inside a cradle on the floor of the drydock.

Two ladders were places on the port side; and without so much as a glance toward the stern (much less a salute), July Roucloux and I strad-dled the gunwale, climbed down, crossed the floor of the drydock, and climbed up another ladder to the walkway that went around the two sides and back.

The subchaser looked small and tired there on her pedestal in that great arena. She did not look like something that had crossed the great Pacific Ocean with two dozen men aboard her.

Mr. Hiller, wearing a wrinkled khaki uniform, complete with tie and cap, suddenly appeared at the door of the pilothouse of the little ship. July and I watched as he climbed to the bridge and removed the megaphone from its holder.

"Now, hear this," he said into it, speaking in a normal voice. "I want all hands to fall in on the double! I've got a few things to say."

"I guess we went to all that trouble for nothin'," said July. "Why did I let you talk me into this?"

No one had talked him into anything. I took off back down that five-story ladder without a word, and I could hear him scrambling behind me. We finally made it to the quarterdeck, out of breath and looking like two recalcitrant school boys tardy for school

"This is not going to be a picnic," Mr. Hiller was saying. "I've just been talking to Base on the landline, and, unsurprisingly, we're at the bottom of the Navy's shitlist. I was informed that there will be a Board of Inquiry convened about Baldini's disappearance. And, to cap that off, the Base Commander here thinks I ran the ship aground deliberately, to get out of the next skirmish. Anyway, we can speed things up by working around the clock on the hull. I want it completely scraped and painted by the time our sonar head has been replaced and the other repairs have been made. We *will* be ready for the big convoy that's preparing to head west, one way or the other!"

Sharkey groaned, "There goes our R and R."

"I'm headed over to Base Headquarters right now to arrange for some replacements, check on our mail, and have a chat with the Base Commander. I want the Port Section to fall in on the dock and, once the scaffolding has been put in place, begin on the scraping. Starboard Section, you can go ashore but you had better be back here by noon. I will be back by then and if any of you want to spend your time in port aboard this ship, just screw up. The Port Section will be ashore from twelve to sixteen-hundred hours."

Already tied up to the starboard side of the drydock, out of sight of us, was a fourteen-foot wooden boat with the words "Base Personnel" painted on the bow. In the stern, propped against the waist-high railing, was a coxswain in undress whites smoking a cigarette and listening to a small radio. He watched the two low-ranking officers making their way down the long, uncertain ladder, thankful that he was not in their shoes. He had watched the sorry little thing that had brought them to this drydock, and it was his considered opinion that such trash should not be allowed inside the harbor.

Having timed exact;u the arrival of his passengers so that he would not have to wait, he finally pulled himself to his feet, threw away his cigarette, bent at the waist and turned off the radio, and started up the motor. All in one admirably fluid movement.

Mr. Hiller and Mr. Howorth were engaged in conversation as they stepped into the boat and prepared to sit down. Before they were fully settled, the coxswain began to work his end of the boat against the landing at the foot of the ladder, which forced the bow outward. Then, without a glance in the direction of the officers, he tossed the line to the dock and full-throttled the engine.

Having to shout to make himself heard, Mr. Hiller said to his Exec, "I want you to punch me in the ribs every time I begin to lose my temper. I'm afraid I'll knock hell out of somebody!"

Mr. Howorth nodded, grinning. "Just remembah that you don't want to be beached heah fo' the duration. If we play ouah cards right, we'll be out of heah inside a week."

"Damn right we will. Let's go by the Officers Club first."

"I don't think that'd be a good idee, Bill. Let's save that till later."

Ten minutes later the coxswain cut his motor and swung the boat expertly in a circle and brought it alongside a dock. The officers stood up and Mr. Hiller stepped out of the boat. The coxswain, timing it right again, the instant Mr. Howorth's weight left the boat, he cut the motor, flipped on the radio, and settled into his spot.

"Sounds like stateside music," commented Mr. Hiller, as they strolled down the long dock. "I wonder where that's coming from?"

Mr. Howorth stopped, held up a hand for the Skipper to wait, and retraced his steps to the boat. Within a minute he was back, "That was Tokyo Rose direct. You know, Bill, I can't understand how the Japs git their hands on the latest Stateside hits. Most of the stuff AFS puts on was around at the beginning of the war." After a time he pointed toward a row of quonset buildings, "I reckon thaet must be the Personnel Office up theah, thaet first one on the right."

"Good. Let's go get this over with."

"Remembah, now."

At the door of Base Personnel, Mr. Hiller hesitated, his knuckles raised. Then with a determined look on his face, he opened the door and entered. Mr. Howorth was right behind him.

A Yeoman First Class in starched and pressed undress whites turned and looked at him across a long, chest-high counter.

"We're here to see the Commander," said Mr. Hiller. And before he could identify himself and Mr. Howorth, the yeoman said:

"I'm afraid he's busy, Sir. If you would like, take a seat over there."

"We have an appointment," said Mr. Hiller, frowning.

"You can either wait or come back later, Sir."

At this point, the Exec said to the Skipper, "Remembah, now," which caused the latter to say:

"Let's go get a drink. So we can put up with this kind of shit."

"Maybe this man could announce us to the Commandah," said Mr. Howorth, approaching the counter. "Let him know weah heah."

"He's not in the office right now, Sir. Like I said."

"When will he be back?"

"I don't have the slightest idea, Sir."

"Let's go," snapped Mr. Hiller, already heading for the door.

"If the C. O. gits in eny time soon, tell 'im we'll be right back," said Mr. Howorth. Without waiting for a reply, he turned and followed the

Skipper. He found him on the little front stoop studying the neat double row of quonset buildings on their right.

"I see it," announced the Skipper. "The one on the right at the end."

The ensign nodded. "Bill, if we start likkerin' up, you know what'll happen. Remembah that night in Noumea an' the buttahfly rum?"

"Yeah, I remember. Okay, we'll stick to beer."

"Two beahs, an' no mo'. Right?"

An hour later they were back at Personnel, having put down three cold Lucky Lagers apiece. The Commander, they were informed, was still not on deck.

"But he'll be here any minute, Sir," said the yeoman, with a glance in Mr. Howorth's direction. "He called from Ship's Stores." After a pause, he asked, "Isn't your ship that subchaser that went into the drydock this morning?"

Mr. Howorth nodded, impressed.

"Well, I just heard Tokyo Rose say that the drydock has been targeted by the Japanese Navy. She didn't say when it would happen, but according to her, there's a sub in these parts, maybe already inside the harbor."

Mr. Hiller was staring at him. "You don't put any stock in such talk, do you?"

"She said the drydock has been targeted, Sir."

"What the hell! They still bombing this far out?"

"I guess they intend to torpedo the drydock, Sir."

"But they can't git inside this harbor, not with those dadblamed nets across the mouth at night!"

"Generally there's a little truth to just about everything she brags about, Sir. When she mentions specific places—"

At that point a bald head with flabby jowls appeared in the open doorway behind the yeoman. On the collars of his khaki shirt were the silver clusters of a full commander.

"Hiller?"

"Yes, Sir."

"Come in here." To the yeoman, who had leaped to attention, he growled, "Get us some coffee, Dewey."

It was on the tip of Mr. Hiller's tongue to decline the offer of coffee, but Mr. Howorth raised one finger at him, just in time. The yeoman lifted a leaf in the counter and they filed through to the open doorway toward the rear.

"Your fellow LCC officers are over at the Supply Depot," said the Commander, making no attempt to shake hands with the two of them. "Why is it you don't play ball with the others, Lieutenant?" He waved them toward a row of cushioned chairs that faced his desk.

"Begging your pardon, Sir," said Mr. Hiller, "but it is a bit difficult to play ball with anybody when you are forced to patrol outside a harbor for which you have no charts and especially when your radar is out."

"I'm aware of what you've been through," snapped the Commander. "And I didn't mean actually playing ball. According to this" (The Commander pointed toward a folder on his desk), "you've been up to something ever since you took command of that—wooden boat. Which, by the way, you ran into the rocks last night."

"We found ourselves in a no-win situation, Sir. We couldn't stay where we were, and visibility was too poor to move."

"Then what in hell were you doing when you hit that rock?"

"We were headed for the open sea, Sir."

The commander and the lieutenant, junior grade, stared at each other for a time.

"I do not understand why any of the subchasers had to stay out, Sir, given what we've been through and the shortness of our fuel supply. Not to mention our vulnerability and—"

"Are you criticizin' Base Operations, Sir?" The Commander's voice was soft and cajoling. The cat was getting ready to pounce.

Mr. Howorth adjusted himself in his chair nervously, managing to elbow the Skipper in the side as he did so. This, however, did not stop the Lieutenant from saying:

"I'm just not clear about why we weren't given an opportunity to turn in a damage report before being ordered to patrol outside the harbor."

"Hiller, you're a young, cocksure, conceited maverick," said the Commander, pulling a cigarette out of his desk and lighting it. "Smoke if you like, gentlemen."

The Skipper and Mr. Howorth declined.

"I suspect you're bankin' on that old man of yours saving your ass from the messes you've got yourself in, going as far back as Auckland."

"'Messes', Sir?"

"Hell, do you think the Navy's that stupid? I refer to that affair in Auckland, which led to your C. O.'s irreconcilable differences with his spouse and your present rank of lieutenant, junior grade. Hell, you would have been a junior grade commander by now if you had kept your record clean. But, no! And how about the theft of two PT-boat motors in New Caledonia, the loss at sea somewhere north of New Guinea of your boatswain's mate, and running your ship aground, right outside my place of business! Hell, even your old man—"

"My father knows nothing about any of this, Sir."

"The hell he doesn't." The Commander carefully sent three smoke rings toward the overhead, all the while studying the Lieutenant out of the corner of his eyes. "But it would take Nimitz to get you out of this last thing."

Mr. Hiller glanced around at Mr. Howorth, rolled his eyes, then turned to the Commander. "I was hoping you might be willing to listen to my side of the story—Sir."

"Hell, there shouldn't be any your 'side of the story'! There shouldn't be any side at all. I laughed when I heard about the damned motors you stole and put in that wooden boat of yours, but I stopped laughing when I heard about that boatswain's mate. What the hell kind of a crew do you have on that rowboat? Did they actually push him over the side?"

"The boatswain's mate was pretty hard on the men, Sir. And twenty men crowded together like that, day in and day out, with no recreation equipment or space to use it if they had any and—"

At this point Mr. Howorth broke in, "I think it's a bit surprisin', suh, that only one man has been pushed over the side. 'Y, Commander, our ship is just a little over one hundred feet long and below decks in the daytime it is quite often like an oven. We have no storage space for fresh water or food, and when we submit a requisition for something, we always seem to end up with crackers and peaches. There's no library or phonograph or much of anything that might give the men something to do. Twenty-one men are billeted in two small compartments that are not even ventilated. And add to this a boatswain's mate that was busted from CPO and therefore out to torment and aggravate every enlisted man aboard the ship. By the time he disappeared, the crew was ready to jump over the side themselves."

"My God!" burst out the Commander. "And, of course, they didn't consult you about pushing him over the side. Did they draw straws?"

Mr. Hiller shrugged, glanced at the ensign, "We have no clue as to what actually happened, sir. It's possible he fell over the side. The ship was rolling badly, and the deck was slick."

"Well, it appears to me your men need some R and R. Now that you're out of the next party, they should be able get plenty. By the way, most of my officers and *all* of the officers of the other LCC's think you deliberately ran aground to get out of—"

At this point Mr. Hiller stood up quickly. "Our main concern, Sir, and I assure you I'm speaking for my entire crew when I say this, is to get the ship ready for the next—party."

The Commander's eyebrows went up: "I didn't say I think you're yellow, Lieutenant. Remember, I know where you came from." He motioned for Mr. Hiller to be seated. "What's the extent of your damages?"

"Our repairs will be minor. We need a new paint job, which will take maybe three days."

"Well, I'll be damned!" The Commander was visibly pleased. "Tell you what, if you can get that thing in shape and get out of here with the convoy, I'll do what I can to have the charges against you cleared up. Now, what do you need in the way of supplies and equipment?"

"Mainly beer and something to chew on, Sir," said Mr. Hiller with a grin. "And I've worked out a requisition for a few other things."

"Okay, I'll give you clearance for Ship's Stores and the Supply Depot for anything you need that we've got." He stood up, shaking his head and smiling. "I'm glad we had this chat." He stuck out his hand to Mr. Howorth, "Where'd you go to school, Ensign?"

"Virginuh, Suh."

"Good school." He turned to Mr. Hiller, his hand extended, "Oh, by the way, I served under your old man back during the first big one. I've heard him speak of you as enterprising and resourceful. Tough old sailor—and one hell of a good poker player."

"Thank you, Sir." Lt. Hiller's face was deadpan.

Outside, the two officers once again faced the neat avenue of quonset buildings. Mr. Howorth was shaking his head in amazement. "All this time and not a word about your old man being an admiral! You're second generation Navy?"

"Fifth. The first Hiller that made it to the States joined the Coast Guard, back when there was no U. S. Navy."

*   *   *

"Hey, Sparks, pipe us some Stateside music down here!" shouted Sharkey, from his lofty perch on the scaffold. "Can't you tune in WGN Chicago? Anything, for Christ's sake! Leavy's about to drive me nuts!"

Leavy was working beside Sharkey, and each time he shifted his massive weight the entire scaffold shuddered and threatened to collapse. But it was his groaning and farting and other body noises that the sonarman found particularly disgusting.

"I'll see what I can do," I said, looking over the gunwale at the two.

A few minutes later I lowered a speaker over the port bow, not far from Sharkey but safely out of Leavy's reach and influence. It was already emitting big-band music.

"I think it's AFS!" I called down. "Sorry, but I couldn't get WGN!"

"Well, hell!" said Sharkey. "An' you call yourself a radio man."

Then a very soft and sexy voice broke into the music, "Hello, American sailors and soldiers so far away from home! This is your second best girlfriend, Rose, bringing you the very best in American music. And today I have vehee important message for the sailor boys way down on Manus Island! I hope you are listening, Admiralty Islands! But relax now and think about your sweetheart back home while I play the hottest thing on the Hit Parade, 'I'll Be Seeing You', just recorded by no other than Mister Frank Sinatra himself."

"Hey, fellas!" yelled Sharkey. "This's comin' from Tokyo Rose!"

"Turn up the volume!" somebody on the other side of the ship called out.

For close to an hour the scrapers on both sides of the ship were entertained by the honey-voiced Rose, and among the songs we heard for the very first time since leaving home were "Now Is the Hour," sung by Gracie Fields, "Polka Dots and Moonbeams," with Johnny Burke doing the crooning, and Nat Burton and Walter Kent singing "The White Cliffs of Dover."

Near the end of her broadcast, Rose broke in with, "Now, lover boys, I've got a song that I want to dedicate to those of you who have received 'Dear John' letters. Here it is!"

The song, 'Don't Sit Under the Apple Tree', went the distance without one wisecrack; and at the end, someone from the drydock repair crew far above our heads on the starboard side yelled, "Get ready! Now comes the shinola!"

"What shinola?" Sharkey wanted to know.

"Haven't you boys heard yet?" came the reply.

"Wouldn't it be wonderful to be home where it is safe?" asked the soft, seductive voice. "Where you could hear such good music all the time? You do not deserve to be killed so far away from those that love you and want you there with them. Have you ever asked yourself why you are way off in the Pacific Ocean? Why the American government has forced you to travel so far from home and fight in a war that you cannot win, a war that hate mongers started?"

"Shit," said Sharkey, grumpily, "who wouldn't want to be home?"

"But now I must tell you some vehee bad news."

"Here it comes!" shouted the sailor high atop the starboard side of the drydock.

"To the lonely sailors on the big sea-going drydock at Manus—" From both sides of the subchaser came startled cries of, "Oh, shit!"

"Shut the hell up!" shouted Sharkey. "Let's hear what she has to say!"

But the noise had blocked Tokyo Rose out. All we heard was the tail end of something about a sub parked on the bottom of the harbor. The voice had hardened, "Go back to your soft life, American sailor, or you will be killed!" Then from a distance, surrounded by soft background music, the old seductive voice purred once again, "Goodbye, now, from your second best sweetheart, Tok'yo, Rose!"

"How does she know about this drydock?" demanded Sharkey, alarmed. "That's weird!"

A dock worker had paused on the runway above Sharkey and Leavy and was looking down at them. "Don't worry about it. She's just tryin' to git us all hot and bothered. Tomorrow, she'll scare the shit out of somebody else."

"Yeah, well, she's sure as hell spooked me!"

*   *   *

The next morning early the Starboard Section of the *995* crew settled in on the recently re-positioned scaffolding, this time with paint buckets and brushes. The main topic of conversation concerned the scuttlebutt that had just reached them, that they would be at it until midnight, or until the entire starboard side was covered with red lead.

My section had knocked off around one that morning, having completed our side of the ship. Now, liberated until midday, we lowlies of the forecastle filed noisily topside, dressed in clean, faded dungarees. Everyone except me was carrying three bottles of warm Griesedieck beer; but, having no stomach for that foul-smelling stuff, I had packed three warm Pepsi Colas and several Hersey Tropical Chocolate Bars into a small cardboard box. We went down the steep ladder on the exterior port side of the drydock and boarded the waiting LCVP.

This was our first trip ashore, and we were headed for the enlisted men's beach at the Navy base.

Sharkey had dug out some ancient cigars from a secret storage place and was offering them for sale to the highest bidders. His minimum price, he told Leavy, was five dollars or one bottle of warm Griesedieck. He found no takers on this occasion, since the Paymaster had not made the rounds since we had been in the drydock.

"I'll give you a Pepsi for two of them," I offered.

"Shit, don't insult me," moaned Sharkey. "These are genuine Havanas, from New Caledonia."

The LCVP, gurgling contentedly, eased away from the drydock and headed up the harbor, weaving its way among the anchored ships. The coxswain, after listening to Sharkey for two minutes said he would bet five-dollars he could guess where the sonarman was from.

"I'll cover that bet with one of these cigars," said Sharkey.

"You got a match?"

"Hell, yes, but you won't need one."

"Hah. It's a bet. My five against one of your cigars. I've got witnesses."

"Put your money where your mouth is."

"Chicago, north side, probably Morningside Heights."

Sharkey's mouth dropped open and he lost temporary control of the cigars. "Well, I'll be goddamned! Who told you?"

"Nobody told me, buddy! That's where I'm from, too!"

The LCVP, on its own, was plowing down the harbor on a collision course with a tanker riding high in the water.

"Watch out!" bellowed Leavy, humping over in the boat and covering his head with his hands.

Roucloux grabbed one of my Pepsis and flung it at the coxswain, yelling, "Turn this sonsabitch to one side or the other!"

The Pepsi missed its mark and went sailing across the bow of a passing boat. At the last possible second the unperturbed coxswain heeled the boat on its butt and missed the tanker by about a foot. At no time did he stop flapping his mouth at Sharkey.

Once we were back on an even keel, I casually reached over and removed a bottle of Griesedieck from Roucloux's cardboard box. July, looking stunned, shouted, "Christ, man, I saved your life back there!"

"Next time save it with somebody else's Pepsi," I told him with a grin. "Besides, you'll never finish off two Griesediecks. Three's too much for any one person to drink."

At that moment, from some distance behind us came a mighty VAROOM! It sounded as if the whole western half of the harbor had exploded! A moment later, as I climbed up on the gunwale to see over the elevated stern of the boat, I felt a powerful puff of wind; and when I looked around, the entire Port Section was flattened out on the deck of the barge. The coxswain was down on all fours, with his hand still on the steering mechanism. It was about this time that I saw a great ball of black smoke down the harbor, from whence we had just come.

"What in hell—!" somebody began, his words interrupted by another ear-splitting explosion.

"It's comin' from around that point!" yelled the coxswain, who had risen and was pointing back the way we had come. "About where the drydock was located!"

Roucloux cautiously poked his head over the tall starboard gunwale, where I was kneeling; but he said nothing. In fact, it had gotten very quiet in that LCVP.

Black, heavy clouds were filling the sky in the western end of the harbor!

Sharkey, hunkered down next to the coxswain, spoke what was on everybody's mind, "Tokyo Rose called it right, fellas! That had to be the drydock!"

I finally said to July, "The whole Starboard Section!"

"Turn this sucker around and take us back!" ordered Sharkey, rising and nudging the coxswain in the back.

"Can't do that, old buddy! I'm gittin' outta here an' you guys are comin' with me! Either that or you can swim!"

"If that's the way you feel about it" yelled Sharkey, "goddamn you, you swim!" And with that he grabbed the surprised coxswain around the legs and hoisted him over the stern of the boat. Then he turned in my direction and began waiving his hands, "Hey, somebody, git up there on the double, before we run into something!" I scrambled up to the controls and, after a bit of wild maneuvering, got the boat turned around.

Explosions continued to occur down the harbor. These were accompanied by new clouds of purple-black smoke, which rose above the outcropping of land that separated us from the drydock and our helpless little ship.

"I think it's a Jap bombing attack!" screamed Roucloux. "The drydock wouldn't keep on explodin' like that!"

With the boat at full throttle, we swept down the harbor between big transport ships, tankers, and landingcraft carriers of one kind or another, narrowly missing a number of small boats headed in our direction.

Rounding the point, where the harbor cut around to the north, we began to wave and shout like madmen: There in the distance, sitting high and safe above the water, was the drydock, a good mile from the billowing smoke of a doomed ship. It was an ammunition ship that had been anchored by itself in the center of the lower part of the harbor, quarantined as it were by custom and Navy Regs from all other ships.

Even so, we were to learn later, the force of the initial blast had been so great it had badly damaged a transport ship and two destroyers and sent a tidal wave the entire length of the long, narrow harbor.

The *SC-995*, resting in the bosom of the drydock, had been unaffected; however, (And this, too, we learned later) at their moorings two miles away, the other subchasers had not fared well at all.

We roared across the final quarter of a mile of rough water at full speed, waving and shouting like a bunch of heathens. My shipmates were completely unaware that the only thing I knew for sure about that LCVP was how to steer it! I had not the foggiest how I was going to bring it to a stop. Frantically, I searched the control panel, very much aware that the big dock was just a short distance ahead, and we were bearing down upon it at full throttle!

At the last possible second, just as heads were coming around in my direction, I found the ignition switch and cut the engine! Dead in the water, we drifted the rest of the way to the landing dock!

The Skipper was waiting for us when we climbed aboard the ship.

"I guess we were lucky after all," he said, looking pale and shaken. "The explosion sent a wall of water straight down the harbor into the dock area where the other subchasers were moored. They all sustained some water damage, but no one was hurt. It looks like the *419* won't be continuing on with us."

My newsletter, which I had named *The Splendid Five*, carried the following lead story that afternoon: "Tokyo Rose was fairly accurate today, October 1, 1944. In yesterday morning's broadcast she said that the sailors aboard the U. S. Navy's largest floating drydock had better go on shore leave because a Son of Nippon was at that very moment maneuvering for a shot at it.

"Apparently what happened was that the tin fish meant for the dry-dock missed its target and hit an ammunition ship farther out in the harbor instead.

"The ammo ship was loaded to the gunwales and took out two other ships, a tincan and an empty U. S. Army transport ship, not to mention a lot of smallcraft. It sent a tidal wave down the harbor all the way to where the other subchasers were either anchored or tied up. We're still waiting for news, but it has been reported by a reliable source that *Splendid Three* is now listing at a sixty-degree angle on a dock not far from where she was anchored; and a preliminary report says that *Splendid Eight* and *Splendid Six* received a lot of water damage, which may keep them out of the next skirmish."

17

Leyte

This time there was little doubt in anybody's mind where we were going. It had to be the Philippines. What was left, except Japan itself? Of course, the Philippines was a mighty big place; so we didn't know exactly where we would land, and we didn't know the when right down to the day and hour; but it was a good guess it would be Leyte sometime around the end of October. We knew this last because our convoy was cruising at twelve knots and two and two make four.

If anybody on the ship worried about running out of food and water on such a long trip (Ace McCormick had estimated it at around eighteen hundred nautical miles from Manus to Leyte Gulf), I heard nothing about it. Of course, we were escorting enough K-Rations and spam to feed the Western world for a decade; so maybe the thinking was that when we ran out of something we would just ease up alongside a big supply ship and holler over for it. That is, maybe our luck would change.

Boredom and apathy were our deadliest enemies now that Baldini was no longer around. We hadn't seen a Jap plane since Peleliu, but the closer we got to the Philippines the more alert we were for dots in the sky.

Some of the men, like Tracy and Milleson and Sharkey, passed a lot of time gambling with their beer futures with dice, and when they weren't doing this they were arguing about who owed whom what. Tabor spent his nights on the bridge and his days writing in his cozy little corner in the bow of the ship. What he was writing was a real mystery to me because, according to Leafdale, our unofficial mail person, he never mailed anything and he never received anything from the States.

I asked him pointblank one night what he was writing. It was such a dumb question, considering the fact he had been at it since New Caledonia and since he had never told anybody anything about himself. I really didn't expect an answer, but to my surprise he said:

"Journal."

"If you're keeping a journal, the Navy will put you away."

He looked at me for a split second, "I'm disguising it to look like a novel."

"What's the novel about?"

"Wooden subchasers and the Japs."

"Sounds interesting. How is it going to end?"

He didn't say anything for a time, and I was about to go back to the pilothouse and listen to McCormick when he said:

"I don't want to give away the plot. You might steal my thunder."

"I give you my word."

"We all git killed."

Tabor had a sense of humor, but it was so close to sarcasm most of the time no one gave him much credit for having one. I think I understood him better than anybody else on the ship, since I had grown up with a Seminole boy that reminded me a lot of him. Sasawaka was this kid's name, and I came to know him so well I could actually tell when he was laughing, when his face was deadpan. Of course, he never made a sound that could be called laughter, but he had a way of looking at you very intently for just a moment and opening his mouth a little. Tabor had just done this very same thing; so I knew he was laughing.

"Hmmm," I said, "a tragedy."

"No, it's a comedy. Don't you think it's funny that the United States would send little wooden boats into war against the Japanese Imperial Navy? I mean if that's not funny I don't know what is. In fact, it's ludicrous.

The only chance we've got of making it through this is our nothin' size and insignificance."

"I'm sure glad we're not on the *Hazelwood*," I said, just to see how far he wanted to go with that line of talk. I happened to know that he thought this Fletcher-class destroyer was the gnat's bristle.

He thought about that for a long time.

"Well, if I have to go I think that would be a good way. This is no way to go at all."

So I still didn't know what he was writing. Perhaps it was a novel. Or, for that matter, knowing what I knew about Tabor, it might have been a book of poetry. One thing for sure, he was not spending all that time in the sack doodling or sleeping. In fact, no one had ever caught him sleeping. When his curtain was drawn, you could imagine him sleeping; but the only time anyone broke his rule of privacy and drew that piece of cloth back, he was exceptionally wide awake—and fighting mad.

It was hard to tell how things were going on the other subchasers, but on the *995* we were becoming more and more like a large family of trailerhouse people. We bad-mouthed each other a lot, and at least once a day somebody grabbed up somebody else and threatened to kill him on the spot. We had stopped looking at each other, and we were no longer amused at anything anybody had to say. We had heard every conceivable thing everybody had to say, and so most of the time when somebody started to talk we would nod and agree or disagree and walk off.

The problem was, there was no place to walk to. We came face-to-face with each other a dozen times a day, and the only thing we hated more than looking at each other was looking at the ocean, the sky, and the ugly fantail of the *1066* leaping and bobbing ahead of us.

We had come to like the people on the other two subchasers more than we liked each other. We thought how nice it would be if a Jap plane would swoop down and kill a few of us, certain ones that is, make a mess of it. I continued to be on reasonably good terms with most of the men primarily because I was stuck away in the radio shack most of the time and when I did circulate I generally had something from Armed Forces Radio about the progress of the war or what was going on back in the States.

It was a curious thing, I thought, that while everybody seemed to be starved for news of the States, nobody talked about going home anymore. Milleson no longer mentioned his colorful women friends in Wichita, July Roucloux had stopped talking about San Antone, and, a real believe-it-or-not, Sharkey had shut up about Chicago.

As for myself, it was getting hard for me to remember anything specific about the States. I remembered flashes of things, little moments in time; but these were like still pictures that had no before or after. I had never gone out with a girl, and so I could not even pretend to have a sweetheart back in the States. When I heard "Peg of My Heart" the first time on shortwave radio, I fell in love with a pretty dark-skinned girl with large innocent brown eyes and long straight black hair that fell about her naked shoulders, covering her nipples. The face was Irish-Filipino, perhaps, because it was round and had a little turned-up nose and there was a hint of the Oriental about the eyes.

All of my imaginary women had the same face, but when Cookie ran out of saltpeter the body of my woman-of-the-moment began to change considerably in the breasts and about the middle. But she still wasn't three-dimensional because I just couldn't remember the real thing well enough. The only clue I had to go on was Sharkey's pin-up of Betty Grable, who had big beautiful legs and a great smile.

Sometime during the night of October 19, 1944, word was passed that we were paralleling the coast of Leyte, headed in a northerly direction. And although I had stood the midwatch, I parked myself on the bow to get a first glimpse of this new land. Roucloux joined me when he got off watch, of course, and we were still there when daylight came.

The convoy stretched for miles in either direction and was easily the largest any of us had ever seen. Only during the past three or four days had we seen anything of the Japanese; and then it was, in each instance, a dogfight in which the three or four Zekes would be trying to get away from half a dozen F6F's or P-38's.

By full daylight we were entering what turned out to be Leyte Gulf, and July and I knew from what the Skipper had said our first day out that we were heading for landing beaches between Tacloban and Dulag.

On the bridge Tabor turned and glanced at the Skipper, who was scanning westward into the heart of dark, mysterious Leyte Gulf.

"That's the *Hazelwood*."

"I think you're right. And if I don't miss my guess, we're about to get a change of orders."

Sure enough, the words were hardly out of his mouth when a tiny flicker of blinker light began to penetrate the heavy fog from the bridge of the destroyer. Tabor sent K and waited. The flashes came at us fast, almost too fast for me. It's one thing to copy CW *dit-dahs* at high speed, using a typewriter; but it's a far different thing to keep up with very fast light flashes and make words and sentences out of them. But when they paused, Tabor rogered without asking for a repeat.

Mr. Hiller lowered his glasses. "What's he saying?"

"Wants us to go to point Three One Five Five dash Twelve and remain there until further orders."

"What the hell?" moaned Mr. Hiller, obviously upset. Into the voice-tube he yelled, "Ace, bring Chart Twelve up here!" To Tabor he said, "See if you can find out what the other subchasers are doing!"

"They're getting changes, too. The *1066* will be at Three One Five Six and the *1318* at Three One Five Seven."

Ace appeared on the bridge with a large chart and spread it out across the Captain's Chair.

The Skipper leaned over it and stared. "Looks like we're going all the way to downtown Tacloban. Hell, this thing doesn't even show Three One Five Five. If there was such a number, we would practically be on the beach!"

"Well," said Ace, "it figures. We always seem to get the short end of it. I guess they found tincans to do our job at the landing beaches.

"Or maybe minesweepers."

The Gulf was full of ships of every description; and very unlike Peleliu, nobody seemed to be going in the same direction! Wave after wave of aircraft, fighters and torpedo-bombers for the most part, swept over; and in the distance off our port bow Tacloban appeared to be in flames. Great columns of smoke marked the most recent strikes in and around the city.

The rain had continued to come down, and now in the Gulf visibility had diminished to about a thousand yards.

The three subchasers, this time led by the *995*, moved down the Gulf, actually weaving among the big transports, most of which were already dead in the water. Tacloban, or what was left of it, was coming up on our port side, as we rounded a point and moved into a long, narrow cove. Behind us was a stretch of water that ended in jungle; and in front of us was a wide, sandy beach that led up to what appeared to be a long grove of palm trees.

"This is hairy," observed the Skipper, scanning the area inland from the park with glasses. "I swear we're not more than a mile from town! And I'm just hoping—"

At that moment three low-flying Jap fighters came in out of the mist, and one of them veered toward us, sending at the last moment a burst of machine-gun bullets along the beach.

"I don't like this!" yelled Mr. Hiller. "We're in a bottleneck in this cove! We have no idea how much farther we can go, and since our number's not on the chart, I think we better not proceed much farther!"

Mr. Howorth, with a pair of field glasses in one hand, observed that it was mighty strange that the *995* had been sent so far down into the cove.

"Engines stop!" blasted the Skipper. At that moment, when the ship was practically dead in the water, those on the bridge felt the keel make contact with something!

"What's the depth in here, do you suppose?" asked Mr. Howorth. "I hate to say it but I think we just touched bottom."

Mr. Hiller's face had blanched white, and he was running from one side of the bridge to the other. Then, leaning over the railing, he yelled, "Tracy, rig something to sound with! Find out how deep it is in here!"

Again those on the bridge felt, rather than heard, something touching the keel!

"I sure as hell hope we've got here at low tide," said the Skipper. "Tabor, call the *1318* and ask them to relay a message to *Splendid Leader*. Tell them we're aground."

"I think I can see the *Hazelwood*." Tabor pointed into the heavy accumulation of smoke and ground fog.

"Okay, see if you can reach her direct. Make *Splendid Eight* an addressee."

The reply from the destroyer was fast and to the point: "Maintain your position, *Splendid Five*. You're just gun shy, after Manus."

"Well, goddamn," said Mr. Hiller, as the ship's keel brushed solidly against the sandy bottom. "The tide is going out, sure as hell. Talk about lousy luck!"

Within minutes the ship had settled into the sand and begun to list to port. Those of us at the three 20mm. guns took it for awhile but eventually had to secure and move to the starboard side of the ship, with the rest of the crew.

"Skipper, I'm not going to be able to use this twenty!" called out Milleson.

I looked at Roucloux and he said, "Milleson never was one to leave a thing unsaid."

Every few minutes Jap fighters zipped in and out, invariably leaving their calling cards on the beach. And with each passing minute the *995* settled deeper into the sand and listed farther to the port, forcing us finally to hang onto something. All of the guns were useless.

"We couldn't get out of here now if we wanted to," the Skipper told the bridge gang. "I wonder if MacArthur brought along a tug for this landing!"

At the lifeline and against the port side of the pilothouse the crew of the *995* waited silently. Five hundred yards down the cove the *1066* was sitting straight in the water, and beyond her the *1318* was actually wallowing a bit in the choppier waters of the Gulf. And it was from that direction that the Jap fighters were coming in, sometimes as many as five or six at once. Generally, they dipped in just past the first subchaser and by the time they reached the third (us) they were leveled out and shooting.

The Skipper, following closely upon the heels of a strafing run by three Zeros, appeared at the bridge railing and looked down upon his crew. "All right, men, let's get to hell off this thing! Make it quick and head for that line of palm trees!"

Once again we were abandoning ship!

I led the way to the starboard side, using the railing around the 'midships gundeck. I leaped to the sand and in less than a minute the entire crew was wading ashore. Halfway up the beach a lone Zero zoomed in, leaving a straight line of sand geysers. "Hit the deck!" I yelled, falling flat. Then I was up and running, and nobody was looking back. A few minutes later, when the strafing run occurred, we were scattered among the trees on our bellies.

Then I heard Pills shout, "Somebody's down on the beach!"

"Who's not accounted for?" groaned the Skipper, dashing toward the beach. I leaped up and followed.

All I could think of was that it could not be Roucloux. He had left the ship with me. Pills was behind me, running clumsily, calling out, "Damn, I knew it!"

"That's not who you think it is, Pills!" I yelled over my shoulder.

The Skipper was blocking my view of the body as I ran up. I looked over his shoulder, feeling light-headed. It was Smitty.

I helped lift the bloody, lifeless body and three of us carried it back into the grove of trees. Sharkey sat down beside it, just staring.

When I joined Roucloux, he said, "Pills is a jinx on us."

I fell to the ground, aware of a lump in my throat, and looked back down the beach. The three little subchasers were lined up like ducks waiting for the kill. Our own ship looked more like a derelict than something that had brought us all this long way. It occurred to me that this was the second time I had seen my own vulnerable little home from something like an objective viewpoint.

Then, once again, above the noise of the big guns exploding constantly and engines of every kind roaring over and around us, we heard fighters coming; and all eyes turned in the direction of the subchasers as a line of Zeroes came ripping in. This time the *1318* did not escape the attention of the fighters. We watched as one of the planes splintered the after gundeck, knocking the gun into the water and cutting the gunner and the loader to pieces. Our eyes went with the plane up the beach to the *1066*, where it practically cut the pilothouse from beneath the bridge. We saw the canvas skirt go sailing off into the water.

Then we watched, in a state of shock, as the lead fighter zoomed upward and cut away once it had passed the *1066!* The other two followed suit.

"They've decided we've already bought it," said the Skipper, "and they don't intend to waste ammunition."

The next time I lookedat the *1066* she seemed to have collapsed from bow to stern. As I watched, her bridge and mast fell into the water; and the after gundeck, what was left of it, burst into flames. Dazed, I glanced at the *1318*. Except for the after gundeck, it seemed to have come through the strafing all right.

We stood up and moved slowly to the edge of the beach. None of us had said a word during this whole time. The crew and officers of the *1066* had been as close as family to us, and now apparently all of them were gone. We could see no one moving on the burning wreck or in the water among the floating debris.

The rest of that day is still a blur in my memory; but I know that it ended after we were finally in deep water again, alone in the cove next to the town of Tacloban. We had watched helplessly while the *Hazelwood* and another tincan gathered up the identifiable body parts of the crew of the *1066*, dragged what was left of the ship out to deep water, and towed the *1318* away. To a makeshift dock somewhere down the Gulf, we learned later.

The tide had returned to the cove just before sundown, but to our astonishment our ship remained stuck in the sand! From the safety of the wooded area we watched and waited, reluctant to return until we were reasonably certain the Japanese Air Force had retired for the day. The Skipper finally decided that he, McCormick, and the motormacks would go out, fire up the engines, and attempt to back the ship into deeper water. We knew that where the *1066* had been was safe water, but no one mentioned that.

All afternoon we listened to the noise of the invasion forces and waited for the Skipper and his little rescue crew to free the ship from the sand. No enemy planes put in an appearance that whole afternoon and early evening; and that night we went out to the ship and tried to strap ourselves into our bunks and get some sleep. But it was still listing badly and, in the end, we took sheets and pillows and bedded down on the beach and listened to the war move inland.

The *Hazelwood* had disappeared without so much as a goodbye. Perhaps, we thought, she was abandoning us for good. After all, this was our second time to run aground. But later we were to learn that she had joined other destroyers and cruisers to fight off a Japanese Naval attack of our landing forces. Admiral Halsey's Third Fleet had been lured north, apparently so that large contingents of the Japanese Navy could move in on us from the south and west.

But nothing ever came of the rumors and scuttlebutt.

The war swept inland on Leyte, leaving Tacloban in a shambles. We spent our days in the little lagoon waiting for high tide or some kind of miracle, like the return of the *Hazelwood*, that would extract us from the sand. Each morning we would wade out to the ship and climb aboard, accepting whatever Cookie could come up with for us to eat. And for a time we would cling to the lifelines and gaze out at the busy harbor.

On the fourth morning, I joined the Skipper and three or four others on the bridge. They were talking about how peaceful it had been in the cove. Since that first day we had seen very little of the Japanese fighter planes; and Tabor, who was pointing his binoculars toward the harbor, suddenly announced, "I think I know why it's so quiet the last couple of days." He had brought the glasses around and was looking at the point of land close to where the *1318* had been stationed a short while before.

"What is it?" asked the Skipper, aiming his glasses in the same direction.

"Is that who I think it is?" asked Tabor.

Several LCVP's had nosed into the shallow water off the point and dropped their landing ramps with great splashes. As we watched, a dozen men in khaki uniforms began spilling out of one of them into the shallow water. Even without glasses we could tell they were High Brass, from all the scrambled eggs and medals. From the other barges came a small army of men carrying large cameras with Mickey Mouse ears.

This entourage moved slowly toward the beach in the knee-deep water, led by a tall man in a peaked officer's cap. He was smoking a ridiculously tall corncob pipe!

"I hope to hell none of those people point their cameras in our direction," complained the Skipper.

Mr. Howorth, who had joined us, smiled and said, affably, "I don't think we have to worry much about that, Skippah. In fact, I suspect they'll make sure of it. What would the folks back home think, us settin' heah like this while history's bein' made?"

18

The Lazaret

The war had come to a standstill finally, with our end of Leyte Gulf secured but in ruins. For approximately ten days, following MacArthur's return and the taking the city of Tacloban, the Subchaser-995 had done nothing but bobble at the end of an anchor chain in an isolated finger of the Gulf. There was nothing on the radio but flyboy chatter and cryptic messages from Army contingents in and around Tacloban. If anybody knew what was going on, he was keeping it to himself.

For four long days we had stayed in that little cove less than a mile from Tacloban. Our pharmacist's mate went into the devastated town on the third day to look for mail and returned with stories about 'miserable-looking waifs' picking through the rubble of what was left of Tacloban. He had seen no females except old, stooped grandmothers in tattered clothes.

"You sure you didn't see any young chicks?" asked Sharkey. "How about taking a bodyguard next time you go in?"

"If I ever need a bodyguard, I won't pick you, Windy," said Pills, looking sour.

"Just thought I'd ask. How about the waifs? Any of 'em split-tails?"

On the fourth and last day in the cove, Leafdale asked me if I would like to go along on the mail run. He had found a large U. S. Army tent full of mail, but it would take a lot of digging to go through it.

"If you want to go, check out a pistol and be ready to go at thirteen hundred hours."

I was waiting at the midships when the LCVP pulled up alongside around twelve-thirty; and when Leafdale emerged from the after crew's quarters with his mailbag he took one look at me and said:

"I've changed my mind about taking you along. I thought you belonged to the United States Navy."

"I do, Pills!" I protested. It was just like this old sour puss to get my hopes up and then dash them.

"Go git some shoes and a helmet, all right? And check out a pistol from the wardroom, like I said."

In no time I was back, with a Navy Colt .45 flapping on my right leg. I was having difficulty getting a helmet on, because my hair hadn't been cut in a good six months.

"All right, let's be off," said Pills. "Did you tinkle?"

Leavy and Milleson were sitting on the gunwale using their bare feet as fenders to keep the LCVP away from the subchaser, and the delay I had caused was beginning to bring forth uncomplimentary words from both of them. So when the I stepped between them and onto the narrow ledge that ran the length of the metal landing barge, Leavy tried to trip me.

Pills, like a mother hen protecting her chick, brought the heavy U. S. Mail bag around and into the deckhand's face. The blow sent the two-hundred-and-fifty-pound Leavy sprawling backward onto the deck and provided a wide space for the pharmacist's mate and me to exit the subchaser.

"Damn, Pills!" complained Leavy. "I think you loosened one of my teeth."

"You asked for it. Do you want any mail today?" he teased.

"Hell, I don't know."

"All right, then we won't bother to look for any addressed to you. Red, I want you to throw any back you might run onto addressed to Leavy."

"That's all right with me!" bawled Leavy. "Nobody back home writes to me anyway!"

"Nobody that knows you knows how to write," said Milleson.

The coxswain wheeled the barge away while Leavy was trying to think of an insult for Milleson. The motormack, who had a wife and several girlfriends back in Wichita, Kansas, was most anxious for Pills and me to be off. It was altogether possible, he had bragged, that he could have thirty or forty letters waiting for him by this time.

To Leavy he confided: "I'm expectin' letters from Charlotte, Mary Anne, and Paulette." In answer, the deckhand expelled a great, exasperated bellyful of air from his chest and then farted. Not put off, Milleson added, "And maybe Sylvia."

"Them your wives?" asked Leavy.

"I have only the one wife, stupid," said Milleson. "Her name's Charlotte; and she's a lovely, soft, sweet-smellin', delicious piece."

"Why do you need the others then?" demanded Leavy, suspiciously.

"Well, Fat, I know you won't appreciate this, but every woman has something a little different to offer. Not one of my girls is like any of the others. Mary Anne not only smells sweet she is sweet. Paulette's built like the proverbial brick shithouse."

*   *   *

On the afternoon of Day Ten or maybe Eleven the rain, having paused for one full day, was back with us; and I, happy to be doing something, had gangway watch from twelve noon until sixteen hundred hours. It was a joke aboard the *995* that the crew was having to stand gangway watches even though there was no gangplank. The duty did not amount to anything, as far as I was concerned. All I had to do was strap on a Navy Colt forty-five and walk around the ship occasionally and keep an eye out for boat people trying to board and any possible blinker messages that might be aimed in our direction.

About once a day an outrigger canoe, resembling the *proas* we had seen in the Solomons, would appear alongside out of the fog and mist, manned by a Filipino man and sometimes filled to the gunwales with old wrinkled women and small emaciated children. And although there did not seem to be much of a threat from them, the gangway watch was supposed to prevent these locals from climbing aboard.

I rather enjoyed the peace and quiet of the afternoon watch because as soon as the crew had eaten their peaches and crackers, they sacked out for most of the afternoon, leaving the topside deserted. Even the officers did not venture out when it was raining.

Aboard our wooden subchaser privacy did not exist, but something resembling it took place on rainy afternoons.

The natives who dropped in on us invariably had something to trade for food. All of them, without exception, wanted something to eat; and they loved to bargain with their straw hats, straw sleeping mats, shell necklaces and bracelets, hand-carved dolls, and Japanese money. Now that their Japanese Government *pesos* and *centavos* (most of which had been run off on ditto machines onto plain paper) were useless as money, the liberated Filipinos were bartering them for considerably more than their face value to souvenir-hungry G. I.'s. I had traded a pillowcase for three "Fifty Centavo" bills to a native who told me he had no need of pillowcases but anything was worth more than Japanese paper money.

They never stopped smiling, even when the bargaining did not result in a trade; and there was a rumor, almost surely started by Sharkey or Tracy, that they would trade anything, even their wives, if you had what they were looking for. They wanted most of all, in this order: flour, sugar, salt, rice; and they were all desperate for anything in a tin can. Not only were they after the contents of the can but the can itself. An empty can was worth more on this market than a pillowcase.

Sometime around two o'clock, halfway through my watch, I heard a light pecking on the starboard side of the ship, back aft. It continued all the time I was zipping along the port side trying to reach the fantail, where I intended to cross. It was the kind of noise that the Skipper hated most during the *siesta* period.

Just as I rounded the corner of the after gundeck and stepped beneath the awning, I saw a large, floppy straw hat bobbing at the starboard gun-wale. I knew at once that it was another Filipino outrigger, and on this one three large straw hats were hovering over it like umbrellas.

To the nearest hat I hissed, "Hey, don't make that racket!" I said this just loud enough to reach across the narrow deck. "The Skipper's trying to take a nap," I explained.

But I realized I was just talking to a hat, which might or might not have a face and a brain beneath it. The pecking noise, I discovered, had been made with a bamboo pole by the one in the center of the boat.

Between the straw hats were bulging straw matting, and underneath this, I was certain, were other straw hats and handicrafts to be bartered.

The hat in the center of the boat began to rise slowly above the gun-wale at my feet. It tilted upward just enough for me to see a very brown, wrinkled face and two shinning black eyes. Whether it was an old man or an old woman I could not say; but suddenly the mouth popped open revealing one ancient tooth, and a thin high-pitched voice called out to me cheerfully:

"Holl-lee!"

"Yes," I nodded, wondering what my attitude should be. I was, after all, in full charge of the ship at this point, protector of the crew and offi-cers of a United States naval vessel. Could this be a raiding party of Japs disguised as old women?

While I stared at that one enormous tooth, the other two hats came up slowly. The one in the stern belonged to the old man of the boat, I decided; so the one standing in the center of the boat immediately beneath me would have to be his old woman. I turned and looked at the one in the bow. What I saw put an end to my breathing. I suppose I had been expecting another old person or perhaps a middle-aged daughter or son; but what I found myself looking at was young and easily the most beautiful face I had ever seen. I stared, dumfounded and speechless.

Almost the moment our eyes met the hat lowered again, and I became aware that the old woman was chattering.

"We trade! We trade! Much things trade."

I nodded doubtfully, still looking at the girl. I would have traded anything I owned for a tiny smile from her; but the truth was I doubted that I had a single thing these people would want or could use.

"I don't know," I finally managed, thinking what terrible luck it was that I had already traded every sheet and pillowcase and skivvy shirt I owned for bracelets and sandals and mats. "Maybe you would like a Navy blanket?"

"No, no!" said the woman quickly, disappointed. "No blanket!"

"How about American money?" I dug out a one dollar bill.

"No, no, no!" whined the woman, beside herself. "No doo-la!"

"Well, I don't think I have anything else."

"You got flour? Sugeer?" As she named off a long list of things, I shook my head to each. "The can goods? Anything eat?" She began lifting the upper layers of straw matting for me to inspect the merchandise.

While she was at this, I remembered that there were some small sacks of sugar and flour in the *lazaret*. Stuff that Cookie never seemed to use; but, I suddenly realized, looking at the things in the bottom of the boat, she had nothing at all that I wanted.

I tried to explain this to her but she would not listen. Then the hat in the bow came up; and although the face did not appear to be sad, there was no smile on it for me. We stared at each other while the old woman rattled on.

"Cans of food! You have cans of food? We trade! Here, look at pretty bracelet, necklace for your gearal!"

I had begun to wonder, *What if I hauled out some of that stuff from the lazaret?* Cookie would never miss it. There might be some canned goods down there. Then I remembered *the cling peaches!* We always had plenty of that, and they were in cans, and nobody aboard the ship, not even Leavy, liked them. These Filipinos, on the other hand, might!

As long as the girl looked at me, I could not pull my eyes away. She was simply the best thing I had ever seen. Beside her my imaginary prototype woman was a Russian peasant. Her unblemished skin sparkled with life, and framing her face was raven black hair that fell to her waist.

The old woman, having had her say, read the truth in my face. For a moment she appeared to be very disappointed. She began to whine and toss her hands in the air, looking first at the girl and then at me.

"What you want?" she whined. "What you really want? We maybe got." She raised the mats and showed me more handmade things, carvings for the most part, but her enthusiasm had disappeared.

I was ready to turn the ship over to the old lady, ready to give up citizenship and home and loved ones, to desert and go with this family back into the hills, if only I could be near this lovely young girl.

"I don't want anything." I glanced at her old wrinkled face, then my eyes went back to the beautiful one in the bow of the boat. She was undoubtedly the granddaughter, for she couldn't be more than sixteen or seventeen.

"You no want the fruit or the mat or the basket?" the old woman whined. "What you want?"

I dug out some American money. "Five dollars for one of those necklaces."

"No want doo-la!" After a long pause and a glance toward the stern of the boat, she whined, "What 'bout dotter?"

Say what? I swallowed, staring at the old woman. Surely, she had not said what I thought I had heard. I was losing my mind.

But she was nodding eagerly at me and using her hands, trying to pull a yes out of me. She had found what it was I wanted, and after a glance at the girl (I was certain she had communicated with her, gotten her approval), she was no longer whining.

"Dotter. She nice gearal. She never lie with man."

For the first time the old man in the stern of the boat spoke, and although his voice was calm and manly there was a hint of desperation in it. "We have no luck with the tradeeng, my son. Many mouths to feed. The dotter will do thees thing if you trade us two sack of flour an' two sack of sugeer—"

The girl's hand went up, stopping her father. She turned to me and nodded, lowering her lovely eyes, "I will do for what my father has said."

I glanced over my shoulder at the hatchway that led to the galley and the after crew's quarters. Somebody could pop out of there any second. I turned and stared at the man, who had stood up unsteadily in the boat and was pointing toward the girl.

"She go along with you! Savee?"

Against internal forces so powerful they garbled my speech, I said, "No. She can't come aboard the ship, Sir. It's against Naval Regulations. She would have to have permission from the Commanding Officer."

"She go aboard with you!" The old man's face had hardened.

"You be nice to her, yes?" pleaded the mother.

The man began to wave frantically at the girl, motioning for her to climb aboard the ship.

"I can't let you do this," I begged. "It isn't up to me." Then I equivocated: "Besides, I don't know whether I could find any of that stuff you want."

The girl stood up, balancing herself in the bottom of the boat. The old man began to work the boat forward slowly until she was at the 'midships.

What was I to do, pull out my Navy Colt .45 and shoot the old pirate? In a daze, I watched him maneuver the outrigger and its valuable cargo toward the spot where I was either going to have to lend a hand or move aside, the spot where the gangplank would have been if we had been tied up to a dock.

I tried half-heartedly a time or two to discourage the boarding, with words like, "I don't think—uh, maybe—" but in the end all I did was move down and wait for her to be delivered up to me.

The instant she was aboard and standing before me, a go-to-hell feeling came over me. Something like this had happened to me before, and I recognized it for what it was; but I was powerless to resist it. Since I had already sinned against the Navy, broken the Number One Cardinal Rule of the Gangway Watch, I might as well be a man about it and make the most of it.

This daredevil attitude scared the hell out of me, but somehow it made perfectly good sense, at the time.

The girl had not helped things any by removing her hat and letting her shimmering black hair fall down over her shoulders to her waist. Prettily, like a little trooper standing at attention before her superior, she held the hat at her side, waiting for me to make the first move. Her eyes, now glued to mine, seemed to be drawing me to her.

I mumbled something, like, "Uh, just a minute. Let me—"

I whirled and headed for the stern, to the galley hatch. I stuck my head inside the open cover and listened. Was that roaring noise I was hearing coming from below or was it inside my head? I thought seriously of going below and checking out the old salts, but common sense prevailed.

I was now resolved to find something to give these people. The old woman had mentioned canned goods. The *lazaret* was my only hope. I dashed back and removed the round hatch cover, placing it to one side.

This was where we kept our supplies and spare parts, even spare mattresses, pillows, blankets. I lowered myself through into the darkness, thinking what the hell?

The heavy cans of peaches, stored in crates, were supposed to be on the port bulkhead. The graham crackers, in cardboard boxes inside other wooden crates, would be somewhere along the forward bulkhead.

I tossed aside rolls of towing line, scrub brushes, boxes of saltwater soap, buckets of red lead.

The picture of that angel standing in the boat, waiting for her father to barter her body to me for food—was etched into my brain. I had to keep telling myself why I was down there in that tiny, damp compartment. Then I became aware that my right hand was trembling as though I had palsy. I had just found an entire crate of cling peaches!

As quickly as I could, I filled a cardboard box with the heavy cans of peaches, another with graham crackers, and a third with small sacks of hardened sugar and flour. These I pushed through the hole to the top deck, being as quiet as possible.

As I strained with the crate of peaches, I found myself looking into the round, innocent eyes of the young girl. She was standing above me, her face glowing with excitement at the boxes of food. I put my head through the hatch opening, tried to smile up at her, then glanced quickly toward the after hatchway. So far so good. I pulled myself out onto the deck and stood up. A quick inspection of the entire deck assured me that none of the crew or officers had made it topside!

The girl stooped and picked up one of the heavy boxes and raced with it to the outstretched hands of the old woman. This lady was smiling and nodding, while trying to balance in the bottom of the boat.

"Flour?" inquired the old woman happily, her head just above the gunwale.

I nodded, lifting another crate and moving around the girl.

"Mostly, though, this is peaches and crackers."

I looked at the old man as I said this. His face was suddenly full of smiles, "Yas, yas! Pitches! Crackers! Very good!"

The girl had straightened up and was standing at attention in front of me again. I lay my hands on her shoulders for just a moment, becoming aware that she was wearing only a thin cotton shift beneath her threadbare raincoat. Slowly, her lips parted as she looked at me. I dropped my hands and rushed back to get the third and last box, certain she would climb back into the boat. But when I turned back, there she was, still at attention!

"Maybe you'd better get back into the boat," I suggested, as I handed the box to the old man. "I'm not supposed to let anybody come aboard, without Skipper's permission."

I heard these stupid words coming out of my mouth and couldn't believe it. Brain-washed, that what I was. I wanted to take this girl in my arms and—

"I come aboard for you," she said, with resolution. "We made bargain."

"No. I can't let you do that," I pleaded (with myself more than with her). "It's all right. The peaches were not mine, and besides I don't like peaches at all. It's a gift from the Navy to you."

"I give you something in return," she said matter-of-factly and headed for the *lazaret!*

My knees almost gave out on me at this point, as the girl stopped and waited for me at the little hatch opening. I wavered toward her, trying to decide what to say. I could not go into that compartment with her. Nobody ever went there, not even Cookie and Tex, who were supposed to store their galley stuff there. It would be worse in the Navy's eyes than swimming with nurses. The brass would not even bother to give me a dishonorable discharge before putting me to death.

She moved close to me and took one of my hands. The top of her lovely black hair came up to my chin, and suddenly her angel's face tilted toward mine! She was wearing a kind of ancient poncho over her light dress, and this fell loosely about her body all the way to the deck. Only her head and her sandaled feet were visible.

"You have a place down there, yes?"

"No! I definitely have no place down there," I said, shaking my head vigorously. "There or anyplace else." When she did not budge, I added, "There is no place in the entire U. S. Navy—for—"

"Down there." She tugged at my arm and nodded toward the glaring hole in the deck.

I said weakly, "Definitely not." But I felt myself being drawn by her tiny brown hand. I could not resist her at all! The Navy, with all of its regulations and no-no's, was suddenly off somewhere else.

"Why not thees place?" She had me by the arm and was drawing me toward the hole. "Do you find me pretty, some?" As she swayed against me, I could not resist putting my hands on her small, strong shoulders. "You are so very beautiful!" I whispered.

We were standing in the center of the stern deck, in plain sight of most of the topside, and yet I could not resist holding her tightly for a moment. And instead of pulling back and running to her mother, she snuggled her head against my chest.

Very softly she whispered, "And you are most beautiful, too."

The girl's body suddenly stiffened and she pushed me back, a move that somehow did not surprise me much. She was finally coming to her senses. Her next move, I figured, would be run to the boat. Perhaps, if I were lucky, she would wave at me as her parents took her away.

Suddenly, she reached up, standing on her toes, and grasped my head with both hands, pulled my face down, and kissed me on the lips!

At this moment, if my heart had not been strong and healthy, I would surely have died of a stroke. I had been caught completely off guard, and for a brief moment I tried to pull back and save myself. But once again I felt a great surge of adrenaline, which wiped out reason and sanity. Gone completely from all serious consideration were the job of gangway watch, Naval Regulations, the Skipper, and what would happen to my decent and honorable parents, once the news of my indiscretion reached the States.

This was indeed my first kiss, ever. It was sweet and warm and moist, full-mouthed, potent beyond words. The very marrow in my bones seemed to be oozing out, and I felt my toes turn inward.

She was suddenly in my arms, like a baby, and we were still kissing and birds were singing—and nothing else in the world mattered.

"I'll go first," I whispered.

And with that I lowered myself to the deck, eased her to a sitting position beside me, kissed her again lightly, and put my feet through the hole. All of this, I later realized, under the direct gaze of the two old people in the boat. About whom I had forgotten completely. Quickly, then, I lowered himself into the dark interior of the *lazaret*, bracing with my elbows at first and then letting go and dropping to the deck below. Once inside the compartment, I looked up and saw bare feet and legs.

She whispered, "Catch me!" and dropped into my arms.

Instantly, I realized that she had left the poncho and hat behind and that beneath her very thin, loose-fitting shift of a dress there was nothing! Indeed, her nude body had slid through my arms!

I pointed toward a stack of mattresses and whispered, "Sit there."

Then, as she turned and surveyed the small compartment, I sat down on a five-gallon can of paint and reached for her hands.

"You have lots of—"she began.

"Peaches!" I laughed, pointing at a wall of wooden boxes. They were lashed down. "More peaches than this crew could eat in a year!"

She removed her hands from mine and put them around my neck. "We must hurry!"

I nodded, standing up and taking her with me. "Can I hold you in my arms for just for a—?"

Sshe pulled my head down and kissed me, wetly, on the lips. "You are good man and very, very handsome," she said. "I like very much to be held by you."

My arms tightened around her, and I could feel her young, firm breasts against my chest. Then, unable to resist, I lifted her off the deck, delighting in the feel of her strong, slender body against me. I felt her tremble; then she became completely relaxed in my arms.

"You're so tall!" she cried.

"Let's get out of here!" I whispered. "You're wonderful, but we have to get you back into that boat before someone—!"

"I give you—!"

"No, you've already given me plenty! You're the most beautiful girl I've ever seen, and I'll never forget you. But right now we've got to get you back into that boat before the Navy finds out about this."

I knew that my tortured mind and body would be unable to resist this lovely young girl much longer, that what I was feeling was much more than animal lust. From out of the fog and mists and rain of Leyte Gulf had come this angel. And from this moment on she would be my Dream Girl.

"You might get into trouble? Maybe I come another time."

"Or maybe I could see you—on the island."

She pulled her head back and looked into my eyes, "Yes, I see you in Tacloban."

"Yes, if you would tell me how to find you."

But I knew, even as she clung to me and nodded happily, that such a thing as a rendezvous on the island was highly unlikely. Even if I could get ashore, what were the chances I would ever be able to find her? And if she ever paid the ship another visit, what were the chances I would be the only one awake on the entire ship?

"I am Alisa Montoya. Ask for the family of Miguel Montoya, in the south part of Tacloban."

I kissed her quickly and helped her up through the hatch. Then, as I pulled myself upward, I heard her exclaim, "Oh!"

"What?" I whispered loudly, pulling myself through the opening to the deck.

My question was answered the moment my head went through the opening, for there lounging about the fantail of the ship were Sharkey, Tracy, and Jines!

"Forget all that stuff we talked about, Bill," said Sharkey. "Our boy needs no help from the likes of us."

Those two were leaning against the K-gun rack on the starboard side of the ship, and Jines was standing at the lifeline on the other side of the ship, grinning stupidly.

Tracy was visibly overwhelmed with what he was seeing and imagining.

"Could I assist the young lady to her carriage?" asked Sharkey. "Redt—"

"That won't be necessary," I said, getting to my feet and taking the girl's hand. I leaned down and whispered into her ear, "Everything's all right. They are harmless."

She nodded, smiling, suddenly quite calm. "Now, tell me your name and promise me you won't forget me."

I whispered my name into her ear and added, "I promise I will look for you when I go ashore."

"Everyone knows my family."

As I was helping her into the boat, I was thinking, yes, and I'll bet every young fellow within a hundred miles knows you.

Between the girl and her mother a very knowing look had passed, producing a metamorphosis in the old lady. Then, while my heart raced along dangerously, I saw the old man's face. He was smiling happily.

"Much thanks, sailair," he said. "You good mon. *Vaya con dios.*"

By his words and demeanor it was obvious that he also knew that nothing had happened.

Still ignoring my shipmates, I watched as the long, fragile outrigger disappear into the rain and mist. For another moment the three large straw hats appeared to be floating on the water; then they, too, were gone. I walked to the lifeline and stood looking into the deep mist of the failing afternoon.

"I want the truth," said Sharkey, from the gunrack. "The whole truth and nothing but."

"I'd appreciate it if you wouldn't say anything about this," I said, taking him by the throat and pretending to choke him.

"Sure. As far as I know nothin' did happen."

I looked first at Jines and then at Tracy. They nodded and I said:

"Nobody hears about this, right?"

"Who would believe us anyway?" asked Tracy. "Hell, we'd be laughed off this ship if we went around claiming that a young, gorgeous brown-skinned virginal female of the human species came alongside in a boat and voluntarily—"

"While her parents waited nearby, approving," put in Sharkey.

"Did go into our *lazaret*—" said Jines.

"From now on," warned Sharkey, "I'm afraid you will be known as 'Peaches'—after Cookie finds out about the missing stuff from the *lazaret*."

"I'd appreciate it if you would not mention that name for me," I said, clamping my hands around Sharkey's throat. "If any of this gets out, I'll blame all three of you."

"How about ole Ace McCormick?" asked Sharkey. "Can we tell him?"

My grip tightened considerably.

19

Lingayen Gulf

There was a feeling of anticipation in the air, something like the feeling one gets before a tornado comes along and changes the landscape for all time. Every night it was more difficult for me to fall sleep because I did not want to miss anything, and when I did drop into something resembling sleep I awoke with a start.

The first invasion of the Philippines had been accomplished, the General had returned to stay, and the Japs' naval and air superiority was history. But, as we were soon to learn on our way through Mindanao Strait, instead of facing reality and giving up, the Japanese had gone into the *kamikaze* business in a very serious way.

On a daily basis a high-flying reconnaissance plane would come snooping around, almost invariably early in the morning and late in the afternoon, causing the entire convoy to sound General Quarters; and, of course, during such times there was always the possibility of a *kamikaze* dropping out of nowhere. But generally, and it could be anytime during the day, a single fast-moving black dot would appear in the sky, heading straight for one of the big transport ships. Every GQ in the convoy would go off, of course, and the sky would fill up with flak; but after this had happened half a dozen times, we knew that the whole thing would be over in about a minute at the most, and that somebody was going to get it, no matter what.

During that first week out of Leyte Gulf it got to be a cruel joke that every morning and every afternoon at chow time, we would have to dash to our battle stations. This colored our attitude toward the Japanese more than anything else had, because we were convinced it was all a deliberate attempt to spoil our appetites.

Once through the Strait, the big invasion convoy turned north into the China Sea; and the air raids continued, getting worse if anything. It was during this time that I realized we had undisputed air superiority. Again and again Japanese fighters and torpedo-bombers would show up only to be chased away by American P-38's, TBF's, and F6F's. And although I must have watched two dozen dogfights, I never saw one in which the Japanese were the winners. Invariably, they were the ones that turned tail and ran.

Something, we knew, was about to come down. Something big, like Manila. As far as Ace was concerned, it had to be Manila. Where else could it be? And while the invasion of Leyte Gulf was not exactly a surprise party, this was going to be a real head-on collision. This time the Japs knew exactly where we were going to hit, and they would be waiting with everything they had.

*   *   *

One early morning when I was relieving Sharkey at the sonar watch, I asked him to fill me in on the news. It was a rhetorical question, of course, because I knew he was much in the dark as I was.

"Hell, there aint no news. We're winnin' the fuckin' war, Tokyo Rose has been arrested for treason, the invasion of Manila is set for day after tomorrow, and I'm gonna be home for Christmas."

Roucloux, at the engine controls, jumped in, "I've got it from real high authority we're headin' back for the States right after this next one."

Sharkey turned his bloodshot eyes toward the source of that remark. "Tex, tell me somethin'. Who is the ears of this ship?"

"What do you mean?"

"Who gets the scoop before anybody else does? Who knows what's gonna happen before the Skipper does?"

"You're not tellin' me it's you."

"Yes, me. Me and Jines and your buddy here. Right, Hall?"

I nodded doubtfully.

"It's the truth. Even the coded stuff we have to decode, these days. Mr. Darling's too wiped out to do it." The sonarman leaned against the door, taking his time, knowing that we know he has more to say. He removed the package of Camels from the sleeve of his skivvy shirt and tapped out a cigarette. "Got a light?"

Roucloux and I shook our heads.

"Shit, I forgot. Neither of you boys smoke." There was a mixture of disgust and disbelief in his voice. "You know, smokin's about the only vice that's possible on this ship. We can't drink, chew, dip, or whore. So what's left? Nobody's been paid for six months so the only thing you can do with dice or cards, provided you had same, is play pretend like." He searched himself and finally found a battered kitchen match. "Here goes nothin'." He tried to strike it on his mildewed dungaree shorts. Finally, in disgust he gave up.

I said casually, "The smoking light is out, Shark."

"Hell, I know that. I was just funnin' you boys."

At that point, the Skipper came into the pilothouse from the bridge. He was in a talkative mood; so I asked him pointblank where we were going.

"It's called Lingayen Gulf. Let's ask Ace where exactly that is."

Ace McCormick stuck his head out of the chartroom. "Just north of Manila. We ought to get in there sometime after midnight day after tomorrow, say about daybreak."

"What the hell is it?"

"Damned if I know, Skipper. I've been past there several times. It looks like nothing but a harbor surrounded by mountains and jungles."

"It's obviously a diversion," said Sharkey, disappointed. "We're going to fake the Japs out. They'll be down in Manila waiting for us."

The Skipper silenced Sharkey with a raised hand. "Of course, we don't know what the strategy is, but Sharkey's probably right. Manila's due to be hit, but it'll probably happen about the time the Japs find out about us at Lingayen. Once we've diverted the Japs from Manila, that's when the ax will fall. Anyway, if we manage a surprise landing, we'll be in real luck. Maybe we'll be able to get in, secure the beaches, and unload before they have time to hit back." After a moment he added with a grin: "I think it's safe to say this will be our last landing—" (He held up a precautionary finger) "before R and R."

*   *   *

The convoy stretched out of sight ahead and behind us. The APA's, AKA's, LST's and LCI's were in three columns in the center; and the escort vessels, which included a large number of DD's and DE's, as well as several PC's, were spaced every five hundred yards or so apart in two columns on both sides of the convoy. Light and heavy cruisers, we knew, were just over the horizon ahead of us, ready to provide real fire power in case of an air attack.

With each passing day after we left Leyte Gulf the tension aboard the ship had increased. A persistent heavy, low-hanging cloud cover kept visibility and spirits down close to nothing; and at night, once we entered the Sulu Sea, it was impossible to move about topside without holding onto something. We were, I knew, traveling just out of sight of the west coast of the Philippines in the South China Sea.

Because of the twice-daily visits by reconnaissance planes, we knew that the Japanese were keeping close tabs on us. They knew our size, speed, and heading; and they thought they knew exactly what our destination was.

Now, after having spent another Christmas and New Years in unfriendly waters, here we were on the morning of January 8, 1945, well past the Manila Harbor entrance, making our way in dense fog and mist to a place we had never heard of two days before. Visibility had been consistently bad all that day and that night, ranging from about five hundred to a thousand feet, forcing us to remain at Condition Yellow.

We had reached the mouth of Manila Harbor sometime during the afternoon of January 8, according to McCormick, having seen not a single Japanese aircraft; and although he had computed our E. T. A. at around daylight the next morning, we on the guns in the cold mist and rain, received little encouragement from this. By this time we had already spent twenty-four hours at our battle stations, soaked to the skin the entire time.

All attempts to while the time away with talk had ended, and only Eddie Jake's deliveries from the galley and McCormick's occasional forays onto the quarterdeck broke the monotony for us. By this time I had heard the life stories of all the men aboard the ship, six times over. We knew each other better than we had ever known our own brothers or other members of our immediate families. So when July Roucloux started in about San Antone, I was forced to do one of two things. I could listen and keep his story straight or close my mind to him and try hard to think about something else.

*   *   *

The long black hump of a mountain had begun to take shape on our starboard side, which we knew had to be the island of Luzon. It reminded me of the Sleeping Giant, on Viti Levu Island, in Fiji. It had first appeared from the darkness and mists far ahead of us as a shapeless black cloud; but as time had passed and visibility had improved, we could see that it was indeed a mountain range, stretching out of sight to the north. Then, just as day was breaking, we realized that we had reached a great natural harbor.

And while a number of us on the 995 gathered along the starboard lifeline to stare into the darkness, the drama began to unfold with the bunching of the convoy in the mouth of the harbor. There had been no "softening of the landing areas," since surprise was obviously an important part of the strategy in this landing.

It was, of course, Lingayen Gulf, and our job was to find our station, an imaginary spot in the shallow water not far from another imaginary rectangle of sand called Osage Beach. As daylight neared, carrier planes began strafing the area back of our beach and, indeed, the entire stretch of wide, flat beach that seemed to go on forever around the vast harbor.

This time, as we moved slowly into the Gulf and formed a ragged line about three hundred yards from the beech, we found ourselves part of a motley assortment of small ships, including two PC's, a minesweeper, and something that looked like a yippy boat. And with engines idling, we waited. The transport ships and troop carriers had by this time positioned themselves out in the harbor, the attack transports farthest out and the LST's, LCI's, and LCM's in closer.

From the bridge of the 995 came the order to remain at Condition Yellow until further notice. We had been at our battle stations so long the order seemed ludicrous. In addition to being malnourished, wet to the skin, sore in every part of our bodies, and so sleepy we could hardly stay awake, we had to treated like children.

The sound of someone moving clumsily up from the stern of the ship reached my ears. It sounded like Leavy but it was still too dark to be sure.

"You boys awake?"

Sharkey had bumped into a number of things on his way from the galley, and it was perfectly clear to everyone about the quarterdeck that his question had been tossed out merely to get someone to give him a point of reference.

"What's up?" I asked. "Is that coffee for me?"

"Hah. Go git your own. Tex there can spell you."

"Just kidding," I said. "I didn't want you to run into me with that stuff."

At my right elbow, Roucloux said, "I think I've got jungle rot."

"It's the same thing Ace's got," said Sharkey. "You been lettin' him feel of you with his toes?"

"God no!" protested Roucloux. "I don't have what he's got. His flesh is fallin' off. Mine just itches until I can't stand it. There're red rings all over my crotch."

"Well, I know it's no consolation to you but my teeth are fallin' out," said Sharkey. "I used to have the best teeth in my family, but I swear I'll be toothless by the time I get back to Frisco."

"I think my hair's falling out," said July.

"It's not the same thing," said Sharkey. "You can git other hair that's better lookin' than that sorry stuff of yours. And if you tell me I can git some other better teeth, I'll belt you one."

"You can! But you're right, it's not the same."

By good daylight it was possible to make out the Jacob's Ladders hanging down the sides of the transport ships. LCVP's were already positioning themselves for the landing troops, waiting for the signal to come in to the beach and rendezvous with us and the other communications ships.

Thus far not a single bogey of any description had been spotted.

Evidently, we had caught the Japanese completely by surprise.

The LCVP's, looking like long, ugly corrugated boxes, began to circle the 995; and young soldiers standing inside along the gunwales were taken by the quaintness of our little wooden ship. Naturally, some of them began to yell questions.

"Anybody aboard from New York?"

"How about Alabamah?"

Roucloux and I waved but neither of us had anything to say. We were thinking of a similar day a million years ago, at a Godawful place called Peleliu.

Tabor, beside his flag box, waited patiently while the distant blinker light spelled out the word *ten*. Without waiting for the rest of the message, he quickly ran up the first of three pennants. Then, glancing at his watch, he readied the second pennant and relaxed.

From the instant the big yellow pennant began its ascent, all merriment ceased in the LCVP's. Suddenly, the young, smiling faces went blank; and what had been a party of goodtime Charlies only a moment before was now what appeared to be a disciplined military unit.

After witnessing this transformation, I remarked to Roucloux that the soldiers all suddenly looked alike. They appeared to be wearing masks.

"That's because they've done this before, and it's not fun anymore. But you're right, they all look as if they come out of the same mold."

Finally, the bark of the Task Force Commander cut through the static of the U. S. Army transceivers: "Execute!" Then, as Tabor's red pennant leaped upward and the LCVP's roared away, the Commander's voice, now high-pitched, rang out, "I say again, 'Execute'!"

With no resistance at all, as far I could tell, along the beaches, the first wave went ashore and fanned out. Two additional waves followed, without major incident; and after that amphibious vehicles of every description and LCVP's loaded with supplies began moving to the beach from the transports like ants toward an anthill. The drama was entering the third act, without a hitch.

By sundown the harbor was quiet, and along the beach as far as the eye could see the Marines and the Army had dug in and settled down for the night.

*   *   *

As soon as we had finished chow on the afternoon of the second day of the landings, July Roucloux and I went topside and, out of old habit, settled at our starboard twenty. All around us the spectacle of hundreds of ships disgorging themselves of men and supplies toward the already crowded beaches was a show we could not resist. Just out from us was the flagship of the invasion fleet, and at anchor beside it was the the *USS Mississippi.*

Before we knew it the sun had disappeared and dusk was moving in. The ships became dark outlines against the water of the Gulf; and although there had been little resistance from the Japanese, not one of them was showing a light.

I had turned and was looking at the sleeping giant of a mountain that ran north and south above the beach and jungle. Suddenly, I became aware of a speck of light moving along the crest of the range, heading north. While I watched, it altered course to the west, and headed for the upper end of the enormous harbor.

I sat up quickly.

"What?" asked July. "Don't start sniffin' out trouble."

I raised my hand for silence.

Although afternoon had turned into dusky dark, it was still possible to make out the silhouettes of the big ships in the Gulf. And, now, as I followed that growing speck of light, I realized that it was circling back toward the center of our enormous invasion force.

"Hear that?" I asked.

"Man, I don't hear anything but the hog snorting of our old worn-out engines," said July, querulously. "What do you *think* you hear?"

"I hear an airplane," I said, pointing toward the upper end of the harbor. "There it is!" We watched it grow larger, without seeming to move much. I realized suddenly why it didn't appear to be moving very much. It was coming toward us fast!

"It's one of ours," said July. "It couldn't have come over that mountain!"

"That's a bogey!" I shouted, leaping up. "Look at it, it's that's not one of ours!"

"How can you tell?" demanded Roucloux, getting to his feet. "It's too dark to be sure!"

I had no time to explain, but I was convinced that what we were seeing was a bogey! I dashed across the quarterdeck to the pilothouse and
checked the I. F. F. gear. Roucloux continued to watch the small orange
glow that was growing larger with each passing second. I could hear
him arguing with me in the dark, then he was shouting:

"I hope you're not plannin' to—do something stupid!"

"That's not ours, July!" I yelled, returning to the gun and motioning
for him to check the ammunition canister.

"That's got to be one of ours! Nobody else in the fleet is payin' any
attention to it! Don't you think somebody would have known if it was a
bogey?"

"It's a Jap, July! Look at that exhaust! What does that tell you?"

Then, not bothering to strap myself to the gun, I whirled the twenty
around and lined it up on the growing strip of orange light. "It's a Jap!
No doubt about it!" I yelled, clamping my fingers over the trigger for
maybe five seconds.

The noise of that first short burst, coming as it did at a time when not
a sound was coming from the beach, was unbelievable. The WHAM-
WHAM-WHAMMING of the twenty instantly caused chaos below
decks on the subchaser, and almost immediately from one ship after
another across the harbor came the angry clattering of General
Quarters!

The bogey was still out of range; but, using the big clumsy sight, I
lined up the barrel on a piece of clear sky that was almost certainly to be
the path that orange streak was taking. When I tried another burst to
see where my tracers were going, July, now beside himself with worry,
shouted, "You're gonna hit one of our ships!"

As the orange streak swept up the gulf, barely clearing the masts of
some of the big transports on the extreme north edge of the harbor, I let
go another longer burst, aware now that the quarterdeck was crowded
with shouting people. Bill Tracy, of course, was doing his dance and
waving his arms for me to cease. Then Roucloux, surprisingly, was also

dancing about and shouting, "Higher, higher!" He was so excited he began to slap me on the head with one of his heavy gloves. "To the right a bit! I hope to hell you don't hit the flagship!"

That's when I realized where the bogey was heading. Up to now I had been convinced that it was just a reconnaissance plane coming by to check our numbers.

I held the trigger down again and, guided by the tracers, sent a series of short blasts ahead of the plane. It did not swerve or alter course at all, surprisingly enough, but kept plodding along toward our end of the harbor. The thought occurred to me that the pilot of that plane knew exactly where he was going.

"Lead him a bit more!" shouted Roucloux, whapping me with his glove.

By this time every ship in the harbor was sounding General Quarters, but still not a single anti-aircraft gun had joined mine. I saw the Skipper and the other two officers milling about before the pilothouse, waving their arms in my direction; and although I could see their mouths flapping, I could not make out a word they were saying!

As the orange glow in the sky swept in, aiming straight as a missile now for the flagship of the invasion fleet, I settled upon an imaginary square box of sky and braced myself. July was going crazy, screaming into my ear:

"Git ready! Hold it till I give you the word!"

But just as the orange glow became a twenty-foot streak of exhaust flames, I pulled the trigger and held it, ignoring the screams of Tracy on my left and the pounding July was giving me on my right shoulder. The long black fuselage, hurtling across the fleet like a comet, could now be seen ahead of the tongue of exhaust fire, which, if I had ever had any doubts, convinced me that it was indeed a bogey—and aimed at the Task Force Commander's flagship.

As the plane neared its target. July began yelling something about the gun barrel, and I knew what he was trying to tell me. But it was either now or never, and I stayed with it.

The brilliant row of tracers that spewed from my barrel lighted up the sky; and as a thousand pairs of eyes watched, the black messenger of death swept squarely into it, drawn as if by a magnetic force.

As my bullets ripped through one of the wings, a giant ball of fire suddenly lighted up the sky, revealing to the entire harbor the long black airplane, heeling and circling counterclockwise, with half a wing flapping. Then it began to nose toward the water, still heeling to the left, a great wounded bird hurtling out of control to its death.

By this time even Tracy had shut up and was watching the spectacle. And suddenly it was all over.

The final WHOOSH-BOOM made by the *kamikaze's* dive into the drink was followed by a short but brilliant bonfire, during which the attention of the entire harbor was focused about one hundred yards from the flagship.

The crew and officers of the *995* seemed to be in a state of shock. No one had anything to say; but all around us the buzz and rattle of General Quarters continued for a time, ours, I think, being the last to stop.

Then Roucloux was repeating over and over, "You shot another Jap plane down!"

Needless to say, I was exhausted; and when my body finally said *enough already*, I went down to a sitting position beside the gun. For a time I thought I was going to pass out; and what was weird, my mind seemed to welcome it. I became aware that July was moving me around and that Tracy was once again doing a James Cagney dance on the quarterdeck. Some of what he was saying had to do with hanging from the yardarm because I shot down an American plane.

Then the Skipper was leaning over me, looking pale and drawn.

"What'n hell came over you, Hall? I'm already in more trouble than I'll ever be able to get out of!"

"Cap'n!" yelled Tracy. "He did that on his own! I did not have a thing to do with it!"

"Stow it, Tracy!" yelled the Skipper.

Tabor shoved people aside to reach me, and I could see at a glance that he was pleased.

"You've got eyes like a Blackfoot woman," he said. "Nobody in the harbor saw that Jap but you."

I sat up, in time to hear Mr. Darling explain to Tabor what I had done was shoot down a friendly. To me he said, "You're in real trouble for this, Hall! The Navy will send you to Mare Island for this."

Mr. Hiller had begun clearing the deck, chasing most of the crew to the fantail, where they bunched up to wait and speculate. Tracy, Jines, and Pills were permitted to go inside the pilothouse with the officers and McCormick. I started to get up but was ordered to stay put.

So I sat there on the quarterdeck, my head in a spin, wondering why the Skipper, of all people, had not identified that plane, or at least was willing to give me the benefit of the doubt. And he had seemed not impressed at all that Tabor was on my side.

It was dark by this time, but I could make out the silhouettes of those in the pilothouse talking about me. Someone came outside and stood over me. It was Mr. Darling.

"Inside. The Skipper wants to say a few things to you."

I went into the pilothouse, sidling past the three officers on the left in the tiny passageway, and took a position in front of the ship's wheel. Without preliminary, the Skipper started in on me:

"Hall, have you lost your mind? I can't believe that you, of all people, would do something like this! Why, the Admiral will put you in' the brig and throw away the key for this!"

"Sir, that was a bogey," I said, nervously. "I swear it was!"

"How can you say that? Will you explain that to me? How do you know? You don't just jump up and start shootin' that gun anytime you feel like it! Who gave you permission to do it? Nobody! You know that the O. O. D. has got to give the order to commence firing!" He was wringing his hands and shaking his head tragically. "My god, you shot down a U. S. plane! Don't you realize that?"

No one said a word for a time.

"Dry up, everybody!" shouted Mr. Hiller. "Not another word out of any of you!"

"Didn't any of you see the exhaust on that plane?" I pleaded. "It had an exhaust! It wasn't one of ours, Skipper!"

The sixteen Army transceivers had sputtered away throughout the confusion, with not a single audible signal coming from them the entire time. Now, a loud, authoritative voice cut through the background noise:

"This is Leapfrog One! I want the name, rank, and serial number of the man that shot down that plane, and I want it on the double!"

Mr. Hiller sighed pathetically. "Well, it's out of my hands, now. I've got no choice."

I started to say something but changed my mind.

Jines lifted a mike and said, "Leapfrog One, this is *Splendid Five*, over."

"Who the hell is this?" snarled Leapfrog One.

"The *SC-995*, Sir. We're an LCC, sir. Landing Craft—"

Mr. Hiller said, "Tell him we're a Landing Craft Communications."

"I did, sir."

Leapfrog One blasted, "Tell me the name of the commanding officer of whatever it is you're calling from!"

The Skipper took the mike, "This is William E. Hiller, sir, lieutenant, junior grade, commanding officer of the *SC-995*."

"Well, Hiller, are you responsible for that plane going down?"

"Yes, sir, I am. One of my men—"

"What's his name? I want a full report of this immediately, you hear? Because, god damn it, whoever he is, I want to shake his hand! As far as I can tell he was the only man in the harbor that was awake and on the ball when that *kamikaze* tried to take out the flagship! Your gunner may have saved my gosling."

The mike went dead with a metallic click. After expelling a great chestful of air, Mr. Hiller said, "Well, if that don't fry your balls! Somebody pinch me!"

Then for an awkward moment things became very quiet in the pilot-house. Ace was the first to speak:

"Skipper, did he say—?"

"Yessireebob!" yelled Mr. Hiller, sounding a bit giddy. "Jines, my boy, draft a message to the Task Force Commander." He grabbed my shoulder, "I would like to kiss you! Not only have you not brought basic and unsolvable problems into my life, you just may have made life easier for—all of us! Now, give Jines your serial number and rank. What are you, by the way? Still a Third Class Radioman?"

McCormick that took me by the arm and led me into the chartroom, followed by Jines, and shut the door and turned on the light.

"'It had an exhaust'!" I heard Mr. Hiller say just outside the door, imitating a young high-pitched female voice. To the others in the pilot-house he demanded, "How many of you knew that if it had an exhaust it couldn't be an American plane?"

"I did," said Tracy proudly.

"The hell you did. You don't know shit, son. Now keep quiet."

Then he added, "And he had the goddamned balls to pull that trigger, without permission!"

With that he dispatched Leafdale to the after quarters and Tracy to the fo'c's'le to relate the good news that we weren't all going down, after all.

While this was going on, Ace and Jines said nothing; and I was still in a state of shock and had nothing to say. Just outside the door, we heard the Skipper say,

"Now, men, I'm going to hit the sack and I don't want any more excitement before chow call in the morning. It has been some kind of a day." He opened the chartroom door a crack and put his nose through it. "Everything under control? Got that message drafted? I want it sent at once to Leapfrog One."

         *   *   *

Later, most of the crew of the *995* gathered on the bow of the ship, reluctant to go into the hot and humid quarters. Ace McCormick led off with:

"So, Hall boy, you checked the I. F. F. gear in the pilothouse."

I laughed, hesitated, then said, "Where else could I have checked it?"

"Our I. F. F. gear hasn't worked since Peleliu."

"Yeah, I know," I said. "But the way I understand that thing is, if you turn it on and it doesn't go crazy you know there are no friendlies in the sky."

Everybody cracked up except Leavy, who said it made perfectly good sense to him, so why was everybody laughing?

McCormick, ignoring the deckhand, asked, incredulous, "And so, Hall kid, because that plane showed an exhaust you concluded it was a bogey?"

"That is correct, Ace, old slug."

"Well, who in the hell ever told you *none* of our planes show an exhaust after dark?" he scoffed. "I know for a fact some of our reconnaissance planes do."

20

The Enola Gay

Lingayen Gulf turned out to be the end of the line for the Splinter Fleet's island-hopping adventures; but, of course, no one aboard the two remaining subchasers could have known this at the time. In fact, we had come to believe that this kind of thing would go on forever. After a little R & R we would more than likely head on toward Japan.

In a big convoy that included three or four wagons, half a dozen cruisers both light and heavy, and eight tincans, we went back down the west coast of the Philippines through the Sulu Sea, and cut through Mindanao Strait, into one of the fiercest hurricanes that area had ever seen.

For two days Ace McCormick had been doing his best to get everybody upset over the rapidly falling barometer, which, finally, by the end of that second day, had dropped lower than he had ever seen one drop. But since there was nothing any of us could do about it, we just went about our duties as usual, occasionally poking fun at him for being such an old woman. We were heading for fun-and-frolic on some peaceful island, and nothing short of a typhoon was going to slow us down. But, as I said, by the end of that second day, we were in the center of the biggest and scariest thing any of us had ever experienced.

By four o'clock that afternoon the winds were so strong we had to crawl from one hatch to another when we were topside, hanging onto something with both hands. Visibility even that early was about two hundred feet, and only then between the great sheets of rain and spray over the bow.

All of the off-duty crew at this time went below and strapped themselves into their bunks; and that was the last change of watch that night. By the time the eight o'clock watch was supposed to go on, our radar and sonar had gone out, leaving us totally helpless in that raging sea. I was in the pilothouse with McCormick and Leafdale; and when the awning was ripped from our bridge, we were joined by the Skipper, the two ensigns, and Tabor.

"I don't know how much more of this we can take!" yelled the Skipper, as he came in. "This little ship wasn't built to take on a typhoon!"

"I can't maintain any kind of heading!" called out Ace. "But I guess it doesn't matter much!"

The noise of the storm was unbelievable. Even yelling at the top of our voices we could hardly make ourselves understood. The wind was howling and screaming around our superstructure, and every five seconds or so there would come a great crash of thunder that would blot out all other noises. We all lined up before the brace of windows (They did not qualify as portholes) in the front of the pilothouse, hanging onto whatever we could find that was bolted down; and, by the almost constant flashing of lightning, we stared in awe out into the black and terrible night, scared as we had never been scared before.

Then someone, the Skipper I think, bawled out, "Oh, my God!"

What had been only an instant before a wall of water and spray that varied in height from moment to moment was now a very solid wall of battleship gray, the top of which we could not see even when a lightning flash would turn the world into brilliant day! Someone shouted, "Would you look at that!" And then we caught a glimpse of the upper bow of a giant warship! We were, in fact, beneath the bow of an aircraft carrier! And with each mighty ocean wave we rose higher and higher, until our mast seemed about ram into the steel hull!

Everybody was yelling. I could make out some of the Skipper's scream-ing at McCormick: "Hard right rudder! Git us away from that thing!"

Somehow, miraculously, we escaped from that monster; and with the help of lightning flashes, which never let up during the entire ordeal, we back-paddled a distance and rode out the storm. And the next morning, our sonar and radar still out, we looked about in vain for the *SC-1318*. Later, we would learn that she had survived better than we had; but two tincans had gone down with all hands aboard, and many of the larger ships had suffered severe damage.

A week later, having rejoined the *1318*, we dropped anchor in Leyte Gulf to await long-overdue orders to head eastward for R and R.

We had been in the War Zone sixteen long months, and almost everybody aboard was in need of a shrink.

Soon after we anchored, near Tacloban again, Pills winked at me and nodded toward the beach. I nodded and headed for the radio shack to tell Jines there would be a mail detail right away. Then I checked out a Navy Colt .45, belt, and holster from Mr. Howorth in the wardroom.

Someone, probably Tabor, had arranged for an LCVP to ferry us to the island. And going in I was struck by the feeling that no time at all had passed since we were doing this mail pick-up on a daily basis. Lingayen Gulf and the worst typhoon in history seemed unreal, as if I had never experienced them.

In a pile of mail higher than my head I found a large cardboard box addressed to me. The only date I could find on it was December, 1944. It was battered and torn, but the mailing address was clear. And visible through the cracks and holes were books! While everybody else was get-ting cake and pogey bait, I was getting the Greek and Roman classics!

Pills had told me to look for letters, never mind about the packages. He would be responsible for those. So when he saw me drooling over my box of books, he said:

"If you don't beat all!"

We found more mail for the *1318* crew and officers than we did for us; but, even so, there was a big pile for the *995*, including a dozen or so letters for Gilberto Martinez, five or six for Smitty, and one for Baldini. Some of the things we found had been following us since New Caledonia.

I kept looking in all directions for Alisa, certain that she had been keeping an eye out for incoming ships. But when Pills backed away from that mountain of mail from home and said I could either go back with him or camp there overnight, I gathered up what I had found and followed him to the boat. On the way back he complained about my taste in literature, saying that it wasn't healthy for a kid like me to read stuff like that in the War Zone.

As soon as I had handed out all the stuff we had found, I took my box and six letters from Mama and the unclaimed mail and headed for the radio shack. Sharkey blocked my way at the pilothouse door, accusing me of the sin of covetousness. He had no doubt about what was in my box, and he just wanted me to know that he planned to read every one of them as soon as he finished all the *billet dous* he had received from Chicago.

Jines came into the shack while I was admiring the gold lettering on the spines of my books and wanted to know where this batch was going to be stowed. "Why don't you ask your mother to send some detective books or maybe a set of Tarzan novels?"

The beach was off-limits for the crew except when there was a work detail, but that was not a great hardship since Tacloban had very little to offer in the way of recreation. There were daily swimming parties off the fantail, and Mr. Howorth made arrangements for the men to start attending movies every night on a nearby transport ship. This lasted only about a week, however, before the transport left for parts unknown.

Tabor was into stainless steel creations. Somehow, with only a pocketknife, he was turning out earrings and bracelets and watchbands with delicate and quite artistic carvings on them. Dressed only in a pair of frayed and disintegrating dungaree cut-offs, he spent his days in the Captain's Chair with his wares. Occasionally, he would be joined by one or more of the officers, who invariably ended up bartering for some of his art work. One day he handed me a stainless steel watch band, and when I had looked at it for a time he shook his head and said I could keep it if I wanted it.

It was a masterpiece. On it he had created a forest scene, complete with a buck deer drinking from a brook, a thicket of Indian sumac, and a naked Indian maiden. A Blackfoot girl, perhaps, except she had an hourglass figure.

"What do I have that you're after?" I asked with a grin.

"I ran out of writing paper."

$$* \qquad * \qquad *$$

From Leyte Gulf we eventually headed due west, to find an island with some R and R facilities on it. At least that was our understanding. No one seemed to know anything. Our orders read: "Proceed to Saipan Harbor for new assignment." That, the Skipper told us, meant that we were finally going to get some real R and R. When we stopped at Guam for a day and found that the Navy base there had an excellent recreation building for enlisted men and a fine beach large enough for baseball, everyone was convinced that we were headed in the right direction.

The next day early we were headed for Saipan, the last leg of our long journey. Saipan and Tinian, according to our resident authority on Pacific geography, history, and whore houses, had cost the U. S. Marines dearly in the initial stages of the occupation back in the early part of 1943; and, also according to that same source, Ace McCormick, the hills just back of the big Navy base on the Saipan were still inhabited by very hungry and chagrined Japanese soldiers and civilians.

However, on that Sunday afternoon in April, 1945, when we limped into Saipan Harbor and tied up end-to-end at Dock G, everything looked as peaceful as a Tuesday afternoon in Middletown, U. S. A. The first thing we learned was that there were no R and R facilities at all on this island. And Tinian, next door, was even less equipped to accommodate us. The U. S. Marines, who had established a perimeter some distance back in the hills and indeed around the fringes of the entire island, advised us to drink our beer aboard ship.

What, we wanted to know, is going on? Where's R and R?

"All hands topside! On the double!"

It was Tabor, shouting into a megaphone, and the word was that the Skipper had a few words to impart on the quarterdeck.

"I'm sorry to tell you this, men, but we've been assigned the job of air-sea rescue in the Marianas Trench, starting tomorrow morning. There's a big air strip on Tinian, and it runs right down to the drop-off into the Trench, some thousand feet below. B-29's take off with heavy payloads from there, headed for Japan; and it will be our job to patrol that stretch of the Trench near the airstrip. When the Super Fortresses take off, they're loaded to the gunwales with bombs, and some of them may not make it. And when they return from Japan, they're shot up so bad some of them will keep going right into the Trench.

"We'll rotate with the 1318, one day on and one day off."

No one had a word to say to this. For a change everybody just stood frozen, not even looking at each other. The enormity of the crime the Navy was committing against us was mind-boggling.

"During our day off you can do as you please, stay in your bunk or go over to the base PX or write letters home to your folks. Hell, fellas, this is a lot better than convoy duty and landing on islands. Think of it this way, we're out of the war. This is our permanent assignment for the duration."

So that Sunday afternoon some of us drifted over to the U. S. Marine base, curious to know if what we had heard was true. We were told that during the daytime trucks equipped with loudspeakers left the Marine compound to broadcast messages of peace and prosperity for all who would surrender, none of which the Japanese were buying. What they were interested in, however, were the food stored in a guarded quonset hut and the Stateside movies at the big outdoor theater.

*   *   *

Although the routine, one day at the dock and the next in the Trench, was not a difficult one, the days and weeks went by slowly for us. But at last we were getting regular mail from the States, and those that drank beer were getting regular rations, so that by laying off it for a few days they could go down the beach occasionally and party. I began to work at a rating increase, from third class to second class radioman. No one on the ship had received a promotion since New Caledonia.

We kept up with the war the best we could. I made it a habit to pipe AFR shortwave broadcasts into the pilothouse and after crews quarters every morning, and I continued to copy high-speed press and pass it around to the officers and crew. We thought we knew everything about MacArthur's progress in the Philippines and the slow but steady move on Japan. But we were not ready for what happened the first week in August.

We spent the day of August 5 at the dock, having coming in about daylight that morning from the Trench. I had the eight-to-twelve deck watch, my responsibility being to keep the noise down so the officers could catch up on their sleep. It passed without incident, and I was relieved by Leavy about twelve-thirty. Instead of going aft with Ace and Sharkey for a big sandwich and coffee, as I usually did, I went forward and lowered myself into the black stink of the forward crews' quarters, for some much-needed shuteye.

It was still hot and humid on deck at, but dropping into that fo'c's'le was like going into a very exotic Turkish bath. Even without

Baldini the smells were stronger and more exotic than a Mississippi
outhouse in July.

I undressed down to my skivvies in the dark, becoming aware of
Eddie Jake's heavy breathing on the starboard side. My mattress and pillow were damp and clammy against my bare skin, but I hardly noticed
this as I settled down.

The next thing I knew (It seemed like no time at all) Tracy's head
appeared in the saucer-shaped piece of sky above my bunk.

"Rise and shine down there!"

"You rise and shine," said Tabor.

"We're on call. Pass the word."

"Pass it yourself."

"Come on!" whined Tracy. "Pass the goddamn word down there. Get
Eddie Jake up and tell him Mr. Howorth wants to see him in the wardroom, on the double."

"We can't be on call," I groaned. "We were just over there today."

"A radio dispatch just came from the *1318*. She's got engine trouble.
We have no choice."

At these words my guts bunched up like I had been hit with a club. I
had no idea how I was going to summon enough strength to climb topside once more and go back to my radio watch.

"Where's Jines?" I called out, but Tracy had already left.

"I think we're bein' suckered," said Milleson, from the starboard side.
"Somebody on that worthless piece of shit's probably fucked up."

A shudder ran through the ship. That, of course, would be
Vanderveen starting the engines. Which meant that we couldn't leave
the anchorage for another thirty minutes.

I slid to the deck, took my time about getting dressed, and went aft to
the galley for some coffee. It was pitch dark but I had no idea what time
it was. July Roucloux was sitting at the mess table, and I could tell by the
look on his face he had something he had to unload on me.
Kwaitkowski, in a dirty white T-shirt and dirty white shorts, handed me

a mug of steamy black coffee without my having said a word. I turned to July and said,

"What's up?"

"We was just in that Trench."

"Maybe Mr. London's homesick for the dock here. Or maybe he knows something we don't know."

"Like what?"

"Like maybe what's coming off that airstrip tonight is something you don't want to be close to when it hits the water."

"Listen, like Pills says, our number's gonna come up one of these days—and every time we go into the Marianas Trench we're gettin' closer and closer to it. All it'd take would be for one of them out-goin' B-29's to fuck-up."

"Well," I said, "it could be worse, old buddy. This is duck soup compared to the landings and all that convoy duty. Now, we sit here at this peaceful dock half the time and act like civilians. Think about it. How many times do we leave this mooring? Once every two days, and then to watch some flyboys risking their necks just to get their planes airborne."

"Yeah," said July. "But my point is that time's runnin' out on us. We ought to be back at Manus or New Guinea playing softball and drinking beer. One of these days the war's gonna be over, and I don't want to be the last casualty."

"I keep thinking about the fellows still facing it, July. It's easy to forget there's a war going on, here in this place."

We sat for a time staring at nothing. Sharkey, who had taken Smitty's bunk in the after quarters, rolled over in his bunk and growled, "Can the shit, you guys! I'm tryin' to git some sleep!"

"You've got it pretty good back here, huh, Shark?" I said. "We're preparing to go out; so I'd forget about taking a nap, if I were you."

He eased up on one elbow, "Yeah, well, you don't happen to be me! Now, clear out of here, both of you."

We continued to sit and sip on our coffee until Vanderveen passed the word to the bridge that the engineroom was ready. The instant this was passed down to us, we dragged Smitty out of his bunk and the three of us went topside. July ran to help Leavy get rid of our mooring lines, and within five minutes we were headed out into the blackness of late night. I joined Jines in the pilothouse, where he was preparing to send a message to the *1318*.

It was always just a bit scary entering the Trench; but on this overcast night, having to rely entirely upon our radar, it was downright spooky. With towering walls of solid rock close in on both sides of us, so high the sky was just a narrow strip of faint light, and us taking a position squarely in the path of those big long-range bombers, it seemed to me that we were offering ourselves to that black hell as some kind of sacrifice.

We met the *1318* on its way back to the mooring and, by blinkerlight, learned that an outgoing flight of B-29's was scheduled for sometime early that morning. We kept bravely on, arriving in the Trench around two.

It was many times blacker in the trench than out, but with the help of the radar we settled on station and began to tread water. When the flight would take place and how many planes would participate, we had no idea; but until we heard the mighty roar and saw a big black bird drop off the end of that airstrip, we had nothing to do but wait and wonder.

Sometime shortly before three, local time, we heard the first plane coming down the strip far above us and watched it plunge out over the Trench. It dipped low but pulled out easily and went on its way. One down. The second Superfort followed almost immediately, and it seemed to me, judging from the sound of its engines, tumbled almost straight downward. For a hair-raising thirty seconds or so we braced ourselves for disaster, convinced that we were going to hear that mighty plane fall to its death. The terrific downdraft of the Trench and the weight of the bombs appeared to be too much for it.

This one, we could tell, was heavily overloaded; and as it dipped lower and lower toward the water, we became convinced that there was no way it could pull out in time! But when there was no crash and when the roar was obviously louder and becoming louder by the second, we began to realize that it had leveled out! It was going to make it!

Or was it too near the surface of the water to pass over us?

Suddenly, the strip of sky, only slightly lighter than the walls on either side of us, was blotted out! And over us swooped that mighty plane with its payload of bombs!

Then, before we had time to breathe normally, the third plane came roaring over that precipice and dipped into the Trench. It was briefly silhouetted against the sky above us, looking like some giant, primordial bird. As it angled clumsily down toward the water then began to level out, the thought occurred to me that this had better be the last one or I was going to have a heart attack.

When it leveled out and almost immediately began to climb, everyone breathed a sigh of relief.

Pills walked by and said over his shoulder, "I can't take much more of this."

I heard Eddie Jake laughing. He had just come up from the galley in time to hear the third one sailing off into the clouds. "No problem! Hey, fellas, is that the last one?"

We returned to Saipan Harbor, arriving at our mooring just as the sun was coming up. In my radio log I wrote the date, August 6, 1945, and "NS" in fifteen-minute intervals and signed my name. I was so bushed I lay my head down on the cool steel of the radio position and went instantly to sleep.

Perhaps an hour later I was awakened by the gangway watch with the news that an atomic bomb had been dropped on a city in Japan. It was Milleson and he was leaning through the hatchway above my head. "Turn the radio on!" he shouted. "Did you hear what I said about the A-bomb? Turn on something and pipe the shortwave through the ship!"

My head was splitting and although I could hear Milleson loud and clear, his words were not making sense. I tried to lift my head. "You want the radio on? It's already on!" I slumped again, like someone drugged. Time passed and suddenly I became aware that Milleson was still staring down at me. He had shouted something about a bomb. "What kind of a bomb did you say?" I managed.

Then Sharkey's head appeared beside Milleson's. "Hoss! Snap out of it! The goddamned war's goin' to be over any minute, man!" He stood up and began dancing a jig around the hatchway and punching at Milleson.

I sat up and flipped on the SX-25 Hallicrafters receiver and stared at it while it warmed up. Eddie Jake appeared at the hatchway with a mug of coffee for me, which I realized with a shock, was an extraordinary thing for him to do, while the ship was tied up at the dock. Something must indeed be up.

"Did you hear about Hiroshima?" asked Tex, his face beaming with happiness. He pronounced it *Hiro-shima.*

"What's that?" I took the coffee and stared at it. "Thanks."

"That's where the bomb fell! The whole city went up in smoke! They're estimatin' eighty or ninety thousand—"

The mug was halfway to my mouth, where it remained for a time.

"Man, that's gonna end the war! What's wrong? You don't seem all that happy about it!"

I took a sip of coffee and nodded, not looking at Eddie Jake. "You actually think one bomb—?" I began. "Tex, the Japs don't give up that easily."

The SPAT-SPAT noise of pistol and rifle fire had begun to reach my ears.

"What's that?" I called out.

"Celebratin'," said Eddie Jake. "The goddamned war is over!"

A machine gun cut loose, clattering in short bursts. It was joined by another and another. And as Tex made his way back up the ladder, the noise reaching me through the hatch sounded like the beginnings of a Fourth of July celebration.

I plugged in the wardroom and both crews quarters. One of the regular commentators was summing up the Pacific news:

"This day will go down as one of the greatest and one the worst the world has ever experienced. It's much too early to say what the long-term effects of the bomb will be, but Washington is already working out the precise terms of Japan's surrender. It will be unconditional, of course, and it will be soon. From Tokyo there has been no word, not even an acknowledgment of the catastrophe at Hiroshima. Armed Forces Radio will interrupt its regular programming throughout the day to bring you news as we get it. I'm Norm Soldalski and this has been an Armed Forces Radio Communiqué."

I had missed something, evidently. One bomb had been dropped on one city and now Washington was expecting immediate capitulation by the Japanese. Okay, so it was a new type of bomb, much more powerful than anything we had used before. But there was no way the Japanese would quit because of just one bomb.

By the time I reached the quarterdeck, guns were going off all around the harbor, and on the fantail of the ship Tracy was loading one of the fifty-caliber machineguns. Roucloux showed up, his big face all smiles.

"The war's over," he grinned. "Hot damn but I've looked forward to saying them words."

"I'm afraid you're just a little premature," I said. "Unless you've heard something I haven't."

Astonished at my attitude, he cried, "The friggin' war's over! Don't you realize that? Listen to what's goin' on around you!"

"Maybe you're right. I sure as heck hope so. But we've been clobbering Japan now for two long years and she has showed no signs of quitting. We've destroyed all of her Pacific island bases, chased her out of the Philippines, knocked out her air force, and reduced her 'invincible' navy to shambles—and still she keeps coming back. I don't think they know how to quit. In case you don't know it, July, we're not the only nation on Earth that has a reputation for never losing a war."

While I carried on, the entire crew of the *995* was running up and down the deck shouting and laughing and pounding each other on the back.

"I don't understand why you're so gloomy," said my friend.

I slapped him on the shoulder, "I'll show you how to celebrate when the word comes that there's a ceasefire. Until Japan declares a ceasefire, the war isn't over."

The machine guns and rifles had been joined by anti-aircraft guns, and out in the harbor somebody on a tincan had cut loose with a five-inch cannon! The sky was full of puff balls by this time, and a great cloud of smoke had begun to settle over the harbor. Then in the distance I heard what sounded like the buzz of a fighter plane.

"Do you hear that?" I asked Roucloux. "I think it's a plane, but there's so much smoke in the sky I haven't been able to spot it."

"There he is!" shouted Roucloux, pointing excitedly. "And the crazy bastard's heading straight across the harbor!"

I saw the small dot in the sky and moaned, "Surely nobody capable of flying a TBF is stupid enough to come directly over all these guns!"

But while we watched, the plane kept a straight course over us.

Out of frustration, I began waving my hands and shouting, "Turn back!"

"The jerks are actually tryin' to hit him!" screamed July. "The lunatics! Don't they know he's a *friendly*?"

Roucloux was right. Suddenly, every gun in the harbor seemed to be aimed at the high-flying plane, even the ones on our ship! Then it was all over. A stream of black smoke began to trail out behind the TBF, and, instantly, as if someone had flipped a switch, all the guns stopped firing.

"We shot down one of our own planes, Red! And the war's over!"

I looked at Roucloux. Tears were running down his face.

THE END

The Crew of the SC-995 (Pearl Harbor, October 1945)

TOP ROW from left to right: Big John Leavy, Harold Jines, July Roucloux, Wesley Hall, Ace McCormick (peering over my shoulder), Bill Cody, Chalmer Jean Tabor, Johnny Olson, Eddie Jake Groth, Hutchinson, Kwaitkowski, and Lt.(jg) Cleary. SECOND ROW: Gilberto Martinez, Pop Law, Carpenter, Dowell, and Blair. FRONT ROW: Beck, Henderson, Leafdale, and Lt.(jg) Lowery, the new Skipper.

Afterword

The celebration of V-E day began for us on that momentous day, August 6, 1945, and lasted until all the alcohol and ammunition in Saipan had been exhausted, which was about the time the second bomb was dropped three days later. Surprisingly, only one casualty occurred as a result of all the celebrating in Saipan Harbor, that lone TBF that flew into the flak from our guns. The two crewmembers made it down safely, and the Subchaser-1318 ended up with the bright yellow inflatable liferaft that they had brought down with them.

Lt. John London, the skipper of the *SC-1318* and the ranking officer of the now defunct *Splinter Fleet*, had yearned for a small boat throughout the last year or so of the war; and, now, when all the fuss and bother had ended and he was being transferred to a cruiser, he was the recipient of a beautiful, roomy, rubber life raft, with oars.

Before the month was out, Lt. (jg) William F. Hiller went to Guam to receive a Presidential Unit Citation for the *SC-995* and a promotion to full lieutenant. He never returned. Scuttlebutt had it that he was transferred to a Fletcher-class tincan; but with his luck I doubt that it actually happened. Mr. Howorth and Mr. Darling became our new skipper and our new executive officer, respectively, and, at the same time, were promoted to the rank of lieutenant, junior grade. None of the crew, as far as I know, received a promotion, although many of them were due one. I had completed all the requirements for Radioman, Second Class, months before the war ended; but for some reason the paperwork was never completed.

No replacement for Mr. Hiller ever caught up with us.

For all practical purposes, the war ended on August 15, but it wasn't until sometime in September that it was official. And since our air-sea rescue service in the Marianas Trench was no longer needed, we began to count the wake-up days until our return to the States. Eventually, we joined a very slow convoy loaded to the gunwales with servicemen on their way home for Christmas. The lights had gone on again all over the world, and so convoying eastward was a new and exciting experience for us. Lights remained on day and night, and we could wear anything or nothing while on deck.

We stopped for a night at Eniwetok and saw a movie about John Wayne winning the war. We had Thanksgiving dinner twice on our way home, once when we crossed the International Date Line and the next day when we arrived at Johnston Island, not far from Hawaii.

In Hawaii, we tied up at the submarine base in Pearl Harbor. There we counted up our "points" in anticipation of a hasty discharge or at least re-assignment to Stateside duty. The Point System worked best for married men with dependents, of course; but length of service overseas also played a role. And since we were heading home, some of the recent additions to the complement of the *Splendid Five* were re-assigned to ships there in Pearl. They did not have enough points for a discharge. All of the original crew stayed with the ship, however, and, on December 5, 1945, we passed beneath the Golden Gate Bridge.

At Treasure Island, in San Francisco Bay, nine members of the crew, the Department Heads for the most part, were assigned the unhappy task of decommissioning the ship. This entailed the inventorying and storing in grease and waterproof paper of every nut and bolt and radio part on the ship. And since Jines was married and I wasn't, the job of inventorying the radio equipment and spare parts fell to me.

Bill Tracy, pleading hardship disability, managed to turn over the Gunnery Department to Julius Anthony Roucloux, who was still just a gunner's mate striker, his rating Seaman, First Class.

These were wonderful, crazy times for me. Like Roucloux and the others in the decommissioning crew, I spent my days mothballing parts and equipment and my nights in San Francisco in tailormade dress blues. In the final days of the inventorying, a package my good friend Roucloux tried to send home was X-rayed and found to contain a Navy Colt .45. Mr. Howorth gave me a choice: I could volunteer to deliver him by Jeep to Mare Island, or I could let the SP's do it.

The ride across the north half of the Oakland-San Francisco Bay Bridge has remained crystal clear in my memory all down through the years. At one point I turned to July and said, "Just say the word and I'll chauffeur you to San Antonio. Or wherever else you want to go."

"That wouldn't solve a thing." For a time he gazed westward toward Alcatraz Island. Finally, he laughed and said, "All they're gonna to do is give me a D. D. I'll be back home by the time you are."

It was December 22 and at that point I was certain neither one of us would make it home for Christmas.

Later that same day, however, Mr. Howorth handed me my travel orders and said, "Go home to your folks, Sparks."

Still in a state of shock from having delivered July Roucloux to prison, I boarded a Southern Pacific iron horse; and three days later I arrived in my hometown, in a blizzard. It was Christmas Eve and every place in town was closed. Worst of all, no one was expecting me, and home was still seven miles away in the River Bend.

About the Author

Wesley Hall, after retiring emeritus professor of English at Southwest Missouri State University, in Springfield, moved to Dragon Fly Cove on the Lake of the Ozarks, where he resides with his wife, Sharon. There he fishes in season and and surfs the Internet regardless of the season.

Appendix A

It was not until sometime after we returned to the States that the news broke about the *Enola Gay*, a B-29 (named for the mother of the pilot, Colonel Paul Tibbets), that had taken off from Tinian on the morning of August 6 with the bomb that destroyed Hiroshima. It did not take me long to remember who was on patrol that fateful night in the Marianas Trench.

This Super Fortress had a wing-span of 141 feet, thirty-one feet longer than the *Subchaser-995,* and was therefore too long to fit into the Smithsonian Institution's National Air and Space Museum, in Washington, D. C.

Its mission from Tinian to Hiroshima, covering 1600 miles of ocean (one way) took twelve hours and thirteen minutes. It was carrying a five-ton payload, fifteen thousand pounds overweight; and because there was a good possibility it might not make it out of the Marianas Trench, the bomb wasn't assembled until the plane was safely airborne. With a force equal to twenty thousand tons of TNT, or the payloads of about twenty ordinary bombers, the atomic bomb was the equivalent of all the artillery fired in both world wars. It instantly killed or seriously wounded eighty thousand people and was responsible for launching the Nuclear Age, as well as the Age of Pushbutton Warfare.

After the war the Enola Gay wandered from air force base to air force base in Arizona, Illinois, and Florida, finally ending up in the Smithsonian warehouse in Silver Hill, Maryland, in 1960.

Appendix B

Books About Subchasers

ALLIED COASTAL FORCES OF WORLD WAR II, by John Lambert and Al Ross (1990, Conway Maritime Press, London). Another reference book on subchasers.

BLACK COMPANY, THE STORY OF SUBCHASER 1264, by Eric Purdon (1972, Robert B. Luce). This is actually the story of PATROL CRAFT (PC) 1264, whose officers and crew were African-Americans. It performed so well it was one of fifty warships reviewed by President Harry S. Truman in the Navy Day Celebration in New York City in October, 1945.

THE CINDERLLAS OF THE FLEET, by William Washburn Nutting, USNR (1920, Standard Motor Construction Company of Jersey City), about WWI subchasers.

DICTIONARY OF AMERICAN FIGHTING SHIPS (1977, the U. S. Naval Institute Press. An 8-volume encyclopedia of U.S. warships, including subchasers.

NINETY DAY WONDER, by Lewis M. Walker, Comdr., USNR, (Ret.), (1989, Harlo Press), about a WWII subchaser in a typhoon.

A SAILOR'S TALES, by Bill Robinson (1978, W.W. Norton), about the SC-743 in the Pacific (among other things).

THE SEVEN, by William Edward Syers (1960, Duell, Sloan and Pearce), about a WWII subchaser.

THE SPLINTER FLEET OF THE OTRANTO BARRAGE, by Ray Millholland (1936, Bobbs-Merrill), about a WWI subchaser.

SPLINTER FLEET; The Wooden Subchasers of World War II, by Theodore R. Treadwell (10/31/00, U. S. Naval Institute Press). Publishers statement: Hastily built at the onset of World War II to stop German U-boats from taking their toll on Allied shipping, the 110-foot wooden subchasers were the smallest commissioned warships in the U.S. Navy yet they saw as much action as ships ten times their size. In every theater of war these workhorses of the fleet escorted countless convoys of slow-moving ships through submarine-infested waters, conducted endless mind-numbing antisubmarine patrols, and were used in hundreds of amphibious operations. This book, written by the commander of one of the subchasers, defines their place in World War II naval history and gives readers a taste of life aboard the wooden warships. Ringing with authenticity, it describes the cramped quarters and unforgiving seas, as well as the tenacious courage and close bonds formed by the men as they sought out the enemy and confronted nature. Long overshadowed by the larger, faster warships and more glamorous PT boats, subchasers have been virtually forgotten in naval history, but this work restores the plucky little ships to their hard earned status as significant members of the fleet. Price: $34.95, hardback. 272 pages.

SUBCHASER, by Edward P. Stafford (U. S. Naval Institute, 1988), about the SC-692.

SUBCHASER IN THE SOUTH PACIFIC; A Saga of the USS SC-761 During World War II, by J. Henry Doscher, Jr., Captain, USNR, (Ret.) (1994, Eakin Press). This is a true story of life aboard a subchaser from the time it was commissioned in September, 1942, until it returned to the states in 1945. It is told by a young officer who eventually became the C. O. During the time Mr. Doscher was aboard this subchaser, it played an active part in the Solomon Islands campaigns in 1943. Along with the *SC-760*, it took part in the first invasion of Vella LaVella in August of that year. This was the first time a subchaser was used in an island invasion. Also, prior to the invasion and working with U. S. submarines, the SC-761 took an active part in returning coastal watchers from Bougainville. Price: $15.95, hardback. 110 pages. Two years after this very exciting book about subchasers came out, Dr. Doscher published **Little Wolf at Leyte**, the story of the heroic *USS Samuel B. Roberts* (DE-413) in the Battle of Leyte Gulf during World War II. It is an excellent job of research, and no one can read it without becoming personally involved in the story. I took part in the first invasion of the Philippines (on Leyte), and this book answers so many questions that I have had down through the years about that very complicated time. Price: $18.95, hardback. 148 pages.

SUBCHASER JIM, by Josef Berger (1943, Little, Brown), a first-person account of chasing submarines on the East Coast.

U.S. SMALL COMBATANTS, by Norman Friedman (1987, U. S. Naval Institute Press). A general reference book on subchasers.

54260190R00221